GREAT AFRICAN AMERICANS

Allison J. Keyes

Gloria Blakely

CONSULTANT
Charles R. Branham, Ph.D.,
Senior Historian, DuSable Museum of
African American History

WEST
SIDE
PUBLISHING

Charles R. Branham, Ph.D., is senior historian for the DuSable Museum of African American History. He was the writer, coproducer, and host of *The Black Experience,* a series of 60 half-hour programs for Chicago's WTTW-TV, which was the first nationally televised series on African American history. He is the author of *The Transformation of Black Political Leadership* and *Black Chicago Accommodationist Politics Before the Great Migration.* A recipient of the Silver Circle Excellence in Teaching Award from the University of Illinois, Dr. Branham was a consultant for Publications International, Ltd.'s title *Profiles of Great African Americans.*

Joyce Ann Joyce, Ph.D. (additional consultation), is the former chairperson and professor of the African American Studies Department at Temple University, where she is currently a professor in the Women's Studies Program. Dr. Joyce was a 1995 recipient of The American Book Award for Literary Criticism for her collection of essays *Warriors, Conjurers, and Priests: Defining African-centered Literary Criticism.* Dr. Joyce is also the author of *Richard Wright's Art of Tragedy, Ijala: Sonia Sanchez and the African Poetic Tradition* and the coeditor of *The New Cavalcade: African American Writing from 1760 to the Present.* She was a consultant for Publications International, Ltd.'s title *Profiles of Great African Americans.*

Allison J. Keyes is an award-winning journalist who reports for both WCBS-AM and WNYC Radio in New York City, and she writes for ABC's *Good Morning America* and *World News Tonight.* A contributing author for Publications International, Ltd.'s titles *Profiles of Great African Americans* and *African American Heritage Perpetual Calendar,* Keyes is a member of the National Association of Black Journalists.

Gloria Blakely is a journalist for a variety of national magazines and metropolitan newspapers. She wrote *Danny Glover (Black Americans of Achievement)* and was a contributing author for Publications International, Ltd.'s *African American Heritage Perpetual Calendar.*

Jennifer Elizabeth Rosenberg (factual verification) is About.com's guide to 20th-century history and has provided factual verification for numerous Publications International, Ltd., titles, including *The Holocaust Chronicle.*

Jean Currie Church (additional factual verification) is chief of the Library Division of the Moorland-Spingarn Research Center at Howard University in Washington, D.C., and she provided factual verification and consultation for Publications International, Ltd.'s *Profiles of Great African Americans* and *African American Heritage Perpetual Calendar.*

Additional contributing writers: **Stan West, David Smallwood, Kimberly Rose**

Additional factual verification: **Rosa L. Anthony**

Cover images: (top row, left to right) Edward "Duke" Ellington, Oprah Winfrey, Lorraine Hansberry, Barack Obama, Medgar Evers, Mae Jemison, (bottom row, left to right) Malcolm X, Condoleezza Rice, George Washington Carver, Michael Jordan, Frederick Douglass, Adam Clayton Powell, Jr.

ACKNOWLEDGMENTS

Page 25: Commentary on the Dred Scott decision by Standish E. Willis, attorney at law. Reprinted by permission.

Pages 106–107: License granted by Intellectual Properties Management, Atlanta, Georgia, as manager of the Estate of Martin Luther King, Jr.

Page 135: Excerpts from the article "Robert L. Johnson: A Business Titan Redefining Black Entrepreneurial Success," by Robert G. Miller, in *The Black Collegian.* Reprinted by permission.

CONTENTS

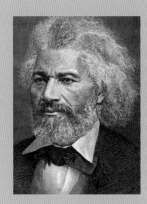

FREDERICK DOUGLASS

MARIAN ANDERSON

ROSA PARKS

EDWARD "DUKE" ELLINGTON

CONTENTS

OPRAH WINFREY

LORRAINE HANSBERRY

MAE JEMISON

MEDGAR EVERS

MUHAMMAD ALI

COLIN POWELL

GREAT AFRICAN AMERICANS

SOJOURNER TRUTH

OPRAH WINFREY

MARCUS GARVEY

EDWARD "DUKE" ELLINGTON

HARRIET TUBMAN

BARACK OBAMA

GEORGE WASHINGTON CARVER

GREAT AFRICAN AMERICANS

I have tracked my bleeding countrymen through the widely scattered documents of American history. I have listened to their groans, their clanking chains, and melting prayers, until the woes of a race and the agonies of centuries seem to crowd upon my soul as a bitter reality. Many pages of this history have been blistered with my tears; and, although having lived but a little more than a generation, my mind feels as if it were cycles old.

George Washington Williams

In 1882, historian George Washington Williams published his two-volume *History of the Negro Race in America* "not as a blind panegyrist of my race nor as a partisan apologist, but for a love for 'the truth of history.'" The last decades of the 19th century brought the first flowering of African American remembrance: Frederick Douglass wrote his *The Life and Times of Frederick Douglass* and Charles W. Chestnutt, father of the African American short story, wrote his heroic biography of Douglass. William Still wrote his history of the Underground Railroad; Joseph T. Wilson wrote *Black Phalanx*, a history

of black sacrifice and courage in the Civil War; and Bishop Daniel A. Payne and former Congressman John Mercer Langston wrote their autobiographies. Perhaps attempting to challenge the uniformly gray psyche of the Industrial era, black writers sought to recall the valor and glory of a more colorful period. Or perhaps they sought a more instrumental history.

Somewhere, perhaps, a young W.E.B. Du Bois or William Monroe Trotter was reading alone, by candlelight, the stories of men and women of courage who dared all, risked all, to keep their covenant with racial justice. Perhaps, just perhaps, the stories of these men and women who helped shatter the fetters of chattel slavery put black men in their nation's blue [Union uniform] and secured and defended their right to the franchise. Perhaps these stories' real life heroes and heroines inspired a new abolitionism and reignited the banked fires of social protest.

What Trotter and Du Bois, Ida B. Wells and Mary McLeod Bethune well understood was that they stood on the shoulders and were held aloft by titans; that Harriet Tubman and Sojourner Truth, Frederick Douglass and Martin

R. Delany had paved the way. They understood the incalculable debt that they—and we—owe these courageous and innovative men and women who broke barriers, fought injustice, modeled excellence, and even made the ultimate sacrifice in the quest for social justice. They understood that theirs was a history forged in struggle but filled with stories of transcendence and triumph; of men and women who challenged myths and misconceptions, hurdled barriers, blazed trails, invented, created, transformed, and reinvigorated our common culture and, in the process, refashioned our common heritage.

The extraordinary weavers of dreams and rewriters of record books that grace these pages are monuments to the pride and persistence that permeates the African American past, but they are only a small sample of the rich reservoir of ambition and energy that marks the diverse and still unfolding story of a people. It is the story of a frail and sickly slave stolen from a Senegal village reading her poetry to our nation's first president and of a brilliant man of letters forsaking the cloistered halls of academe to pursue a lifelong struggle for civil rights. Here is the story of a boy, once traded for a horse, who would

GREAT AFRICAN AMERICANS

discover thousands of uses for the peanut and sweet potato and of a man who was an apostle of nonviolence but was cut down by an assassin's bullet.

There is irony here. "Moses" was a woman who led 300 slaves "out of the House of Bondage." A brash young officer who challenged racial segregation in the army later demonstrated remarkable patience and forbearance in the face of catcalls and death threats as he shattered the color line of professional sports. A great composer died unheralded and unknown; a half century later his music would provide the score for an Academy Award–winning movie and revive public appreciation of a forgotten musical genre.

Here Sojourner Truth asks plaintively "Aren't I a Woman?" and Marcus Garvey commands "Up you Mighty race! You can accomplish what you will!" Here DuSable explores, Ellington composes, and Michael Jordan soars high above the rim. Here Malcolm X undergoes a spiritual conversion in a dank prison cell, Ralph Bunche brokers peace in the

> They are all here, the famous
> and the little known,
> the men and women whose
> lives have touched our lives
> and subtly, sometimes
> imperceptibly, reshaped
> our world.

Middle East, and Paul Robeson sacrifices a career for the cause of peace and social justice.

Here Madam C. J. Walker trains a generation of black women in entrepreneurship and self-reliance; Mary Church Terrell, at age 90 and supported by a cane, walks a picket line; and an Illinois State Senator with a difficult name and an unusual past galvanizes a nation with his story of faith and hope. They are all here, the famous and the little known, the men and women whose lives have touched our lives and subtly, sometimes imperceptibly, reshaped our world.

Of course, no selection of the "Greatest" is without controversy, and it is hoped that this list will be a starting point for discussion and debate. Any list is at best an approximation, and the reader is invited to weigh in on the relative merits of the choices or to make suggestions for future editions. History is an argument, and wisdom begins with an admission of the possibility of error. But the real question is: Who's next? What man or woman, undiscovered or unacknowledged, will someday make the list. Who are the deserving, the special, the pioneers who will influence our lives and remake our history?

Who will help create a future worthy of this legacy?

Charles Branham, Ph.D.
Senior Historian
DuSable Museum of
African American History

GREAT AFRICAN AMERICANS

LOUIS ARMSTRONG

CAROL MOSELEY-BRAUN

HANK AARON

ALTHEA GIBSON

THURGOOD MARSHALL

CRISPUS ATTUCKS

CRISPUS ATTUCKS epitomized all that was best in colonial America. Born a slave in Massachusetts, he escaped and became an educated man. He eventually helped begin America's armed resistance against British rule. Attucks was the first to die in the Boston Massacre, and he became a beacon for the American struggle for independence.

Attucks was born a slave around 1723 (he has no known birth date), in Framingham,

Attucks had the highest regard for liberty and freedom from oppression, not only for African American slaves but for America itself.

Massachusetts. He was the son of an African father and a Native American mother. As a child, he was repeatedly sold from one master to another, but he escaped from slavery in 1750. Attucks became a sailor and a whaler; following the sea became his destiny.

This muscular mulatto learned to read and write, and he joined the American struggle for freedom from the British. Attucks attended

Crispus Attucks carried the torch for freedom as the first man to die in the historic Boston Massacre. A runaway slave who became a sailor and taught himself to read and write, Attucks was the ultimate symbol of the American battle for independence.

meetings with other patriots to discuss ways to fight the burdensome taxes levied by England. He then wrote a letter of protest to Governor Thomas Hutchinson, who was the top Tory politician of the province.

According to most accounts, on March 5, 1770, Attucks spearheaded a noisy crowd of protesters who confronted a company of British soldiers stationed at the Custom House on Boston's King Street. Witnesses say Attucks led the demonstrators, who were armed with banners and clubs, and that the crowd began throwing snow and ice at the soldiers. Attucks then grabbed one British soldier's bayonet and knocked him down. The frightened soldiers fired into the crowd, leaving Attucks dead on the ground. Four others also died. The *Boston Gazette and Country Journal* for March 12, 1770, reported that Attucks was killed instantly. His death became a symbol of the Revolutionaries' struggle.

According to testimony at the later trial of the British soldiers, prosecutors said Attucks had been "assaulted with force and arms, feloniously, willfully, and of malice aforethought." But defense lawyers for the soldiers, including patriot John Adams, accused Attucks of not only having formed the patriots' attack party

but also said "it was Attucks to whose mad behavior, in all probability, the dreadful carnage of that night is chiefly ascribed."

After the Revolutionary War, Attucks continued to be a symbol for the fight for freedom. African American military companies called themselves the Attucks Guards. And from 1858 to 1870, African Americans in Boston held a Crispus Attucks Day every year. By 1888, blacks convinced city and state officials that Attucks's contributions warranted a monument on the Boston Common. That statue bears the name of all five men who died for the cause.

The five heroes are buried in historic Granary Burying Ground, along with other famous Revolutionary War figures, including John Hancock, Governor William Bradford of Plymouth County, and, ironically, John Adams.

In 1770, leading a revolt against burdensome taxes imposed on the colonies by England, Crispus Attucks was killed by British soldiers. This made him a martyr and an American symbol of freedom during the Revolutionary War.

JEAN BAPTISTE POINTE DUSABLE

JEAN BAPTISTE POINTE DUSABLE founded the settlement of Chicago in 1772. DuSable epitomized the forbearance and spirit of early African Americans, whose accomplishments represent the incredible diversity of the African American experience.

The details of DuSable's early life are based on much conjecture, but he is believed to have been born in St. Marc, Haiti, in 1745. He was a free black of African heritage. Since many free blacks in Haiti were educated in France, it is possible that DuSable was educated there. DuSable moved to New Orleans and ran his father's business. The Spanish occupied Louisiana in 1764, and DuSable fled to French-controlled areas on the upper Mississippi River.

During this time, DuSable created what became a lifelong connection with several Native American nations, most notably the Potawatomie. The handsome frontiersman spent four years, 1765 to 1769, trading furs with the Indians in St. Louis; he then moved farther north into their territory, onto land controlled by the English and Spanish. He lived, at that time, with boyhood friend Jacques Clemorgan, another Haitian who had received large land grants in return for doing favors for the Spanish Government.

DuSable, who remained faithful to the French, left to live among the Potawatomies. His fur-trapping expeditions took him across North America, to the sites of what are now Chicago, Detroit, and Ontario, Canada.

DuSable was described in the "Recollections" of Augustin Grignon of Butte des Morts, Wisconsin, as "a large man. . . . He was a trader, pretty wealthy, and drank freely." Others who knew him described him as "venerable, about six feet in height, with a well-formed figure and very pleasant countenance." DuSable was described by many as a respectable man.

In 1772, DuSable established a historic fur trading post on the Chicago River near Lake Michigan, the first permanent settlement in the area. He bought land and built his house on the north bank of the Chicago River, just where the waterway turned south, on a finger of sand that extended between the river and Lake Michigan. The ambitious businessman lived a prosperous life with his Native American wife, Catherine, and their daughter, Suzanne.

The first child born in Chicago was born on his property, which also hosted the city's first marriage and housed its first court and post office. He traded heavily with the Native Americans in the area and became known for acting as peacemaker between various warring tribes.

During the Revolutionary War, DuSable seems to have tried to play a role as peacemaker, but his intentions were questioned by both sides. DuSable was jailed on suspicion of treason by British Colonel Arent de Peyster, who described DuSable as "a handsome Negro, well-educated and settled at Eschikagou." DuSable's captor, a Lieutenant Bennett, reported that he had many friends who gave him good character references. DuSable was freed after proving that he was a citizen of the United States.

DuSable later served as liaison officer between white officials and the Indian nations in the Port Huron area on the St. Clair River, appointed at the request of Native Americans.

After acquiring and developing an 800-acre property in Peoria, Illinois, DuSable returned to Chicago in the early 1780s, creating a trading post and home that became legendary for its furnishings and modern conveniences. DuSable's business was so prosperous that it included two barns, a mill, a bake house, a poultry house, and large livestock holdings.

By 1800, DuSable sold his post to a French trader and moved to Missouri. He later moved to St. Charles, Missouri. He was possibly disappointed over his defeat in an election to become chief of the Native American nations in the Mackinac area. DuSable spent most of his time hunting and fishing. Even though his holdings brought the then-unheard-of sum of $1,200, DuSable died a pauper in 1818, apparently forsaken by his relatives. Still, his life and perseverance stand as a symbol of African American ingenuity and self-reliance.

This is the view of what DuSable may have seen when he decided to settle in Chicago. DuSable realized that the waterway he settled on would be a strategic location from which to capitalize on trade throughout the surrounding areas. He was Chicago's first businessman, and Chicago has since become the black business capital of America.

PHILLIS WHEATLEY

STOLEN FROM A SENEGAL village, Phillis Wheatley is the mother of the African American literary tradition. The first black to publish a book and only the second woman in the United States to publish a book of poetry, she became an icon to those trying to prove that blacks and whites are intellectual equals.

Wheatley is believed to have been brought from West Africa on a ship called the *Phillis,* which landed in Boston in 1761, when she was seven or eight years old. A wealthy merchant's wife bought her, taught her English, and gave her a classical education. She was a child prodigy and was fluent in English within 16 months.

Wheatley's poem "On Being Brought from Africa to America" was part of a series of works published in her 1773 book, *Poems on Various Subjects, Religious and Moral.*

> *Twas mercy brought me from my*
> *Pagan land,*
> *Taught my benighted soul to*
> *understand*
> *That there's a God, that there's a*
> *Savior too:*
> *Once I redemption neither fought*
> *nor knew.*
> *Some view our fable race with*
> *scornful eye,*
> *"their colour is a diabolic die."*
> *Remember Christians, Negros*
> *black as Cain,*
> *May be refin'd and join th' angelic*
> *train.*

Except for a single poem published in 1760 by Jupiter Hammon, another slave, Wheatley's book was the first published by an African American. She wrote her poems, mostly elegies and honorific verse, to commemorate friends,

Wheatley arrived in America in 1761 and quickly became fluent in English. In fact, she had mastered the language so well that she produced a book of poetry, which was published in England in 1773. Boston publishers refused to print it.

famous contemporaries, and important events. She wrote her poetry in a style and with references that reflected her African heritage.

Wheatley published her first poem in 1770. Her writings set off a storm of criticism from those who couldn't believe a black woman was capable of creative thought and from those who saw her as a black genius and proof that African Americans were capable of reflection and were not intellectually inferior.

Before *Poems on Various Subjects* was published, the fact that Wheatley had written it was considered so extraordinary that 18 of Boston's movers and shakers questioned her to find out if she had written the poems. When *Poems* was published in 1773, it began with a signed "Attestation" by these men, including John

Hancock and Massachusetts governor Thomas Hutchinson, asserting that a slave woman had written it. Her work was published in England with help from Wheatley's patrons, the Countess of Huntington and the Earl of Dartmouth, after publishers in Boston refused to publish it.

On doctors' advice, she sailed to England in 1773 with her mistress's son when her book was to be published. Wheatley was so well received that her owners were shamed into granting her freedom. In 1774, Wheatley tried to publish another book of poetry in America. She failed despite public acclaim.

Wheatley married a free black man, John Peters, in 1778. During the upheaval that followed Boston's fall to the British, Wheatley lived in poverty with her husband and three children, two of whom died. Wheatley died at age 31, trying to support her remaining child.

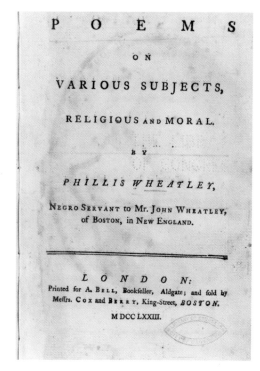

Wheatley had her first poem published in 1770 in a Rhode Island newspaper. In 1775, she wrote a poem honoring George Washington, prompting him to invite her to visit him.

BENJAMIN BANNEKER

Banneker was mostly self-taught. He studied the workings of clocks so he could construct one himself. His clock struck the hour every hour for over 50 years.

BENJAMIN BANNEKER was a walking refutation of the theory of his day that blacks were inferior to whites. Considered the first black American man of science, Banneker was a math wizard, astronomer, and inventor.

Banneker was born a freeman outside Baltimore on November 9, 1731. His grandmother had been a white dairymaid who came from England as an indentured servant. His grandfather, a prince when taken from Africa, had been her slave. They married.

His grandmother, Molly, began a small farm after fulfilling her service. His father, a freed slave from Guinea who married Molly's daughter, Mary, expanded the farm. Banneker was raised on the farm, and he spent most of his life there, pursuing his scientific studies.

When he was young, his grandmother and mother taught him to read the Bible, primarily so he could read it to them as they relaxed in the evening. Later, he bought what few books he could afford and borrowed others. He taught himself literature, history, and math.

In his twenties, Banneker built a clock, a testament to his mathematical wizardry. He had never seen a wooden, striking clock before, but he had seen a pocket watch. Banneker used math ratios to determine the relationship of the gears and wheels, which he carved from wood with a pocketknife. The clock only stopped running when Banneker's house caught fire and the clock burned, 50 years later.

Banneker took over the family farm. He kept a large vegetable garden for his personal use, and he tended beehives for honey. He also learned to play the flute and violin. After his parents' deaths, Banneker sold portions of the farm for money to allow him to continue his studies.

In his forties, after reading math books lent to him by neighbors, Banneker could solve any problem submitted to him. He also wrote a treatise on bees, conducted a mathematical study on the cycle of the 17-year locust, and correctly predicted a solar eclipse in 1789.

Banneker had befriended the Ellicotts, a Quaker family of surveyors and industrialists. They lent him books on astronomy and instruments to work out calculations. After they saw his abilities, they enlisted Banneker's help.

In 1790, President George Washington hired the Ellicotts to survey a 10-square-mile area that would become Washington, D.C. Banneker helped them mark base points using calculations and astronomical instruments. Banneker was the first black federal employee.

When Banneker returned to his farm, he was even more interested in astronomy. For the next ten years, Banneker made accurate studies of the stars. He published his results in his popular almanacs. More than 29 editions of the almanacs were issued. In them, he was the first to propose the establishment of a department of peace to replace the Department of War.

Thomas Jefferson was a fan of Banneker's almanacs. Jefferson sent almanacs overseas to scientists and leaders, who learned of, studied, and praised Banneker's work.

In the latter part of his life, Banneker lived alone on his farm. He often entertained friends and visitors who were aware of his great repute. Banneker also became involved with the abolitionist movement, especially after the invention of the cotton gin entrenched the institution of slavery in the South in 1793.

Banneker died quietly at his home on October 9, 1806. He was 74 years old.

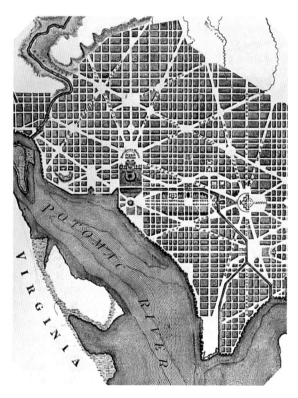

This is an early map of Washington, D.C., which Banneker helped the Ellicotts survey.

RICHARD ALLEN

RICHARD ALLEN was a slave who had a religious conversion experience at the age of 17 that led him to pursue the ministry as his life's work. In so doing, he became the first African American licensed to preach, in 1782, and the first ordained as a deacon, in 1799. He also founded an independent church denomination.

During the War of 1812, Allen, along with Absalom Jones and James Forten, enlisted about 2,500 African Americans to help build Philadelphia's defenses.

Allen was born on February 14, 1760, in Philadelphia, where his family was owned by Quaker lawyer Benjamin Chew. He was by all accounts a kindly master, but when Chew's law practice failed, he sold the Allen family to a Dover, Delaware, plantation owner.

Methodist preachers were active in the area. Allen heard the teachings, and in 1777 he converted. With his master's permission, he joined the Methodist Society, taught himself to read

and write, and soon began leading the meetings. In 1781, Allen's master allowed him to purchase his freedom, and he returned to Philadelphia.

During the Revolutionary War, Allen used his job as wagon driver to preach at regular stops. In 1786, he joined the mostly white St. George's Methodist Episcopal Church in Philadelphia, where he was allowed to hold separate prayer meetings for blacks.

But one Sunday morning, Allen and some black friends were met at the church door and directed to the upstairs gallery. When they entered the main floor anyway, they were not allowed to kneel in prayer. Allen and his group walked out. Such difficulties were becoming a growing problem for black Methodist worshipers everywhere.

The next year, Allen and Absalom Jones organized the independent Free African Society, a beneficial and mutual aid organization. By 1794, the Society had saved enough money to build the Bethel Church, which Allen established as an independent African Methodist Episcopal (AME) congregation.

However, a legal struggle ensued between the church members and the Methodist Society over control of Bethel Church. But, in 1816, the Pennsylvania Supreme Court ruled that Bethel could become independent of the Methodist Society.

Along with other AME congregations that had sprung up in Baltimore, Wilmington, and elsewhere, Bethel's congregation established the African Methodist Episcopal Church as an independent denomination in April 1816. The newly formed denomination consecrated Allen as its first bishop.

Afterward, Allen opened day schools for black students, supported moderate antislavery activities, and encouraged moral reform. He used the basement of Bethel Church to give safe haven to fugitives as they traveled the Underground Railroad. Allen also led the call for the first national black convention to protest the assault on free blacks launched by the American Colonization Society.

Allen and his wife, Sara, were entombed long after their deaths in that same church basement in 1901. In 1876, a monument to Allen was erected in Philadelphia's Fairmont Park—it is thought to be the first statue erected for a black man by other black Americans.

Allen worked as a master shoemaker in order to save enough money to buy a lot on which to build Bethel Church, later renamed Mother Bethel African Methodist Episcopal Church, shown here.

JOHN RUSSWURM

John Russwurm was not only a pioneer of the black press in America, but he also helped settle the African nation of Liberia, founded partially by repatriated African Americans.

THE PREMIER EDITION of the first black newspaper, *Freedom's Journal,* under the editorship of writer John Brown Russwurm and minister Samuel E. Cornish, hit the streets of New York City on March 16, 1827. Russwurm and Cornish became the fathers of the black press and among the first champions of a free press, which, at that time, was a constitutional guarantee only for whites.

"It is our earnest wish," they said in their first issue, "to make our *Freedom Journal* a medium of intercourse between our brethren in the different states of this great confederacy; that through its columns an expression of our sentiments, on many interesting subjects which concern us, may be offered to the public; that plans which are apparently beneficial may be candidly discussed and properly weighed. We wish to plead our cause. Too long have others spoken for us!"

Their controversial column took issue with the ambivalence of white liberals who said one thing and did another. It was because of the disenchantment Russwurm noticed in liberals and conservatives alike that he decided to pack his bags and go to Africa, from where his West Indian mother's family had been kidnapped.

Russwurm, who was also one of this country's first black college graduates—he graduated from Bowdoin College in 1826—gave up his editorship and moved to Liberia. While living there, he edited the *Liberia Herald* and served as governor of the colony of Maryland, according to historian Lerone Bennett, Jr. Russwurm also worked for some time as the first superintendent for the colony's schools.

Russwurm moved to Liberia under the auspices of the American Colonization Society, a proslavery organization. Later, Russwurm and others distanced themselves from it, especially when abolitionists of both races were calling him a "black traitor." Russwurm's critics contended that a mass exodus from America would strengthen the bonds of slavery by depriving American slaves of support.

Disenchanted with the white male privilege in America, he said: "We consider it a waste of words to talk of ever enjoying citizenship in this country." Referring to Liberia, which he helped settle, Russwurm proudly said: "This is our home and this is our country. Beneath its sod lie the bones of our fathers; for it some of them fought, bled, and died. Here we were born; and here we will die."

Like fellow back-to-Africa enthusiasts Paul Cuffee and Martin R. Delaney, Russwurm was an intellectual and an entrepreneur. He sought to use his resources and talents to better the lot of the millions of American blacks who

suffered under slavery. Russwurm and his colleagues were also heavily influenced by the example of Touissant L'Ouverture and the Haitian revolutionaries. The equal rights philosophy, and the prudence, thrift, and sobriety maxims of Benjamin Franklin also guided their actions. But most importantly, Russwurm's legacy lives on with the black press and the role the press has played historically as a champion of black advancement and a forum for black public opinion.

The National Newspaper Publisher's Association (NNPA), a black newspaper syndicate reaching 10 million African American readers, gives the John Russwurm Trophy and Merit Award every year. The award and trophy go to a newspaper that "represents excellence in journalism," according to Bill Reed, managing director of the Washington-based NNPA.

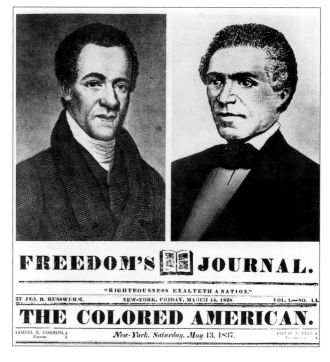

Russwurm cofounded the United States's first black newspaper, Freedom's Journal, *along with minister Samuel E. Cornish (left). Cornish also edited* The Colored American, *circa 1837.*

JAMES P. BECKWOURTH

JAMES P. BECKWOURTH was a tireless pioneer who helped tame the Wild West—one of the many frontiersmen who battled an unfriendly land. The curmudgeonly but talkative man led several expeditions, including one that opened up a barren patch of land in the Sierra Nevada mountains. Beckwourth epitomizes the myth of an American hero.

Born in Fredericksburg, Virginia, the son of a white Revolutionary War veteran and an African American mother with Native American blood, Beckwourth was the third of 13 children. As a child, he lived on the banks of the Missouri River. Beckwourth endured only four years of education before running away to New Orleans. Chafing under the strictures of the South, in 1823 he became a scout for the Rocky Mountain Fur Company.

An explorer, trader, and scout, James P. Beckwourth was a mountain man in the legendary tradition of pioneers who conquered the West. He discovered a pass between California and Reno, Nevada, that became part of a major emigrant route.

From there, the hardy man known for his strong legs and his ability to travel quickly became almost a legend, working for the next 13 years as a miner, guide, trapper, army scout, soldier, and hunter. Beckwourth was accepted as an equal by Native American nations, including the Blackfoot and Crow, who respected his wilderness skills. By 1842, he sided with Native

Rather than live the urban life on the East Coast, James Beckwourth, born in 1798, in Virginia, opted to travel ever westward, conquering the new frontiers of America.

Americans during the Second Seminole War and was on the side of other Native Americans in battles to preserve their lands, which they ultimately lost.

Beckwourth was also an entrepreneur, building and operating three trading posts in the headwaters of the Arkansas and South Platte rivers. By 1840, he had established trading posts, first in what is now Taos, New Mexico, and later in present-day Los Angeles. But he was caught up in the battle for western land, fighting in the California revolution against Mexico and in the war with Mexico, where he served as guide and dispatch carrier.

After the wars ended, Beckwourth made his final trip to California. It was in 1848 that Beckwourth made a historic discovery while working as chief scout for the exploring expedition of General Charles Frémont. The canny frontiersman found a pass winding through the Sierra Nevada mountains that led to the Sacramento Valley. The route, named Beckwourth Pass, later became a popular way to emigrate to California.

In 1866, the U.S. government needed a liaison with the Crow, and Beckwourth was the logical choice. Beckwourth had married into several nations, including the Crow. Some accounts say Beckwourth's devotion to his Native American friends led to his murder by those who were once enamored of his courage and strength. Reportedly, the Crow wanted Beckwourth to stay with them and restore them to their preeminence among the Native Americans. When he refused, it is said that they poisoned Beckwourth in 1886, even as they honored him with a grandiose farewell feast usually reserved for great chiefs.

Green River, Utah, was where Beckwourth hunted while he was a trapper. As "beaver waters" go, the Green River was very lucrative.

NAT TURNER

NAT TURNER was either a hero or a madman. In 1831, Turner led a violent insurrection against whites in Southampton County, Virginia. Its repercussions spurred major debates over slavery that eventually ignited the Civil War.

Nat Turner said he felt the pain and horror of slaves like him who had been kidnapped, raped, abused, and tortured. So he set out with his band of insurgents and killed at least 55 whites. That insurrection stirred slave owners to increase atrocities on hundreds of blacks who remained in bondage in order to teach any would-be "Nat Turners" a lesson.

To some, Turner avenged the holocaust committed on his fellow blacks by whites who were profiting from human flesh. To others, Turner was a demented madman who left a trail of terror lined with the slaughtered bodies of whites during his rebellion in 1831.

Turner, born a slave in Southampton County in 1800, actually escaped when he was 21. He returned to his master to fulfill his religious destiny. Turner came to the view early in his life that God chose him for a purpose. He believed that purpose was to lead an uprising against slavery. He kept to himself, fasted, prayed, and avoided tobacco, liquor, and money.

By the time he reached maturity, his religious dedication was known and respected among slaves. Turner saw visions and heard voices. One such vision showed black and white spirits fighting until the sun darkened and streams ran with blood. There was a solar eclipse that day in 1825, but Turner believed it was a sign.

The final sign happened on August 13, 1831, when atmospheric disturbances caused the sun to look bluish-green and a black spot to appear

Some people, who knew that without a war slaveholders would not be separated from their human property and the comfortable existence it brought, celebrated the violent actions of Nat Turner and his rebels. He became a much-touted martyr for the abolition of slavery.

on it. Turner met his disciples in the woods near his slave master's farm. Before dawn on the morning of August 22, 1831, they attacked Turner's slave owner, named Joseph Travis, hacking him and his family of five to death.

For the next few days, the group, originally consisting of seven slave rebels, rampaged the countryside. They went from house to house, village to village, gathering more slave warriors on the way as they liberated several zones in Southampton County. They sent slave owners and their families to hell, while gleefully singing the praises of bloody insurrection.

News spread quickly throughout the state of Virginia and surrounding areas. Soon, some 3,000 armed whites, including soldiers from as far away as North Carolina, converged in Southampton, adding to the atrocities by slaying innocent blacks at will.

Apparently the goal was not merely to put down the insurrection but to terrorize the slave population so they would never again raise axes against their white masters. Turner was finally caught on October 30. On November 11, this bold man, who some considered a prophet, dangled from a tree as if he were a strange fruit.

The voice of abolition strengthened in the wake of the Turner revolt. Abolitionists organized the New England Anti-Slavery Society the following year. William Lloyd Garrison's *The Liberator* newspaper gave voice to the abolition movement.

Meanwhile, the well-established fears of many white Americans, particularly slave-owning aristocrats, rose to irrational heights. Blacks congregating to practice religion or to socialize, blacks possessing arms for hunting, and blacks acquiring an education now seemed much more threatening.

At least 12 states instituted stricter laws governing almost every aspect of the lives of blacks, whether free or enslaved. The punishments associated with those laws were savage and sometimes fatal. Some states additionally barred free blacks from their borders and gave black residents a short time to get out of the jurisdiction, while other states charged free African Americans a fee to enter. Many slave owners actively sponsored the return of free blacks to Africa. No state north, south, or west was immune from those fears.

Turner's death was a turning point in America. Slavery debates raged from that time until the bitter Civil War, which tore the nation in two and finally led to the abolition of the inhuman practice of owning human beings.

FREDERICK DOUGLASS

After some early lessons in reading from the plantation owner's wife, Douglass taught himself how to read and write by using any piece of paper with writing on it to practice. In fact, he took his last name from a character in the novel Marmion *by Sir Walter Scott.*

THE FIGHT AGAINST SLAVERY is best exemplified by the words and deeds of one man—Frederick Douglass. In the years that spanned the abolitionist movement, the Civil War, Reconstruction, and the post-Reconstruction period, Douglass championed the cause of all oppressed people. The granite Douglass's preeminence as race leader was to persist until his death in 1895. That was the very year Booker T. Washington was thrust into the role of the nation's most famous Negro by his celebrated Atlanta Compromise address, "signaling a strategic retreat with a changed national attitude," wrote Richard Bardolph in his 1959 *The Negro Vanguard.*

Douglass was born in one of the darkest periods of slavery on a plantation owned by Colonel Lloyd of Talbot County, Maryland, the white man who raped Douglass's mother. When Douglass was an infant, he was taken from his mother and placed in his grandmother's care. According to Douglass, hunger was his constant companion. "He used to run races against the cat and the dog to reach the bones that were tossed out of the window, or to snap up the crumbs that fell under the table," said his biographer, J. A. Rogers, in 1947's *World's Great Men of Color.* Douglass would later be beaten for sneaking away to get meat.

At age eight, two years after his mother died at a neighboring estate, young Douglass was sent to live with the Auld family, where his life's ambition to learn how to read was fulfilled. Not knowing it was against the law, Mrs. Auld gave him reading lessons. Her husband scolded her when he found out, causing her to stop her literacy crusade. Douglass continued his lessons on his own, grabbing scraps of newspapers, banknotes, or any piece of paper with writing on it to teach himself.

After a life-altering physical confrontation with a "slave breaker," 21-year-old Douglass plotted his 1838 escape. He somehow acquired a sailor's uniform and a passport, climbed on a ship, and sailed away. He arrived in New York the next day and found work shoveling coal. He took on the last name of Douglass, after the hero in Sir Walter Scott's *Marmion.* He married

At age 21, after many beatings for trying to organize slave revolts, Douglass escaped from slavery. He found sailor clothes, climbed onboard a ship, and sailed away from the South.

a freed woman, Anna Murray, and increased his desire to help those still in bondage by reading *The Liberator,* published by the famous abolitionist William Lloyd Garrison. Three years later, he found himself in front of a crowd speaking forcefully against slavery at an antislavery meeting in Nantucket. He had the uncanny ability to transport his audiences to Slave Row. Historian Lerone Bennett, Jr., said, "He could make people *laugh* at a slave owner preaching the duties of Christian obedience; could make them *see* the humiliation of a Black maiden ravished by a brutal slave owner; could make them *hear* the sobs of a mother separated from her child. Through him, people could cry, curse and *feel;* through him they could *live* slavery."

FREDERICK DOUGLASS

Militant abolitionist Frederick Douglass was the most famous of all antislavery orators and the most effective. He challenged liberals and conservatives to accept the rights of blacks to defend themselves with or without anyone else's help.

In 1845, he published his first autobiography, *Narratives of the Life of Frederick Douglass, An American Slave,* which put slavers on his track after the book had huge sales and subsequent controversy.

Douglass prepared to flee to England. On his getaway boat, he made a speech so fiery that Southerners nearly killed him by throwing him overboard. His life was saved by crew members. This event garnered huge publicity in England. Lords, ladies, and earls welcomed him to their suburban estates.

The now famous baritone orator, with his impressive mane of hair, addressed the Parliament. After 19 months in Great Britain, English friends gave him $2,175, and he used $750 to buy his freedom.

His liberty now purchased, Douglass went to Rochester, New York, and started his anti-slavery paper, *The North Star,* later renamed *Frederick Douglass' Paper.* He wrote his second autobiography, *My Bondage and My Freedom,* in 1855. He returned to this form 26 years later and wrote *The Life and Times of Frederick Douglass.*

The most important aspect of his writing is that it crystallized the abolition movement and

HENRY HIGHLAND GARNET

Prior to the appearance of Frederick Douglass, Henry Highland Garnet was the foremost black abolitionist. These great men were not friends, but they both worked for the dissolution of an American system that treated human beings as livestock.

Although Douglass and Garnet agreed on the need for African Americans to breathe freely, they did not always agree on how that should be accomplished. In particular, they disagreed on the concept of overthrowing slavery with violence and on the issue of permanent emigration from the United States.

Of the two, Garnet maintained the most radical views, but he knew militancy was not enough. He promoted the doctrine of the Free Produce Movement, a blueprint for boycotting goods produced by slave labor, and he worked to develop a viable economic system in independent black communities and nations.

One year after the harsh Dred Scott decision, Garnet and Martin R. Delaney founded the African Civilization Society to promote black emigration from America to freer destinations. They preferred the newly independent African state of Liberia.

During the postbellum era, Garnet continued to lobby for land reform, women's rights, and world peace. An erudite Presbyterian minister and world traveler, he became the first black man to preach to the U.S. House of Representatives in the Capitol rotunda, which he did immediately following the passage of the Thirteenth Amendment that officially ended slavery. He later dispensed aid and relief from the Freedman's Bureau to help African Americans build better lives.

In 1881, Garnet was given the diplomatic post of U.S. consul-general and minister to his beloved Liberia, where he died the following year and was buried.

mobilized both blacks and whites to fight slavery. A secondary result of these stellar works was the stimulation of black scholarship; they created an audience for slave narratives and black literary and historical works.

In his words and deeds, Douglass challenged liberals, who felt he should merely "stick to the facts" in his oratory and "leave the philosophy to them." He challenged conservatives who thought they were empowered by God to enslave black people. And he fought both whites and blacks who thought his terse verse did not fit into the commonly held notions of what a black man should be and say.

Douglass challenged himself and his people. In the process, he emerged as the African American community's first national spokesperson. He taught everyone that freedom is never free—that it is born of and born in "earnest struggle."

WILLIAM WELLS BROWN

WILLIAM WELLS BROWN was a light-skinned man who apparently could have passed for white. He chose not to in order to fight the institution of slavery. Brown had been a slave for almost 20 years before escaping to freedom and becoming an impassioned abolitionist and precedent-setting author.

Brown wrote the first black novel, play, travel litany, and military study of black America. In his written work, he was detached, calm, and objective. His autobiography, *Narrative of William W. Brown, a Fugitive Slave,* was published in 1847. It reportedly sold more than 10,000 copies in only two years.

He was born simply as William in 1815, in Lexington, Kentucky. His father, according to his mulatto mother, was the cousin of their slave owner, physician John Young, who was a distant relative of Daniel Boone. In 1816, Young moved to Missouri, and William spent his next 19 years working the gamut of slave jobs while being hired out to more than 10 different owners. He escaped in January 1834.

William made his escape over eight harrowing days before he was befriended by Quaker Wells Brown, who housed the youth for two weeks while he recuperated from his journey. Grateful for Brown's assistance, William adopted his name. He then departed, settling in Cleveland. He stayed there for two years, where he married and began raising a family. He then moved to Buffalo, New York.

As a steamboat worker, Brown safeguarded and spirited scores of slaves to freedom in Canada by way of the Underground Railroad. In just seven months in 1842, he safely shepherded 69 passengers along the route. An intelligent man with an engaging sense of humor, Brown became a lecturer dedicated to speaking

Brown was remarkable because he went from slave to boat steward, speaker, novelist, historian, doctor, reformer, and sociologist, even though he wasn't able to read or write until he was in his twenties. Though he escaped from slavery, Brown was never able to settle down, moving from one cause and adventure to another until he died.

against slavery. He taught himself to read and write, and he pursued studies in English, math, history, and literature.

In 1843, Brown became a full-time antislavery lecturer. He worked closely with abolitionists Wendell Phillips and William Lloyd Garrison. Brown soon gained national renown. In 1849, he was sent to represent the American Peace Society at a Paris conference, which led to a tour to win British support against slavery.

While Brown was abroad, America passed the Fugitive Slave Act of 1850. This meant that he could be returned to slavery upon coming back to America. Brown remained in England until 1854. He wrote and lectured until friends there raised enough money to purchase his freedom.

During this period, Brown reportedly addressed more than 1,000 meetings and learned French,

German, and Latin. He wrote a book, *Three Years in Europe; Or, Places I Have Seen and People I Have Met* (1852), making him the first black American travel writer.

In 1853 he wrote *Clotel; Or, The President's Daughter: A Narrative of Slave Life in the United States.* Though published in England, it is the first novel written by a black American. *Clotel* focused on the sexual exploitation of female slaves. While fictional, it was no doubt based on the experiences of his mother. The president in question in the book was Thomas Jefferson, who allegedly had a number of children by his black slave Sally Hemings. Well-received in Europe, *Clotel* caused so much furor in America that it wasn't published in its original form until 1969. It was, however, revised and republished under different titles for 14 years after Brown returned to America.

Brown sensed that the country was moving toward war, and he endorsed slave uprisings. In 1858, he wrote the first play published by an African American, called *The Escape; Or, a Leap for Freedom.*

After the Civil War, Brown devoted himself to medicine, which he had learned from his former master, and he continued writing. He wrote *The Black Man: His Antecedents, His Genius, and His Achievements* in 1863 and *The Negro in the American Rebellion: His Heroism and His Fidelity* in 1867.

Brown's last book was *My Southern Home: Or, The South and Its People,* written in 1880, which was about the devastating conditions under which African Americans found themselves. It was also a prelude to W.E.B. Du Bois's legendary work *The Souls of Black Folk.*

Brown died in Boston on November 6, 1884.

Delaney, the first African American field major in the United States Army, felt that blacks should return to Africa and create their own state.

MARTIN ROBINSON DELANY spent his life championing the cause of African American empowerment, freedom, and self-elevation. Delany was an editor, an author, a doctor, a colonizationist, and the father of 19th-century black nationalism. He attempted to create a self-governing African American state in Africa, believing that emigration was the only way to protect blacks from racism.

Delany was born May 6, 1812, in Charles Town, Jefferson County (present-day West Virginia), the son of a slave and a free black woman. Early on, his grandmother regaled the young Delany with grand tales of his homeland and his regal forefathers from the Mandingo and Golah tribes. Delany and his four siblings learned to read, possibly from a Yankee peddler, causing such consternation among their white neighbors that the family fled to Pennsylvania.

At 19, Delany moved to Pittsburgh, studying medicine briefly and getting involved with the Anti-Slavery Society and the Underground Railroad. He married Catherine Richards, and they named their seven children after prominent African Americans. Delany was an advocate for black self-reliance through education, labor, and property ownership, but he needed a venue to promote his views among the people. He published a weekly called *Mystery.* In 1847, he and black abolitionist Frederick Douglass coedited *The North Star* in Rochester, New York.

Douglass once said of Delany, "I thank God for making me a man simply, but Delany always thanks Him for making him a black man."

In 1850, Delany was accepted to Harvard Medical School, but he left after just one term when white students protested his admission. Despite limited training, he returned to Pittsburgh a practicing physician, where he helped the city through a deadly cholera epidemic in 1854.

The enactment of the Fugitive Slave Act, which Delany saw as a threat to the security of African Americans across the country, made him decide that perhaps blacks would be safest elsewhere. Delany then published *The Condition, Elevation, Emigration, and Destiny of the Colored People of the United States, Politically Considered* (1852), which listed black achievements. It also attacked abolitionists for not fighting harder for the rights of blacks. In addition, it advocated emigration as a solution to discrimination. He continued fighting for a black independent nation for the rest of his life.

Delany moved to Canada, then, in 1859, he led an investigation into the Niger River Valley in West Africa as a place for a possible black settlement. He successfully negotiated an agreement with Alake of Abeokuta, in present-day Nigeria, permitting a settlement there. But the Civil War disrupted his plans to emigrate to the "motherland."

Two years after the Emancipation Proclamation, Delaney spoke to President Lincoln about forming black regiments behind enemy lines. Lincoln made Delany the first African American army major. Delany recruited ex-slaves for regiments in South Carolina. Following the war, while still advocating emigration, he tried to help emancipated slaves begin their new lives with just treatment through Reconstruction programs.

This anonymous painting of Delaney being "promoted on the battlefield for bravery," hangs in the National Portrait Gallery of the Smithsonian Institution.

Perhaps due to the demise of black hopes after Reconstruction faded into a tapestry of appalling atrocities against African Americans, Delany got involved in one last failed attempt to return to Africa, purchasing a Danish ship, the *Horsa.* Unable to realize his dream of a free black American state in Africa, Delany died in 1885, in Ohio, still advocating pride of self and of race.

SOJOURNER TRUTH

At the end of Sojourner Truth's long struggle for social change, the American reformist was given medical attention in Battle Creek, Michigan, by Dr. Harvey Kellogg, who founded the company that makes breakfast cereals.

WEARING HER TRADEMARK turban and sunbonnet, ex-slave Sojourner Truth crossed the country for 40 years, drawing on her experiences and deep faith to preach against the cruelties of slavery and to support human rights for African Americans and women.

She will best be remembered as an abolitionist, suffragist, and feminist. For more than 40 years, Sojourner Truth was also a preacher and a teacher. The great and the near-great sang her praises and quoted her strong and striking utterances.

Truth believed it was her Christian duty to further the cause of black people. That sense of mission won her an audience with President Abraham Lincoln. Ushered into Lincoln's presence on October 29, 1864, she showered him with unabashed praise. Truth assured him in her deep-toned voice that he was the greatest president this country ever had, a man to be likened unto Daniel, the biblical standard of courage and faithfulness.

Sojourner Truth and Harriet Tubman were twin mountain peaks in the tradition of black women. These deeply religious women practiced what they preached. They honored the human rights of black people, many of whom were held in the bonds of slavery.

Born Isabella Bomefree in Ulster County, New York, in 1797, Sojourner Truth had a succession of cruel slave masters. Her first master relegated her family to the cold wet cellar during Truth's early childhood. Much later, under the ownership of John I. Dumont, she met her husband, Thomas, and had five children, three of whom were sold away.

When Dumont reneged on a promise to free Truth in 1827, a year before New York's Gradual Emancipation Act became law, Truth escaped with her infant daughter, Sophia. She found shelter with Isaac Van Wagenen, who purchased her remaining time as a slave.

During a trip back to the Dumont home, Truth had a spiritual encounter with God. Around the same time, she learned one of her sons had been sold illegally into slavery in Alabama. Swinging into action, she persuaded Dutch, Quaker, and Methodist residents across the county she was born in to successfully help petition for her son's freedom.

Truth and her two children moved to New York City in 1829, where she found her brother and two sisters attending the same Methodist church she did. Truth was also involved in her employer's Perfectionist religion, for which her talents in preaching, praying, and singing were in great demand. Following an unpleasant separation from the Perfectionists, she took up residence in the Ossing, New York, commune for five years before returning to New York City.

Truth underwent a spiritual conversion after suffering the loss of her son Peter during his first voyage as a sailor. She walked away from urban life with 25 cents and a new name that reflected her destiny to spread God's truth.

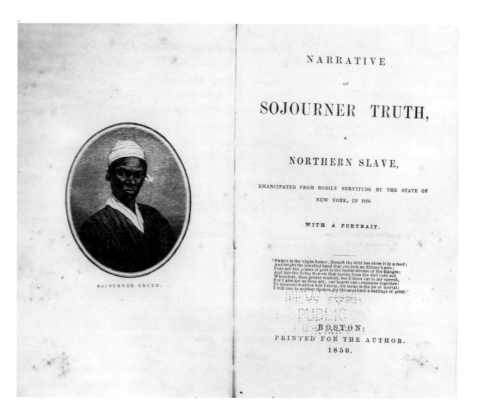

Truth's biography, Narrative of Sojourner Truth, *provided her with some income in her later years. The book was written by abolitionist Olive Gilbert, and Truth published it in 1850.*

SOJOURNER TRUTH

In 1843, an illness led her to the water-cure establishment of black abolitionist David Ruggles. Though Truth was illiterate, her forthright "turn of a phrase" so impressed the residents of Southampton, Massachusetts, that three years later she was a full-time member on the abolitionist lecture circuit, traveling with Frederick Douglass and William Lloyd Garrison, among others. Her popularity as an advocate of women's rights grew among feminists.

The six-foot spokeswoman worked tirelessly for emancipation, desegregation, and women's suffrage. To Truth, the race and gender movements were both of highest importance. With each speech, she broke societal conventions for women, fending off stones, beatings, and hecklers in the process.

Once, a proslavery heckler told her, "Old woman, why I don't care any more for your antislavery talk than I do a bite from a flea." Truth smiled and replied, "Perhaps not, but the good Lord willing, I'll keep you scratching."

She refused to let antagonists stop her. In doing so, Truth helped define womanhood in a way that embraced African American women's experiences as well as addressing issues of gender, race, and class. "Nobody ever helps me into carriages, or over mud puddles, or gives me any best place!" she declared at a women's rights convention in Akron, Ohio, in 1851. "Ain't I a woman?"

Lectures and the sale of her biography, *Narrative of Sojourner Truth,* provided a modest living. The book was written by abolitionist Olive Gilbert and was published by Truth in 1850.

Truth was a resident of Battle Creek, Michigan, by the time the Civil War was at hand. She initially recruited and supported soldiers in

MARY ANN SHADD CARY

Mary Ann Shadd Cary was one of the earliest advocates for women's rights. Though a fellow abolitionist and suffragette, she contrasted with Sojourner Truth in many ways. Cary was a well-educated lawyer and journalist—a highly articulate woman of means whose family had never spent a day in slavery. This grand lady, who was light in skin tone, rather slender, and tall, often carried her haughty beauty as a weapon—lashing into anyone who stood in the way of her belief in education and self-reliance for all.

Cary's activities paralleled many of Sojourner Truth's, such as her work with the Underground Railroad prior to the Civil War. Cary also felt compelled to contribute to the Civil War, which promised the end of slavery. She served as a recruiting officer. After slavery was abolished, Cary's struggle for civil rights continued, making her and Sojourner Truth the inspiration for many young women to pursue nontraditional careers.

In 1855, Negro Convention-goers in Philadelphia received first-hand experience of Cary's ire when the gender-biased among them tried to block her participation. She fought and prevailed in becoming the organization's first female member.

The *Provincial Freeman,* a weekly newspaper published by Cary and her brother, Isaac Shadd, was another weapon she used against social and economic oppression as well as the source for some of the most progressive views on the place of blacks and females. Its publication in 1853 made Cary the first black newspaperwoman.

Cary was an avid emigrationist, just not in the typical black nationalist style. From her home in Canada, she preached leaving the United

States permanently and taking up life as an equal but not segregating into black nations or black enclaves. Her lifelong activities on the Underground Railroad helped many African Americans find the path to freedom, and her education efforts allowed them to compete on the same footing with whites.

Cary had the strength of will to help John Brown write a new U.S. Constitution prior to his defeat at Harpers Ferry. When the Civil War was finally at hand, she felt compelled to participate, serving the duration of the conflict as a recruiting officer. Although they differed in style, Cary's and Truth's lives defied convention, demonstrating that a woman's place was anywhere she could make a contribution to social justice.

Michigan's black regiment. Later she intensified her contribution in the nation's capital and in Virginia. She alternately nursed injured soldiers and freed slaves at Freedmen's Hospital. Under other relief programs, she counseled freed women and established an employment service for free persons willing to relocate.

She even found time to desegregate trolley cars. First she asked the president of the street railroad to eliminate the "Jim Crow" car. When she sued a belligerent conductor, resulting in his arrest for assault and the loss of his job, the

rest of the D.C. trolley staff practically invited blacks into their cars.

Following the war, she encouraged former slaves to move West and often preached to these newcomers throughout Kansas and Missouri. Although no action was taken, she petitioned Congress for land allocations in the West.

Truth remained an outspoken advocate for social reform and temperance until she died on November 26, 1883, at the age of 86.

HARRIET TUBMAN

UNQUESTIONABLY THE BEST known conductor on the Underground Railroad, Harriet Tubman led a life dedicated to freedom. With stops in the South, the Underground Railroad operated primarily in New England and the Ohio Western Reserve, where secrecy in helping runaway slaves was essential in the pre–Civil War era.

Tubman was also the first, and possibly the last, woman to lead U.S. Army troops into battle. Working in South Carolina and other states, Tubman organized slave intelligence networks behind enemy lines and led scouting raids.

A graphic account of the battle she led appeared in the *Boston Commonwealth* on July 10, 1863. In glowing language, the article noted how Colonel Montgomery and his gallant band of 150 black soldiers, under Tubman's guidance, dashed into enemy country. They destroyed millions of dollars' worth of commissary stores, cotton, and lordly dwellings, "and struck terror into the heart of rebeldom, brought off near 800 slaves and thousands of dollars worth of property, without losing a man or receiving a scratch."

Despite working for four years off and on in the service of the Union Army as a nurse, spy, and scout, Tubman was never duly rewarded after the war. Yet she was never bitter. She was truly a humanitarian. A big-souled, God-intoxicated, heroic black woman, Tubman's mission was to save others. That mission guided her to freedom and back into slave states, where she brilliantly planned and executed escapes for approximately 300 slaves.

At great personal risk, Tubman led many to freedom with an operation that she funded primarily by her work as a domestic. In doing so, Tubman inspired peers and future genera-

tions of African American women to continue the long-standing tradition of self-help and self-improvement prevalent in the black community.

Dark-complexioned and short, Tubman had a full, broad face, and she often wore a colorful bonnet. She developed extraordinary physical endurance and muscular strength as well as mental fortitude. She was unpretentious, practical, shrewd, and visionary. A deeply religious woman with a driven sense of purpose, she credited the Almighty and not herself for guiding her during dangerous journeys. She also had a superstitious side, believing deeply in dreams and omens that seemed to put a protective umbrella over her perilous exploits.

She was born on a slave-breeding plantation in Maryland, around 1821, one of 11 children of Harriet and Benjamin Ross. Originally named Araminta, she was renamed Harriet by her mother. In an attempt to stop a nearby runaway slave, Tubman's master threw a two-pound weight on her head as a child. The weight crushed her skull and caused her sleeping fits and headaches that plagued her all her life. After the master died, it was rumored that the slaves were to be sent to the Deep South.

Fearing the often deadly consequences of such a move south, Tubman and two of her brothers decided to escape. Fearful of what would happen if they were apprehended, her brothers turned back, but Harriet kept walking to freedom. She later returned to get three of her brothers and returned again for her mother and father. Infuriated slave masters offered a $40,000 reward for her capture, dead or alive.

Tubman once said, "There was one or two things I had right to, liberty or death; if I could not have one, I would have the other; for no

man should take me alive; I should fight for my liberty as long as my strength lasted, and when the time come for me to go, the Lord would let them take me."

For her heroic work, Tubman received many honors, including a medal from Queen Victoria of England. When she received a $20 monthly pension for her nursing services during the Civil War, she used the money to help needy, elderly freed men and women.

Tubman died in Auburn, New York, on March 10, 1913. After her death, a campaign was launched to collect funds for a monument in the town square. The monument stands in testimony to her indomitable will.

Shrewd and tough, both mentally and physically, Tubman is possibly the only woman to have led U.S. Army troops in battle, which she did in the Civil War with Union soldiers. In addition to her heroic work on the Underground Railroad, where she conducted slaves to freedom, Tubman also served the Union Army as a nurse, scout, and spy.

DRED SCOTT

DRED SCOTT, a short man scarcely five-feet tall, has cast a long shadow as the principal in a case that many historians believe was one of the most significant events in American legal history.

Most schoolchildren know him as a man who sued his master for his freedom and took his case all the way to the Supreme Court. In 1857, Judge Roger Brook Taney gave the majority decision that Scott's removal to a free state did not make him free; that the state of Missouri determined Scott's status, which ruled that he was not free; and that Scott was not a citizen of Missouri, so he could not sue in federal court against a citizen of another state. In essence, he ruled that constitutionally a black man had "no rights that a White man was bound to respect."

During the 1830s and 1840s, Sam (he was later renamed Dred) Scott accompanied his master, a surgeon in the U.S. Army, on many trips to military posts around the country. These trips included visits to the free state of Illinois and the territory of Wisconsin. In 1846, Scott sued his master for his freedom, asserting his trips in states carved out of the Northwest Ordinance, where slavery was expressly forbidden, made him free. A St. Louis paper described Scott as "illiterate but not ignorant" with "strong common sense."

Many northern states followed the English precedent in *Somerset* v. *Stewart,* that a slave became free after setting foot in a free jurisdiction. After many delays, trials, and retrials, Scott's case reached the Supreme Court in 1856.

The court responded with nine separate opinions, and Chief Justice Taney delivered the majority opinion. Taney's ruling was consistent with an earlier ruling he had handed down when he was Andrew Jackson's attorney general; it said that black sailors on English vessels could be imprisoned in America when their ships docked. In other words, even foreign blacks had no rights in this country.

The Supreme Court could have avoided the issue altogether, but for a variety of reasons the justices wanted to make a statement. The decision confirmed the North's worst fears; the ruling gave impetus to the new Republican Party.

The ruling was both complex and controversial in that it unfolded against the background of several ominous developments—all of which underlined how black people had lost ground in America. Dred Scott overruled the Missouri Compromise of 1850 on the grounds that Congress did not have the authority to limit the expansion of slavery; slavery was found to be legal in the territories until the citizens voted for or against it. It said that Africans and their descendants were ineligible for citizenship in the United States, as the framers of the Constitution had not viewed Africans as citizens and they had not become citizens since.

There soon followed a second "final" compromise, the Kansas–Nebraska Act, which opened northern territory to settlement by slaveholders unless its settlers adopted an approved state constitution that prohibited it. The net effect of all this was the de facto nationalization of the slave system. The Dred Scott decision was the first instance in which major federal law was declared unconstitutional, and it was a landmark in the growth of judicial power.

Civil rights attorney Standish Willis described the legal impact of the Dred Scott decision this way: "Justice Taney based his harsh conclusion upon the pro-slavery clauses of the United States Constitution. He argued that under the

Scott actually won an early trial under Judge Alexander Hamilton in 1850, which granted him freedom because he had been taken to free states and territories. But the Missouri Supreme Court overturned Hamilton's ruling two years later and remanded Scott and his family back into slavery.

Constitution slaves were property, and consequently, the Constitution permitted no distinction between types of property. In essence, slavery could not be abolished anywhere without first changing the U.S. Constitution."

Dred Scott fought his court battle for 12 years, until Taney's Supreme Court decision went against him. He was 51 when the litigation was started on his behalf and 63 when he lost the case. Scott died from tuberculosis 18 months later, on September 17, 1858.

For a few years before the Civil War, Dred Scott was the most famous black man in America. Not until the Thirteenth Amendment abolished slavery and the Fourteenth Amendment guaranteed black men the right to vote were the injustices of Dred Scott finally undone.

EDMONIA LEWIS

Edmonia Lewis first learned to create Native American artifacts and moccasins with her hands when she lived with her mother's people, the Chippewa. She transformed those skills into fame as a sculptor.

MUCH OF THE LIFE of Edmonia Lewis is draped in mystery and conjecture. What we do know is that Lewis is widely recognized as the first African American sculptor to study abroad and the first to gain international renown.

In 1871, Lewis was the first African American artist to have an exhibition in Rome, Italy. Her fame quickly spread, and her studio appeared in the well-established guidebooks of Rome. She sketched many tourists from America and elsewhere who ordered busts of family members or celebrities to decorate their homes.

This prolific artist was born in either Greenhigh, Ohio, in upstate New York, or in New Jersey around 1844. She and her older brother were the offspring of a Chippewa Indian mother and a black father. The children alternated between family life in town society and surviving close to nature in the idyllic freedom of their mother's people. This dual childhood continued even after their mother's death.

During stays with her Native American relatives, Lewis was called Wildfire and her brother was known as Sunrise. Lewis enjoyed fishing and romping in the great outdoors as well as creating moccasins and other artifacts.

Lewis's brother found success in the California gold rush. Wanting the best for his sister, he suggested she attend Oberlin College, the first institution of its kind in the United States to accept blacks and women. He provided the financial means for her to do so. There she studied Latin and Greek, along with painting and drawing, which aroused her interest in sculpting even though the school offered no courses on that art form.

Life at Oberlin proceeded well for Lewis until a rather bizarre incident during her senior year. Two of her girlfriends became ill after consuming hot drinks Lewis had prepared. Lewis was abducted and beaten by an irate mob. An acquittal vindicated her of the attempted murder charges, but the ordeal left her with an unshakable need for change.

A few months shy of graduation, she moved to Boston, where she studied with sculptor Edward Brackett. Lewis developed a group of politically active friends in addition to forging relationships with local artists. Patrons of the arts soon followed. Sales rose for her medallions and busts of celebrated abolitionists, including her friend William Lloyd Garrison. In particular, demand for copies of her bust of Robert Gould Shaw, the commander of the heroic black 54th Massachusetts Volunteer Regiment, helped finance her relocation to Rome in 1865 to study the neoclassical style.

Lewis settled easily into a studio in Rome. Her outgoing spirit attracted many friends, although some acquaintances found her peculiar style of dress, tomboy behavior, and other personal habits slightly eccentric.

In addition to commissioned busts, her inspiring sculptures reflecting black and Native American experiences became hot commodities in European social circles. Her "Forever Free" sculpture of a slave couple hearing of emancipation was one such major work. Her acclaim in America reached its zenith at the 1876 Philadelphia Centennial Exhibition, where her dramatic "Death of Cleopatra" was unveiled to the nation.

Lewis's celebrity waned as the popularity of neoclassical art faded in the 1880s. It is believed that she lived the rest of her days in Rome. After her death, which was perhaps around 1909, her artistic creations continued to be highly valued. Equally worthy of celebration is a life that defied the conventions of race, ethnicity, and gender in 19th-century America.

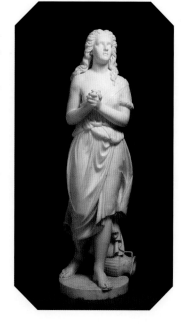

Edmonia Lewis's acclaim as a sculptor reached new international heights after she moved to Rome, Italy, to perfect her neoclassical technique. Pictured at right is her sculpture of the biblical figure Hagar.

The first Medal of Honor given to a Buffalo Soldier went to Sergeant Emanuel Stance, who saved two kidnapped white children. Twenty-one Buffalo Soldiers received such medals for heroism from 1870 through the Spanish-American War. With the help of retired general Colin Powell, a monument was erected in Fort Leavenworth, Kansas, to memorialize the deeds of all who served under the Soldiers' banner.

MMEDIATELY FOLLOWING the Civil War, the American West was a largely unmapped, undeveloped, and lawless territory. Too few U.S. marshals and military troops existed to stop the encroachment of the Mexicans from the south and to bring order to the lands west of the Missouri River. Amid political controversy, six African American volunteer regiments were established to patrol and develop the Great Plains.

The 9th and 10th calvary units, as well as four infantry units, the 38th through the 41st, set out to develop the West and protect newcomers from warring Native Americans, Mexican revolutionaries, and outlaws. Because of the hard work of these brave troops, later reduced to two infantry units, large tracts of unexplored land were mapped. Hundreds of miles of telegraph lines rose across the western horizon.

Railroad crews expanded tracks from coast to coast with black soldiers keeping guard against hostilities.

General Philip Sheridan recruited the first unit, the 9th Calvary, in 1866, mostly from Civil War veterans. Other regiments soon followed. Each man enlisted for five years and received $13 per month in addition to room, board, and clothing. Although supplies and equipment were often from the dredges of the military or, like their salaries, were frequent no-shows, the soldiers persevered. Prior to the 1890s, these soldiers comprised 20 percent of all U.S. calvary troops.

Living conditions for the troops were harsh. They had to grow some of their food, and their work rarely seemed to end. After-hours schooling and holidays on the Fourth of July and Christmas offered a change from their routine.

Furloughs in villages and towns were usually problematic. Black soldiers had just as much to fear, if not more, from the racist townsfolk they protected as from the Indians and lawless predators that they were sent to fight.

The soldiers helped the United States end the 300-year struggle against Apaches by pushing the Apache chieftain Victorio and his warriors into Mexico and by pursuing Geronimo, Mangus, and the Apache Kid. While patrolling the desolate plains for six-month periods, the soldiers managed to contain scattered groups of Cheyenne and other nations, preventing them from amassing into forces too overwhelming for U.S. troops to battle. The African Americans' fearlessness and bravery earned them the respect of their Native American combatants, who named them the Buffalo Soldiers because of their black, curly hair.

Due to military discrimination, Buffalo Soldiers were initially led by white officers. Second Lieutenant Henry Ossian Flipper, who was born a slave, was the first black officer to survive the hostilities of West Point and, after graduating in 1877, became the first black officer assigned to the Buffalo Soldiers. Major Charles Young later served gallantly with the 10th Calvary during the Pancho Villa expedition into Mexico.

Buffalo Soldiers once again proved their mettle while charging up San Juan Hill in Cuba in 1898. They also helped secure the Philippines from 1899 to 1902, but by the 20th century, black soldiers were given predominantly non-combatant jobs, such as moving supplies, tending horses, and erecting military camps. They had served their nation gallantly but were then pushed to the margins of military life.

When Colonel Young, the highest ranking African American in the armed forces, thought he would lead his calvary into World War I, he was dropped from active duty, presumably due to health reasons. Benjamin O. Davis, Sr., who joined the 9th Calvary in 1899, rose to brigadier general in 1940. Davis became the first African American to achieve that commission.

Despite the restrictions, the Buffalo Soldiers continued to serve their country until military units were desegregated by President Harry Truman during the Korean conflict.

HENRY MCNEAL TURNER

Henry McNeal Turner was an abolitionist minister, a chaplain to Negro troops during the Civil War, and one of the earliest African American elected officials during Reconstruction. Later, he became an AME bishop in Atlanta. He was one of the fathers of modern-day Pan-Africanism. His belief that ex-slaves should be paid for their labor is the foundation for the Black Reparations Movement.

THE BLACK CHURCH has always been and probably always will be the most autonomous institution within the African American community. Never was the influence of the black church so powerful as during the late days of slavery.

It is said that of all the groups and individuals working with the missionary movement to aid southern blacks, none were more important than the northern churches of free blacks. Not only did they collect money, clothes, and food, but they also sent social workers and teachers to their downtrodden brothers and sisters languishing under the harsh dictate of southern slavery.

One of the most famous leaders of the black clergy was the Reverend Henry McNeal Turner of Israel Church in Washington, D.C. He was born in Abbeville, South Carolina, in 1834. Like most militant black intellectuals at the time, Turner was educated in the North. He studied to be a minister.

Turner used his pulpit to urge his parishioners to join the Union Army. In 1863, shortly after Turner's historic report about the jubilant effect of President Lincoln's Emancipation Proclamation on blacks and whites, Lincoln made him chaplain of the black troops. President Andrew Johnson made him a chaplain in the regular army in 1865.

Following the end of the Civil War, Turner went to Georgia, working in the African Methodist Episcopal Church—a church founded by blacks who had been denied the right to worship in white churches.

After the passage of the Reconstruction Acts, Turner became a member of the Georgia State Legislature, but only after a bitter fight, which

After the Civil War, Turner was assigned as an agent of the Freedmen's Bureau in Georgia, but he quit to organize area churches as a base from which to help freed slaves participate in politics. He also served as president of Morris Brown College in Atlanta for 12 years.

lasted from 1868 to 1870. The fight left him battered publicly, but he was still defiant. He was finally seated in the statehouse as a Republican despite attempts by white Democrats to prevent it. In defense of himself and 23 other black representatives who had been temporarily denied their rightful seat in the Georgia legislature, Turner made a historic speech before the body that began at 9 A.M. and ended six hours later. He said, "We are told that if black men want to speak, they must speak through white trumpets!"

Turner and the others were finally admitted to the legislature in 1869. But by 1876, radical Reconstruction in the South was dead.

In the next few decades, disenchanted with increasing white supremacy, Turner and others found refuge in theories discussed by Pan-Africanists who felt life for blacks in America was futile. He and other emigrationists, including Edward Wilmot Blyden, called their concept "Africa for the Africans." Turner also supported legislation to provide financial support for black repatriation. He is the father of the current Black Reparations Movement.

Turner called for "two or three million" blacks to return "to the land of our ancestors, and establish our own nation, civilization, laws, customs, style of manufacture, and not only give the world, like other race varieties, the benefit of our individuality, but build up social conditions peculiarly our own." Despite his passionate leadership in the back-to-Africa movement, Turner preferred the word "Negro" to "African" when speaking about blacks in the Western Hemisphere.

Refusing to die on American soil, Turner died in 1915, in Windsor, Ontario, Canada.

LEWIS HOWARD LATIMER

Lewis Howard Latimer was one of the innovative giants of the electrical age. A self-educated engineer from a family of escaped slaves, Latimer made electrical lighting more efficient and more accessible to millions of people.

THE INVENTIVE GENIUS of Lewis Howard Latimer helped bring electricity and related appliances into the common American household. His contributions stand tall among those of the original Edison pioneers at the forefront of the age of electricity. He brought light to cities as far away as London and Montreal and as near as New York City and Philadelphia.

Counted among his early achievements is the inexpensive and long-lasting carbon filament that transformed Thomas Edison's electric lightbulb. Prior to Latimer's invention, the lightbulb burned out in a mere 30 hours; with his carbon filament, it became a practical convenience.

Latimer was a prolific inventor whose creations were not widely credited to him. He often sold his patents to manufacturers and submitted patents under the name of his employer, which left the name of Lewis Latimer relatively unknown to the public—the very beneficiaries of his designs.

Born on September 4, 1848, the fourth child in a household of escaped slaves, Latimer's childhood was more focused on subsistence and maintaining freedom than on formal education. He worked odd jobs after elementary school in his father's barbershop until his father moved out of the house. An escaped slave, George Latimer was forced to keep his family safe from slave hunters by living apart. So ten-year-old Lewis quit school to help support the family.

Against those odds, Lewis Latimer grew into an accomplished engineer by educating himself in art, math, science, and French. The arts brought him personal enjoyment and helped develop his talents as a playwright, poet, and musician.

After serving in the Civil War in the navy on the U.S.S. *Massasoit,* he acquired a job with patent solicitors Crosby and Gould, where he worked his way up to draftsman. He supervised the creation of models to accompany patent applications. In that position, Latimer assisted many inventors, including Alexander Graham Bell and Thomas Edison, helping them get critical patents.

Latimer's own first patent, which he shared with Charles W. Brown, was in 1874 for improvements to the water closet (bathroom) on trains. While in the employ of Hiram S. Maxim at the United States Electric Lighting Company in Bridgeport, Connecticut, Latimer accelerated his creative work in the science of electrical lighting. He gave the world several life-changing inventions, topping the list with a lasting filament for incandescent lightbulbs and a patent shared with Joseph V. Nichols for an electric lamp.

Latimer traveled the country establishing factories for the production of the filament and supervising the lighting of commercial properties, railroads, and even more importantly, entire cities.

In 1884, he helped sustain the growth of Edison's company, General Electric, through his engineering and drafting skills. As an expert

Although he either sold most of his patents, submitted them under his employer's name, or simply faced patent infringements, Lewis Latimer can be credited with the original patents on a number of inventions, including the process of manufacturing carbon filaments for lightbulbs.

witness, Latimer also saved the company millions of dollars from patent infringements. He later served on the Board of Patent Control formed by General Electric and Westinghouse and was a patent consultant with the Hammer & Schwarz law firm in New York until his vision became impaired.

This Renaissance man, who oversaw the installation of the first electric lights in New York City, made life safer and more convenient for people around the globe. Through it all, he found time to share his knowledge. Latimer wrote a textbook about electric lighting—one of the first—and he taught immigrants mechanical drawing skills. He also supported philanthropic and civil rights efforts until his death in 1928.

ISAAC MURPHY

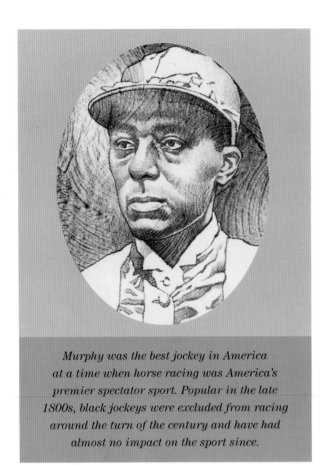

Murphy was the best jockey in America at a time when horse racing was America's premier spectator sport. Popular in the late 1800s, black jockeys were excluded from racing around the turn of the century and have had almost no impact on the sport since.

LITTLE ISAAC MURPHY was the closest thing to perfection that any jockey has ever been—he set amazing records that in most cases have never been topped.

Named Isaac Burns, he was a slave born in Lexington, Kentucky, possibly on January 1 (the birth date given for all Thoroughbred horses), in 1866. His father died in the Civil War as a Union soldier. After the Emancipation Proclamation, his family moved to the Lexington farm of his mother's father, Green Murphy. Isaac took his grandfather's surname.

The story goes that when Murphy was 12, the family added two years to his age so he could get an apprentice jockey's license. Murphy ran his first race in Louisville in May 1875, but he didn't win a meet until 16 months later. That win began an unparalleled string of successes.

Murphy became the first jockey to win the Kentucky Derby three times—1884, 1890, 1891—and the first to win back-to-back Derbies. He also won four of the first five runs of the American Derby at Washington Park in Chicago (1884 to 1886, and 1888). In 1882, at Saratoga Downs in New York, he had an incredible string of 49 victories in 51 starts.

Murphy's three Kentucky Derby wins went unmatched for 39 years, until Earl Sande tied the mark in 1930. The record went unsurpassed until 1948, when Eddie Arcaro won his fourth of five Derbies.

During his career, Murphy won 628 races out of a total 1,412 mounts—an astonishing 44 percent clip. It's little wonder that, in 1955, he was the first rider voted into the Jockey Hall of Fame.

Track aficionados suggest that Murphy knew how to pace a horse better than anyone the sport of racing had ever seen. It was said that he rode only with his hands and heels and only used the whip to satisfy the crowd. Like most of the young riders of his day, Murphy virtually lived and slept at the track. He became proficient at the art of hand-riding, which made the rider more in tune with his mount. Legend has it that a horse could jump straight up and down, but Murphy would never raise off its back. He seemed to be part of the horse. Newspapers and trainers of the day called him the greatest jockey.

Murphy was also noted for his integrity, honesty, honor, and character. He was the undisputed king of his profession, which had the largest spectator attendance of any sport in America at that time.

By 1882, his salary was $10,000 a year. It is estimated that Murphy earned more than $250,000 in his career—an amazing sum of money in those days.

Murphy was the head-to-head winner of one of the most publicized races of the late 19th century. Murphy raced Snapper Garrison, the best white jockey at that time, to settle a debate. Murphy emerged from the race victorious.

Interestingly, Murphy almost didn't participate in his first Kentucky Derby victory. The horse he was to ride, Buchanan, had almost thrown him in a race only a few weeks before, and Murphy wanted nothing more to do with the animal. The horse's owner threatened to suspend him, so Murphy rode Buchanan in the Derby, and he won.

Unfortunately, Murphy's career virtually ended following his third Derby victory in 1891. He was prone to putting on weight during the off-season and would balloon up to 140 pounds or more over the winter. Then he would diet before the spring races.

This unhealthy practice eventually weakened his body and made him prone to infection. He caught pneumonia and died on February 12, 1896, at the age of 30.

Murphy was considered the best of the black jockeys. In the first Kentucky Derby in 1875, 14 of the 15 riders were black. In fact, from 1875 to 1911, 11 black jockeys won 15 Kentucky Derbies and many other major races throughout the South. The black jockeys rode so well, however, that their white peers arranged for their ejection from the sport. They created a governing body that refused to relicense the black jockeys. There has been almost no participation in the sport of horse racing by black riders since that time, despite the acclaim Murphy received throughout America in his heyday.

T. THOMAS FORTUNE

TIMOTHY THOMAS FORTUNE spent his life fighting to free African Americans from racial discrimination. He also worked to keep infighting among blacks from costing them hard-won political and economical gains. As editor and founder of several African American newspapers, Fortune attempted to convince black power brokers to consolidate their forces to achieve equality for the race.

Fortune was born to slave parents in Marianna, Florida, in October 1856, with the blood of blacks, Native Americans, and Irish whites flowing through his veins. His family's political activities forced them to flee to Jacksonville, Florida, where Fortune had a limited education through the Freedmen's Bureau. He briefly attended Howard University in 1876, and he began his love affair with journalism while working on the *People's Advocate*.

In the late 1870s, Fortune moved to New York, working first as a printer, then he became part-owner of the weekly tabloid *Rumor*. Fortune became editor of the newspaper and changed its name to the *Globe*. He then became sole owner of his first newspaper, *The New York Freeman*, which later became *New York Age*, arguably the greatest black newspaper of the 19th century. His purpose was to counter negative coverage of blacks by the white press.

"The great newspapers, which should plead the cause of the oppressed and the downtrodden, which should be the palladiums of the people's rights, are all on the side of the oppressor, or by silence preserve a dignified but ignominious neutrality," wrote Fortune. "Day after day they weave a false picture of facts—facts which must measurably influence the future historian of the times in the composition of impartial history. The wrongs of the masses are referred to sneeringly or apologetically."

Fortune's New York Age *was his forum for countering negative press from white papers and demanding equality for blacks. He also worked to convince black leaders to consolidate power rather than fight among themselves.*

Fortune's editorial policies advocated black self-reliance, demanded full equality for African Americans, and condemned all forms of discrimination. In an 1883 editorial, Fortune blasted the U.S. Supreme Court for its decisions in several cases, noting that "We are declared to be created equal, and entitled to certain rights, . . . but there is no law to protect us in the enjoyment of them."

Two general circulation papers, the *Boston Transcript* and the *New York Sun*, hired Fortune as a reporter and editor; in the 1880s it was unusual for a black man to be hired by white newspapers. Fortune traveled the South, reporting on the conditions there. Fortune was an early advocate of the term "Afro-American." He considered "Negro" to be a term of contempt.

Fortune also wrote three books. *Black and White: Land and Politics in the South* (1884), a historical essay on land, labor, and politics in the South, which called for the unification of workers of both races. He also wrote *The Negro in Politics,* which was published in 1885, and then *Dreams of Life,* published in 1905.

Fortune later founded the National Afro-American League, an organization that pioneered programs and methods used by many modern-day civil rights groups. He told the delegates at the Chicago event that "before the rights conferred upon us by the war amendments are fully conceded, a full century will have passed away. We have undertaken no child's play. We have undertaken a serious work which will tax and exhaust the best intelligence and energy of the race for the next century."

The League was short-lived. In 1898, however, Fortune's National Afro-American Council held a conference emphasizing civil rights, women's suffrage, and concern for the fate of Latin Americans after the United States defeated Spain.

Despite his racial militance and liberal—even radical—social and economic views, Fortune remained a lifelong admirer of the far more conservative Booker T. Washington. Political infighting over Fortune's support of Washington weakened his organization. The legacies of Fortune's groups helped set the platform for the NAACP.

Fortune suffered a bout of mental illness in the early 1900s, possibly related to alcoholism. When his health returned, Fortune returned to his profession and wrote fiery editorials for Marcus Garvey's *Negro World.*

Fortune died in Philadelphia in 1928. Kelly Miller of Howard University eulogized him as "the best developed journalist that the Negro race has produced in the Western World."

DANIEL HALE WILLIAMS

Dr. Daniel Hale Williams was a physician and surgeon who performed the world's first successful surgery on the human heart. He founded Chicago's Provident Hospital, the first interracial facility in the country, and he started training programs for African American nurses and interns.

DR. DANIEL HALE WILLIAMS was a pioneering surgeon who saved the life of a stabbing victim by performing the world's first heart surgery. He founded Provident Hospital in Chicago because other area hospitals refused Emma Reynolds, an African American woman, a nursing education. Provident is the nation's oldest freestanding black-owned hospital.

Williams created training programs for African American nurses and interns, and he was the only black in the charter group of the American College of Surgeons. He also helped organize the National Medical Association, a professional organization for black doctors.

Williams was born in Hollidaysburg, Pennsylvania, on January 18, 1856, one of seven children. He and his sister left home to pursue career opportunities elsewhere and eventually made their way to Janesville, Wisconsin.

At 17, Williams found part-time work in a local barbershop, where he met Dr. Henry Palmer. He was fortunate enough to take a two-year apprenticeship with Palmer, a legendary surgeon and former U.S. Surgeon General.

In the 1800s, many doctors began practicing after two years of training. But Williams went on to graduate from Chicago Medical College (later Northwestern Medical School) in 1883, opening his first office at 3034 South Michigan Avenue in Chicago. He was on the surgical staff at several institutions, he taught anatomy, and he was physician to the City Railway Company. In 1889, he was the first black appointed to the Illinois State Board of Health.

Upon hearing educational doors were still closed to aspiring nurse Emma Reynolds and most African Americans pursuing a medical career, Williams decided it was time for a change. Together with social activist Fannie Barrier Williams, Dr. Williams assembled an interracial staff of prestigious medical professionals to form Provident Hospital and Nursing Training School in 1891. It became the first black-owned hospital in the United States.

In 1893, Williams gave a stabbing victim 20 more years of life by performing heretofore untried heart surgery. Williams opened the patient's chest to suture wounds to the pericardium and a blood vessel. His actions on that hot July night were history-making. Historians agree that Williams performed the first successful surgery on the human heart. However, he did not perform the first open-heart surgery, as is often commonly believed. That honor goes to C. Walton Lillehei.

A year after Williams's surgical feats, an African American institution acknowledged his considerable skill by appointing him surgeon-in-chief at Freedman's Hospital on the campus of Howard University in Washington, D.C. In 1899, Williams was visiting professor at Meharry Medical College in Nashville. Returning to Chicago, Williams was on staff at Cook County Hospital from 1900 to 1906.

Dr. Williams helped combat racism in the field of medicine by organizing the National Medical Association for African American physicians, who, at the time, were not allowed to join the American Medical Association.

Ironically, leadership at Provident Hospital had passed to Dr. George Cleveland Hall, Williams's longtime antagonist. As a response to the increased segregation of black life, the hospital board, under Hall's direction, required all physicians to bring all their patients to the hospital. Because many of Williams's patients were white, board policy forced the hospital to sever William's relationship with the very hospital he founded.

In 1913, Williams became the first black appointed as associate attending surgeon at St. Luke's Hospital in Chicago. He was also the only African American among the founders of the American College of Surgeons.

Williams suffered a series of strokes in the 1920s that ended his medical career, and he died on August 4, 1931.

PAUL LAURENCE DUNBAR

PAUL LAURENCE DUNBAR was a brilliant, popular poet, beloved by the black community, who put his experiences into lyrical language. He was one of the first black poets to become nationally recognized by white America.

Dunbar wrote until the very end, releasing the poetic collections Lyrics of Love and Laughter *in 1903,* The Heart of Happy Hollow *in 1904, and* Lyrics of Sunshine and Shadow *in 1905. A final complete collection of Dunbar's poems was released in 1913, seven years after his death.*

Even early on, Dunbar was seen as a black prodigy in a white world. He was the only African American in his Dayton, Ohio, high school class, but he was immensely popular. In his senior year, he was elected president of the literary society and served as editor of the school newspaper.

Dunbar wanted to go to college, but he did not have the financial resources. He was born in Dayton on June 27, 1872, to ex-slave parents.

His father died when Dunbar was only 12, and there were other children to support.

Dunbar took one of the few jobs available to a young black man at the time, operating an elevator. He continued writing poems and sending them off to publications.

Paul Laurence Dunbar was the first African American poet to gain national stature. Though he only wrote professionally for 14 years before his untimely death from tuberculosis at age 33, this popular artist turned out four novels, four collections of short stories, and six volumes of poetry.

In 1893, he paid to have 56 poems published in a slim volume called *Oak and Ivy,* which he sold to his captive audience of elevator passengers. Thinking there would be opportunities available at the World's Fair of 1893, Dunbar moved to Chicago, where he became Frederick Douglass's clerical assistant.

In 1895, Dunbar was able to pay to publish a second collection of his verses, called *Majors and Minors,* which presented poems he had written in standard English and in black dialect. The book became his major breakthrough after being favorably reviewed by William Dean Howells, reigning literary critic of the day for *Harper's Weekly.*

Howells encouraged Dunbar to take the best poems from his two books and reissue them in 1896 under the title *Lyrics of Lowly Life,* for which Howells wrote the preface. The book made Dunbar a star in white literary circles and gave him the financial security to write full-time.

Offers streamed in from prestigious magazines and publishers for anything that came from his pen, and Dunbar didn't disappoint, turning out a great amount of work, including four novels, four volumes of short stories, and three more books of poetry.

Because of the necessity of surviving financially in the literary world, Dunbar compromised his art. Although he preferred to write verse in standard English, he wrote uninspired prose and poems in black dialect, which his readers seemed to prefer. Despite his success, Dunbar was riddled with disappointment that his greatest works had gone unappreciated.

However, when Dunbar died from tuberculosis on February 9, 1906, at the age of 33, the American public widely considered him the dean of black poets.

Pictured is Dunbar's office at Dunbar House, his last residence, in Dayton, Ohio. The site is operated by the Ohio Historical Society.

IDA B. WELLS-BARNETT

A journalist and civil rights leader, Ida B. Wells-Barnett fearlessly fought for black self-reliance and against the violence and economic repression that kept African Americans and women oppressed.

IDA B. WELLS-BARNETT was a formidable force in the battle for equality and economic parity for blacks. Her scathing editorials denouncing lynchings and other white violence against blacks alerted the country to the atrocities common in the post-Reconstruction South. This "crusader for justice," as she was called, spent her life lecturing against discrimination and persecution, and she exhorted blacks to use their economic power to change racist white behavior.

Wells-Barnett was born a slave in Mississippi, in 1862, to a family with a strong faith in education. They were all emancipated by the Civil War. Her mother and father were able to use their respective skills in cooking and carpentry to provide for eight children. Then her parents and youngest brother died of yellow fever in 1878, after which the young teenager dropped out of high school to begin teaching so she could care for her siblings. Wells-Barnett later moved to Memphis, Tennessee, where she lived with an aunt and continued to raise her two youngest sisters. While maintaining her teaching job, she furthered her own education in summer school at Fisk University, in what turned out to be the beginning of a lifelong quest for equality.

Wells-Barnett was a crusading journalist who became one of the nation's foremost authorities on the atrocity of lynching. Her lifespan, from 1862 to 1931, coincided with the period in America when lynchings were at their zenith. Through her many studies and documentations, Wells-Barnett estimated the number of blacks killed by lynching to be in the tens of thousands.

In 1884, Wells-Barnett refused to accept a seat in a smoke-filled Jim Crow car and was forcefully removed from the ladies section. She filed a successful lawsuit in the circuit court against the Chesapeake & Ohio Railroad Company, but the ruling, with its $500 award, was overturned by the Tennessee Supreme Court. This event gave her the impetus to seek justice through other means. Her militant actions, along with some editorials she wrote that were critical of inadequate African American schools, caused her to lose her teaching job.

Wells-Barnett, under the pen name Iola, launched a full-time career using her mighty pen to call the country to task for its treatment of blacks. After editing several small black papers,

Wells-Barnett became part-owner of *The Free Speech and Headlight,* a Memphis paper. In 1892, three black men who were her friends, Thomas Moss, Calvin McDowell, and William Steward, were lynched because their grocery business was competing with a white firm. Wells-Barnett fired off a series of blistering editorials, accusing whites of using lynchings to punish financially independent African Americans. She declared, "The city of Memphis has demonstrated that neither character nor standing avails the Negro if he dares to protect himself from the white man or become his rival. There is nothing we can do about the lynching now, as we are out-numbered and without arms."

She called for blacks to leave the towns that refused to protect them. Many followed her advice, while others staged a boycott of white establishments. In response, furious white citizens burned down her paper's presses and threatened her life if she returned to the South. She was in Philadelphia at the time of the backlash, and returning to Memphis was not an option. Perhaps the best-kept secret of the postbellum "chivalrous" South is that black women, as well as black men, were being lynched. Had Wells returned, she certainly would have been killed.

Wells-Barnett transferred her talents to New York, continuing her angry attacks on lynching in the pages of militant journalist T. Thomas Fortune's *New York Age.* She published pamphlets on the lynching problem and traveled to Britain to drum up international outrage.

Wells-Barnett relocated to Chicago in 1893, where she published a pamphlet titled "The Reason Why the Colored American Is Not in the World's Columbian Exposition," which denounced the exclusion of blacks from

IDA B. WELLS-BARNETT

the acclaimed World's Fair. Two years later, she married the founder of the *Chicago Conservator* newspaper, attorney Ferdinand Barnett, with the intention of settling into a quiet family life. They nurtured four children, but Wells-Barnett could not turn her back on the critical social issues of the time: the oppression of American blacks and women. She and Jane Addams prevented the creation of segregated schools in Chicago. Wells-Barnett openly opposed Booker T. Washington's practices of accommodation, such as limiting black education to trade courses.

This tireless crusader helped form and worked with many important groups, including the

To honor her work to end discrimination and the horrors of lynching, the United States Postal Service issued a commemorative Ida B. Wells stamp in February 1990.

ANNA JULIA HAYWOOD COOPER

Anna Julia Haywood Cooper was born into slavery. As a young nursemaid in book-filled surroundings, Haywood Cooper grew to relish the field of letters. After emancipation, Haywood Cooper steadfastly refused to let the double standard in America prevent her from sharing her love of education with fellow blacks.

The freedwoman remained in her hometown of Raleigh, North Carolina, and attended Augustine's Normal and Collegiate Institute. There she initiated her dream of tutoring and teaching students, but she got the added benefit of finding a husband. His unfortunate death came just two years after their marriage, leaving Cooper to follow her dreams alone.

She continued her education by obtaining bachelor's and master's degrees from Oberlin College in Ohio. Her entire life was devoted to ending racism and sexism in America.

Cooper took a bold step as principal of M Street High School, later renamed Paul Laurence Dunbar, by expanding college prep courses for young black students of both genders in Washington, D.C. Those educational pursuits went well beyond the prevailing emphasis on vocational training by accommodationists. Her innovations resulted in charges of misconduct and insubordination leading to the loss of her job.

This backlash neither dampened her belief in nor curtailed her strides toward the highest quality education for blacks. Following several teaching positions, she embarked upon her doctorate in Paris and at Columbia University. This 60-something educator and defender of equal rights received her Ph.D. from the Sorbonne in 1925.

Cooper eventually returned to Washington, D.C., to top off her educational career as president of Frelinghuysen University, serving from 1930 to 1940. She continued to voice progressive opinions through her love of letters, until her passing in 1964 at the age of 105.

Ida B. Wells Club and the Negro Fellowship League. Wells-Barnett was also instrumental in creating the National Association for the Advancement of Colored People (NAACP) and making antilynching legislation its focus. She may have been unable to save her three friends in Memphis from a mob, but she dedicated her life to bringing the racial holocaust to a stop. In the case of Steve Green, she personally saved him from extradition to Arkansas where a lynching probably awaited him.

Wells-Barnett supported existing organizations for women's suffrage. But she had no problem holding those groups to proper standards of racial equality. During a march in Washington,

D.C., organized by the National American Women Suffrage Association in 1913, she would not walk in the rear where black delegates were assigned. In addition to forging beneficial relationships with feminist groups, she assisted in founding the National Association of Colored Women as well as the Alpha Suffrage Club for black women, the first suffrage organization in the nation.

In 1930, Wells-Barnett ran for the Illinois State legislature, becoming one of the first women to run for political office in America. Her powerful voice was silenced on March 25, 1931, when she died of uremic poisoning. She remains a jewel in the crown of the struggle for equality.

BOOKER T. WASHINGTON

Washington was a controversial black leader who admonished African Americans to pull themselves up by their own bootstraps to overcome the limitations placed on them by a racist society.

AT THE TURN of the 20th century, Booker Taliaferro Washington was the most powerful and the most controversial black leader of his time. Arguably no black American, before or since, has wielded such power within the African American community. His influence over black leaders and white philanthropists, his disdain for criticism, his network of spies, and his power to dispense patronage funded by white philanthropists and politicians made him the most powerful black in history.

His supporters say he tirelessly toiled for black pride and educational and economic advancement and that he used his influence with white industrialists to get huge amounts of money for black colleges. His critics say he cozied up to the white power structure, using federal patronage and the favor of white philanthropists to create his own political machine. Historians say they are both right.

Washington was born a mulatto slave in 1856 on a small Virginia farm. He spent his early years of freedom working in coal mines and salt furnaces. He attended Freedmen's Bureau School and Hampton Institute, then a secondary and industrial school.

In 1881, Washington founded Tuskegee Institute in the black belt of Alabama—something many cite as his crowning achievement because of the thousands of blacks whose careers were made possible thanks to the opportunity they were afforded at Tuskegee. The school specialized in vocational and agricultural careers—jobs nonthreatening to an increasingly hostile white workforce.

Washington spent the next 15 years building this landmark institution by accommodating local whites and raising money from northern ones, who were attracted to his emphasis on thrift, hard work, and good moral character. They viewed industrial education as no threat to southern white labor.

At this time, militant abolitionist Frederick Douglass was deemed the most articulate black spokesman. Douglass died in 1895, the same year that Washington catapulted into national fame with a speech known as the Atlanta Compromise Address delivered at the Cotton States and International Exposition. In his speech, Washington implied a scaling back of black voting rights in favor of white support for black businesses. He used the parable of the open hand and the empty bucket to illustrate his point.

His accommodationist, self-help philosophy was clarified in his auto-biography, *Up From Slavery,* published in 1901. The book quickly became a best-seller, and Washington became a household name. He was constantly hailed as a "credit to his race." The book even earned Washington a White House audience with President Theodore Roosevelt that same year, and he remained an important advisor to the president.

Washington then perfected his political prowess by building an organization that more often than not yielded principle to expediency. Washington secretly funded lawyers and pressed court suits to protest segregation in public transportation and prevent black sharecroppers from being driven from their land. He maneuvered bad situations and made them into situations that worked for him. This was perhaps his greatest skill.

His program of industrial education and promotion of small business as the primary way blacks could move up the ladder might have seemed pragmatic, given the racial hatred that existed

Washington founded Tuskegee Institute in 1881, when he was only 25. Through the years, the school has put thousands of black graduates onto productive career paths.

BOOKER T. WASHINGTON

at that time. But critics then and today cite it as taking people of African descent several steps backward. One critic of the Atlanta Compromise speech was noted educator John Hope. "I regard it as cowardly and dishonest for any of our colored men to tell white people or colored people that we are not struggling for equality."

Others praised Washington's industrial philosophy. Industrialist Andrew Carnegie and feminist Susan B. Anthony were among the most prominent speakers who appeared at Tuskegee Institute. Washington's biographer, Louis R. Harlan, said that Washington never stopped working for black pride, material advancement, and every kind of education.

Washington's most vocal critic was W.E.B. Du Bois, who called for "ceaseless agitation" when fighting for racial equality. According to Du Bois, in his book *The Souls of Black Folk,* "Mr. Washington represents in Negro thought the old attitude of adjustment and submission." Washington's rule was "bossism." He rewarded his friends and punished his enemies. He used spies, bribes, and anything short of violence to bring down opponents, who mainly came from progressive quarters of the black community.

Meanwhile, poverty, lynchings, and other assaults to the human dignity of blacks flourished at the hands of southern and northern whites, who in the 1890s began a movement to take back all the rights blacks had achieved.

A little known fact about Washington is that for years he secretly funded court challenges of segregated accommodations in interstate transportation and of attempts by whites to swindle black farmers of their land. His most scathing attack on racial segregation was published posthumously. In his final years he addressed many of the civil rights questions that the NAACP had raised and he had previously rejected. In his last few years, Washington differed from their approach, not their goal.

Washington's supporter, William H. Lewis, memorialized his mentor by saying: "He knew the Southern White man better than the Southern White man knew himself, and knew the sure road to his head and heart." At age 59, Washington died at Tuskegee in 1915. Three days after his death, one of the largest crowds in the Institute's history gathered to honor him.

Washington's successor was Robert R. Moten, his former secretary. Moten was more accommodating to the protest movement, signaling that it had become acceptable for some of Washington's old supporters to join forces with the NAACP. Ironically, during the Depression, W.E.B. Du Bois advocated economic policies similar to those proposed by Washington. This caused a split between Du Bois and Walter F. White within the ranks of the NAACP.

Washington will remain a controversial figure. Each community and hamlet would create their own Washington, a black man who could speak for his community as the voice of Negro opinion. Still, Washington remains admired by many black nationalists and black radicals, who view him as a symbol of black empowerment, of the philosophy of "doing for self."

JOHN HOPE

Booker T. Washington and John Hope understood the importance of education to the national advancement of African Americans. Both dedicated their lives to achieving that end by developing institutions of higher learning that would breathe economic life into the black community, but similarities between the two acclaimed educators ended there.

While Washington was an accommodationist in public and a desegregationist only in secret, on both fronts, John Hope exhorted education and civil rights without racial limits.

After experiencing the boundlessness of white America as the son of a wealthy Scottish industrialist, John Hope's fortunes changed following the death of his father. He saw his mother denied her rightful inheritance simply because she was a woman of color.

Hope was determined to put a stop to such deprivation. He took his place among the black

Throughout his life, blond, blue-eyed John Hope always made his African American heritage public knowledge. In the patrician style to which he was born, he boldly pushed open the doors of the highest levels of education for fellow blacks to follow.

militants at the Harpers Ferry Conference in 1906, a predecessor to the National Association for the Advancement of Colored People (NAACP). He carried the demands of "equality now" into his role on the advisory board of the NAACP, the executive committee of the National Urban League, and the classroom.

His crowning glory was the way Morehouse College and subsequently Atlanta University flourished while he served them as president. Matriculation in the classics by hundreds of blacks on those campuses contrasted dramatically from the trade school approach at Booker T. Washington's Tuskegee Institute.

In 1929, when John Hope helped establish the consortium of Morehouse and Spelman colleges, with Atlanta University as the postgraduate pinnacle, he gave African Americans choices for equal education unparalleled in the first half of the 20th century.

GEORGE WASHINGTON CARVER

George Washington Carver was a famous black scientist who revolutionized farming in the South with his crop combinations and new uses for peanuts and sweet potatoes.

WHO WOULD HAVE GUESSED that a little African American boy kidnapped from his owner's plantation and ransomed by his master in exchange for a racehorse would later revolutionize agriculture? But those were the humble beginnings for Dr. George Washington Carver. This famous African American scientist looked at the damage America's one-crop system was doing and revolutionized farming. He developed an agriculture made for the problems of the South, which saved the South's dying farming system by introducing the right crop combinations and finding and promoting markets for them.

Carver pressed for the introduction of vegetables that did not rob the soil of nitrates as cotton does. Since fertilizer was scarce, his idea of planting peanuts made sense.

Carver was born a slave, possibly in 1860 or 1861. At 13, he ventured off by himself to make his way in a troubled world. He had no money, support, or education. All he had was a dream—education at all costs. He courageously worked for his high school diploma. That whetted his appetite for higher education.

After several rejections, Carver became the first black student at Simpson College in Iowa and at Iowa State University. He paid his tuition by opening a laundry business. In 1894, he received a bachelor's degree in agricultural science and, a few years later, a master's degree. This was the same year the Supreme Court embraced segregation with its ruling supporting the *Plessy* v. *Ferguson* decision, which declared "separate but equal" was constitutional. That same year, Carver became the first black faculty member at his alma mater. Simpson later awarded him a science doctorate.

Carver went on to make a big name for himself with his teaching and research activities. In 1896, Booker T. Washington, head of Tuskegee Institute in Alabama, offered Carver the top position in the school's agriculture department. Carver accepted.

He stayed at Tuskegee, turning down publicity and royalties for his inventions, except when he could talk about Tuskegee, the school he loved. He received several lucrative job offers, including ones from Henry Ford and Thomas Edison, but he preferred to stay at Tuskegee.

By 1921, when Carver appeared before the House Ways and Means Committee to discuss the many uses of the peanut, he was on the verge of becoming a nationally known scientist. He soon became known as the "Wizard of Tuskegee." Carver first experimented with peanuts in 1903. In a decade and a half, he developed more than 300 products, including foods, beverages, dyes, and cosmetics made from the peanut.

Because of Carver's testimony, the U.S. government imposed a tariff on imported peanuts, which delighted Southern peanut farmers who were producing 40 million bushels annually by 1920. Another effect of Carver's appearance before the House Committee was his emergence as a folk hero. He became the subject of several biographies and a movie, and for years he was one of a handful of African Americans ever mentioned in textbooks.

Books about Carver note his discoveries of several uses of the sweet potato and also how he made his scientific crop knowledge accessible to the average person. Farmers needed to understand the information about new crops in order to use it effectively. Additionally, at the suggestion of Tuskegee founder Booker T. Washington, Carver took his science show on the road in a wagon outfitted for agricultural demonstrations and exhibitions, called the "Jesup Wagon."

Carver died in 1943, and he left his estate to the George Washington Carver Foundation as his unselfish way of giving back all the love, knowledge, and attention he had received.

Carver conducts experiments in his laboratory at Tuskegee Institute. He and his students began experimenting with peanuts in 1903; the work resulted in peanuts becoming a huge cash crop for America's South.

MARY CHURCH TERRELL

MARY CHURCH TERRELL waged a struggle against injustice in all forms. She remained active in the struggle for civil and women's rights for 70 years, although she was born into a life of relative privilege. Active in many associations, Terrell also led the fight to desegregate the nation's capital in the 1950s.

Mary Church was born in 1863 in Memphis. Her parents were former slaves. Her father, Robert R. Church, had a successful saloon business, along with considerable real estate holdings. Her mother, Louisa, ran a successful beauty salon.

Terrell earned her bachelor's degree in 1884 and her master's degree in 1888 from Oberlin College. This made her one of the first black women in America to earn a graduate degree. Afterward, she toured and studied languages in Europe for two years. She then married future judge Robert H. Terrell in 1891.

Oberlin offered Terrell a job that would have made her the first black registrar at a white college. She turned it down to marry. She did accept an appointment to the Board of Education in Washington, D.C., in 1895. She began teaching in that school system in 1887. Terrell became the first black woman to hold this type of position. She resigned from the school board in 1901, but she was reappointed in 1906 and served on the board until 1911.

Active in the women's rights struggle, she organized minority women in the fight against racism and sexism. In 1892, she headed a new group called the Colored Women's League. That organization combined with other black women's organizations in 1896 to form the National Association of Colored Women.

Terrell was elected the first president of the group, which established kindergartens and

Well-educated, wealthy, and prominent, Terrell was one of black America's first female upper-class activists. She disdained the role of socialite, which was the slot generally imposed in her day on any woman of means. Instead, she used her position and connections to fight for equal rights for women and African Americans.

day-care centers for black working mothers. The organization also pushed for economic opportunity and voting rights for black women. That work led Terrell to join Susan B. Anthony and Jane Addams in the suffrage movement.

Terrell was also important in the international women's movement; she represented American delegations at congresses in Berlin, Zurich, and London. Usually the lone African American at these gatherings, she impressed fellow delegates by giving her addresses in fluent German and French, as well as in her native English.

Terrell was poised, gifted, and articulate. These traits put her in demand as a speaker, a vocation she enjoyed for about 30 years. She spoke on many topics, from racial injustice to crime and culture. Writing speeches led Terrell to write articles on the same themes, which were

published in America and abroad. The culmination of her writing career came in 1940 with the publication of her autobiography, *A Colored Woman in a White World.*

In 1909, Terrell was one of two black women at the founding meeting of the NAACP. She also attended the 1910 meeting, which formalized the organization. For many years she served as vice-president of the Washington, D.C., branch. However, her three crowning accomplishments didn't come until Terrell was 86 years old.

She chaired the National Committee to Free the Ingrams, a family of Georgia sharecroppers accused of murdering a white man. The incident was self-defense. Terrell appealed to the United Nations and Georgia's governor. The Ingrams were eventually freed. That same year, after a three-year battle, Terrell gained membership in the Washington, D.C., chapter of the American Association of University Women. This ended the group's policy of excluding blacks.

Finally, in 1949, Terrell chaired the newly organized Coordinating Committee for the Enforcement of District of Columbia Anti-Discrimination Laws. The "Lost Laws of 1872–73" prohibited discrimination in restaurants, but owners often ignored the laws. The group fought to have the laws enforced.

For almost a year, Terrell's group boycotted department stores whose restaurants refused to serve blacks. At age 90, supported by a cane, Terrell headed the picket lines. Several stores finally yielded, and in 1953, the U.S. Supreme Court upheld the laws, thus forcing other restaurants to comply. Terrell had won.

Terrell died on July 24, 1954. Born before the end of the Civil War, she died in the landmark year of *Brown* v. *Board of Education,* at the dawning of the civil rights era.

SCOTT JOPLIN

THE RAUCOUS, intoxicating music form that was the worldwide rage from the turn of the century until about 1917 was largely the result of the work of Scott Joplin. Others may have called ragtime "jig piano," but Joplin preferred the term "syncopated piano music."

Joplin was born November 24, 1868, in Texarkana, Texas. His father was an ex-slave who played the fiddle and deserted the family early in Joplin's life. His mother was free-born, and she played the banjo. Joplin showed improvisational talent on the keyboard at an early age. Once his father left, Joplin's mother gave him music lessons. She did this despite raising six children by herself. His mother took him along to houses where she did domestic work so that Joplin could hone his skills practicing on pianos in those family parlors.

Joplin's talent, especially in improvisation, soon led him to become the talk of the area. Volunteers instructed him in formal piano and harmony. They also instilled in the young man a lifelong interest in music education.

In the mid-1880s, Joplin left Texarkana. He became an itinerant piano player, becoming a "professa" (a pianist who plays by memory) in honky-tonks and bordellos. It was during this period that he learned to rag. He also played in churches, at respected "socials," and in vaudeville with the Texas Medley Quartette.

In 1894, Joplin settled in Sedalia, Missouri, attending the George R. Smith College for Negroes. He also resumed his "professa"-ship at Sedalia's Maple Leaf Club.

Once his major compositions began to be published, in 1899, the richness, originality, and painstaking craft that marked Joplin's music garnered great appreciation.

Joplin's legacy includes 32 ragtime piano solos, 7 rags in collaboration with others, 9 songs, 2 syncopated waltzes, 2 operas, 1 instruction book, 2 arrangements, and 11 miscellaneous works. There are also 11 surviving unpublished manuscripts. Several more of his works are probably lost. Some people believe Joplin destroyed them himself because they didn't meet his rigorous standards.

His "Maple Leaf Rag" sold more than a million copies of sheet music and fueled the ragtime explosion. It earned Joplin the title "King of Ragtime" and brought him the financial security to break away from the honky-tonk circuit.

He continued to produce great rag piano works, such as "The Entertainer," which was later immortalized in the popular 1973 film *The Sting.* Joplin began turning to different forms of music composition that brought him less success and more depression.

He produced a folk ballet called *The Ragtime Dance* in 1899 and a ragtime opera in 1903 called *A Guest of Honor,* which received lukewarm public reaction. He went broke trying to stage *A Guest of Honor,* forcing him to return to rag music, a source of financial success.

He wrote the opera *Treemonisha,* an ode to his mother, which he published in 1911. Repeated unsuccessful attempts to mount a full-scale production caused Joplin severe bouts of depression. In the autumn of 1916, he was committed to the Manhattan State Hospital, where he died on April 1, 1917.

With renewed interest in Joplin and ragtime in the 1970s, he has finally begun to receive the status of a serious classical composer. In 1970, a classical label released a collection of his rags performed by musician Joshua Rifkin. After the New York City Library published a two-volume set in 1971, *The Collected Works of Scott Joplin,* artists began including his compositions in their performances.

Treemonisha was revived in concert by the Atlanta Symphony and a full-blown production was staged by the Houston Grand Opera in 1975. Joplin was issued a special Pulitzer Prize in 1976.

Joplin's "Maple Leaf Rag," which sold over one million copies of sheet music, brought him enough financial security to break away from the honky-tonk circuit and allowed him to pursue other forms of composition.

HENRY OSSAWA TANNER

A RELIGIOUS PAINTER who swept the French off their feet at the turn of the century, Henry Ossawa Tanner was an African American who overcame incredible personal and racial obstacles to create beautiful art, which is still proudly exhibited today.

Tanner is generally regarded as one of America's finest painters. However, because of the racism he experienced in the United States, Tanner relocated to Paris, where he spent the rest of his life.

Tanner was born in Pittsburgh, Pennsylvania, in 1859. His father was an African Methodist Episcopal bishop. By his early teens, Tanner had already made up his mind that his life's work would be that of a great painter. His vocational inspiration came from an artist he once saw working in the field. But it seems that his spiritual inspiration came from his home, where his minister father played a pivotal role.

When Tanner's career finally started to get off the ground, he was bothered with financial and health problems. He was forced to stop and restart his career several times.

Tanner decided his natural talent needed formal instruction if he was ever going to get past selling his paintings for $15 and watching them bring in $250 days later. He became a student at the Pennsylvania Academy for Fine Arts in Philadelphia, where from 1879 to 1885 he endured harassment from white students. Before the Academy reluctantly accepted Tanner, other Philadelphia art teachers had rejected his work merely because he was black.

Hoping to succeed in Europe, Tanner put on an exhibition to raise money. It was a failure. With a borrowed $75 in his pocket, black themes in his work, dreams in his head, and paintbrushes under his arm, he boarded a boat to Italy. But he made a stop in Paris and didn't leave. It took him five years to sell a painting to the Salon; that painting was "Daniel in the Lion's Den." But in 1906, even his beloved Salon awarded Tanner only the second-class Gold Medal for "The Disciples at Emmaus." Tanner's biographers, in a 1992 book published by the Philadelphia Museum of Art, *Henry Ossawa Tanner,* noted that was because only French artists could receive the Gold Medal.

Tanner's next expedition took the biblical painter to the Holy Land. He used this ancient setting for his artwork, including "Christ and Nicodemus" and "The Repentance of St. Peter."

France became his new home. And why not? He was insulted when he returned to America.

When Tanner arrived in Chicago to exhibit his work, the Art Institute's prestigious Cliff Dweller's Club made him a member but would not let him in the dining room when white women were present.

Meanwhile, he won major awards, such as the Walter Lippencott Prize in 1900 and the Gold Medal at the Panama-Pacific Exhibition at San Francisco in 1915. He was also named chevalier of the Legion of Honor by the French government. He died in Paris on May 25, 1937.

Tanner is generally considered the first great African American painter. However, a great deal of 19th-century black art is lost, shrouded in mystery, or painted anonymously. Most 19th-century black artists painted landscapes and white portraiture—anything and everything but their own faces. Tanner was an exception. His black religious themes anticipated Langston Hughes's Harlem Renaissance manifesto that black artists record the beauty of their own world.

Pictured is Tanner's painting "The Thankful Poor." Tanner's paintings often dealt with religious themes.

JAMES WELDON JOHNSON

Historian, novelist, poet, educator, diplomat, lawyer, musician, lyricist, administrator, literary critic, editor, newspaper columnist, field organizer—Johnson's versatility and ability to excel in all of his endeavors made him one of the foremost leaders of his day.

JAMES WELDON JOHNSON had a storied life. He supported the advancement of blacks through his literary, musical, and educational contributions, his organizational accomplishments with the NAACP, and his service as a diplomat and U.S. counsel to foreign nations.

Johnson believed in racial assimilation. He considered it the major responsibility of blacks to lift themselves up by their own bootstraps. Johnson believed that to remove the label of "inferior," blacks needed to prove their intellectual and physical equality.

Johnson was a true Renaissance man: historian, novelist, poet, educator. He excelled in all his endeavors. His accomplishments made him the most popular leader in the African American community in his day, behind Booker T. Washington himself.

Johnson is best known for writing the lyrics to "Lift Every Voice and Sing," which is considered the black national anthem. Also, his 10-year stint as the first African American head of the NAACP ushered in a period of tremendous growth.

Johnson was born on June 17, 1871, in Jacksonville, Florida. His mother encouraged him and his brother, John, in music, art, and literature. There was no high school for blacks in Jacksonville, so Johnson moved to Atlanta to complete his education through college.

After college, Johnson returned to Jacksonville and established courses that would lead to a high school degree for blacks. He then became principal of that high school. He also studied law, and in 1898, he became the first black lawyer to pass the Florida bar.

The racial climate at the time led Johnson and his brother to move to New York in 1902. While there, they were successful in writing musical comedies, and they penned a string of 200 songs for the Broadway stage.

While in New York, Johnson studied literature at Columbia University. His interest in politics began to grow at this time. In 1904, he became treasurer of New York City's Colored Republican Club and developed an association with Booker T. Washington.

At the urging of Booker T. Washington, President Theodore Roosevelt appointed Johnson U.S. counsel to Venezuela in 1906 and to Nicaragua in 1908. His consular positions gave Johnson enough free time to pursue writing. In 1912, he published *The Autobiography of an Ex-Colored Man,* one of the first accounts of a black passing for white. He also became an editor and a popular columnist for the *New York Age* in 1914.

Johnson believed success in literature and arts, as well as in politics, would help African Americans break down racial barriers. He became an advocate and literary critic of black artistic works and compiled such pioneering anthologies as *The Book of American Negro Poetry* and *The Book of American Negro Spirituals.* In *Black Manhattan,* Johnson promoted Harlem as the center of black culture during the Harlem Renaissance.

His works of poetry included two collections—*Fifty Years & Other Poems* and the book for which he is most remembered, *God's Trombones.* The last book is a group of sermons that were written using black vernacular.

In 1916, W.E.B. Du Bois urged Johnson to accept an offer to become a national organizer for the NAACP. Johnson was particularly successful in opening new branches in the South.

In 1920, he became executive secretary of the NAACP, the first African American to hold that post. For the next decade, Johnson was one of the most prominent black leaders of his time.

In recognition of his large body of literary work, Johnson was appointed to the Adam K. Spence Chair of Creative Literature and Writing at Fisk University in October 1930. He resigned from the NAACP in December of that year. Working at the university allowed him to write, travel, lecture, and mentor other promising African Americans.

Johnson died on June 26, 1938, when a train struck his car during a blinding rainstorm.

WILLIAM MONROE TROTTER

WHILE TURN-OF-THE-CENTURY whites elevated Booker T. Washington as the "good Negro," *The Guardian* newspaper editor William Monroe Trotter was the militant black leader at the time. He was a crusading journalist who became a significant thorn in the side of segregation and the champion of his people.

After President Woodrow Wilson said segregating government employees in federal bureaus was "in blacks' best interest," Trotter, on November 12, 1914, demanded an audience with the president. Trotter had once supported Wilson, but he felt that for the president to say that, especially when there were lynchings and increased attacks, was not only calculating but "insulting." Virginia-born Wilson reportedly dismissed Trotter for shaking his finger at him.

Trotter was born April 7, 1872, in Chillicothe, Ohio, but was raised in a predominantly white suburb. There he was steeled in the traditions of abolitionists.

Trotter's father, James, the Mississippi-born son of a white slave owner, was a federal officeholder who was successful in real estate. Trotter's mother was a fair-skinned woman related to Thomas Jefferson.

Raised in an upper-class Negro household, Trotter was admonished to do better than whites as a way to break down color barriers. The lessons he learned from his parents helped him develop into a human-rights activist.

Trotter was the only African American student in his high school class. He led the class academically and was elected student body president. He won scholarships to Harvard College, which he entered in 1891. He was elected Phi Beta Kappa in his junior year—the first African American to earn that distinction at Harvard.

Trotter entered the real estate business after graduation. Jim Crow segregation laws forced Trotter to move his business several times, leading to his growing militancy.

In 1901, to rail against such injustices, he started *The Guardian* newspaper in Boston with George Forbes. Their offices were in the same building as William Lloyd Garrison's *Liberator,* an abolitionist newspaper with the same message of total equality and struggle.

Trotter launched his activist journal in part to show a viable alternative in black leadership to the accommodationist Booker T. Washington. Trotter felt that Washington, the most revered black leader of the day, was a traitor to the African American cause. He believed that Washington consistently tried to paint American race relations and opportunities for blacks in the best possible light. He viewed Booker T. Washington as the "Great Apologist"

Trotter was a tenacious, militant bulldog of a journalist who dared to question the conservative black leadership of the day through his newspaper, The Guardian. He even shook his finger in the face of the president of the United States for segregating black federal employees.

for Southern injustice and someone who pandered to the worst Southern prejudices.

Trotter bashed Washington in *The Guardian,* portraying him as a self-serving political hypocrite. Trotter was able to build considerable public criticism against Washington in the black community. Washington, in turn, filed several lawsuits against Trotter. He also funded another newspaper that he hoped would drive *The Guardian* out of business.

The feud escalated. It culminated in July 1903, when Trotter organized a disturbance, including hecklers, at a speech given by Washington. The disturbance turned into a riot. Trotter was arrested and served a 30-day jail term.

Washington's intimidation seemed only to spur on Trotter. Washington helped make Trotter a hero in the black community among those who favored Trotter's more militant views over the accommodationist leanings of Washington. The incident also drew W.E.B. Du Bois more closely to the anti-Washington camp. Trotter teamed up with Du Bois and Ida B. Wells-Barnett to form the Niagara Movement in 1905. It became the forerunner of the NAACP.

Trotter, with his editorials in *The Guardian,* and Du Bois, with his columns in *The Crisis,* were two men of letters who created a new, intellectual-based journalism.

Trotter attended the founding conference of the NAACP in 1909. But, while Du Bois became an instrumental force in the organization, Trotter never embraced it because he could not go along with the white money and white leadership that directed the NAACP.

He founded the National Equal Rights League. As the NAACP grew, Trotter's leadership declined. He died on his 62nd birthday in 1934.

W.E.B. DU BOIS

WILLIAM EDWARD BURGHARDT Du Bois was born poor in 1868 in Great Barrington, Massachusetts, but rose from his meager roots to become the brightest black mind of the 20th century.

Showing remarkable brilliance even as a youth, W.E.B. Du Bois won scholarships that took him through Fisk and Harvard universities. He earned his master's and doctorate degrees from Harvard, and he later studied at the University of Berlin.

His first works of importance included *The Suppression of the Slave-Trade of the United States of America, 1638–1870,* published in 1896, and *The Philadelphia Negro; A Social Study,* published in 1899. The latter is a classic about the social conditions of turn-of-the-century blacks in that city. He wrote several reports about Atlanta a few years later, from 1899 to 1913, with Atlanta University. These social studies were published for the university's Conferences for the Study of Negro Problems. During this same stormy period, when whites' hostility against blacks reached a fever pitch, Du Bois also wrote the oft-quoted classic *The Souls of Black Folk,* which identified the color line as the principal problem of the 20th century.

His uncompromising opposition to injustice and Jim Crow impelled him to write scathing reports about the Atlanta Riots of 1906 and found the Niagara Movement. He later cofounded the National Association for the Advancement of Colored People, which demanded full citizenship for blacks. Du Bois became the NAACP's chief spokesperson through his editorship of *The Crisis* magazine. During his stint as editor, Du Bois greatly advanced African American literature by edit-

W.E.B. Du Bois was unquestionably the 20th century's greatest black intellectual. His work, including helping to found the NAACP and editing its journal, *The Crisis,* has stood the test of time. He was a pioneer in sociology, history, and anthropology and a major contributor to the Harlem Renaissance.

One of the brightest intellectual minds of the 20th century, W.E.B. Du Bois was a scholar, educator, writer, editor, and orator.

ing many of the important voices of the black arts revival known as the Harlem Renaissance.

Through his moving editorials, he stirred the emotions and awakened the sense of outrage in both blacks and whites—an act that drew the ire of Booker T. Washington, the more accommodationist black leader at the time.

Washington said Du Bois was an agitator who was always stirring up trouble. Du Bois said Washington's strategy would perpetuate oppression of blacks. Their debate was legendary and to this day represents the fight between accommodationist and integrationist schools of thought within the African American community.

Du Bois was also critical of black nationalist Marcus Garvey. Their conflict symbolized the differences between integrationist and black nationalist schools of thought.

Throughout Du Bois's life, including periods when he embraced Pan-Africanism, socialism, and communism, he believed in three basic goals for blacks: the right to vote, civic equality, and education of the youth. One of Du Bois's most often quoted philosophies was the "talented tenth." It said that blacks' salvation would come through the accomplishments of the black elite.

Hardly modest about his own achievement in defining and transcending caste and class in this country, Du Bois boasted in his autobiography, *Dusk of Dawn:* "I was the main factor in revolutionizing the attitude of the American Negro toward caste."

Du Bois had a universal outlook. He was concerned, as was Garvey, with the treatment of the darker people of other lands. In 1909, he began thinking of creating an *Encyclopedia Africana.* He finally did work on it in his later years, while in self-imposed exile in Ghana. He was also an organizer of the Pan-African Congress, which brought together, for the very first time, influential blacks from Europe, Africa, and America. Its first conference was held in Paris in 1919.

W.E.B. Du Bois

Du Bois traveled to the Soviet Union in the 1930s, praising the communist nation as being virtually free of racial discrimination. Ironically, he left the Communist Party in America, which he had joined in 1961, because he felt they discounted blacks with their insistence that class and not race was the problem.

Nevertheless, like other blacks such as Paul Robeson and Langston Hughes, Du Bois would be harassed by the United States government for his views on the Soviet Union. In 1950, many were shocked when he ran for the U.S. Senate on the American Labor Party ticket.

Du Bois's universal outlook helped make him one of the few influential African Americans

associated with the founding of the United Nations. Like his colleagues Ralph Bunche and Mary McLeod Bethune, who were also U.N. cofounders, Du Bois linked the struggle of Africans with that of African Americans—another reason why many whites and even some blacks criticized him. This resentment and harassment made him increasingly isolated.

In 1963, Du Bois became a citizen of Ghana, and when he died, on August 27, 1963, he was buried in Accra, Ghana. Born shortly after the Civil War, Du Bois died during the March on Washington, D.C.

W.E.B. Du Bois chats with fellow visionaries Mary McLeod Bethune and Horace Mann, president of Lincoln University, after receiving the University's Alpha Medallion Award in 1950.

CLAUDE McKAY

Most good writers start with what they know, but the American art establishment consistently assumed no worthwhile interest existed for literature among black writers. W.E.B. Du Bois dismissed such notions by encouraging young black intellectuals to write. Then he touted their artistry to audiences far and wide during the course of his work as a civil rights advocate and scholar.

Du Bois was the perfect example of the older guard influencing young blacks to pen their world in all its truth and color. Claude McKay fanned the flames of the same movement with the *The Liberator,* a new-wave literary journal, which he coedited. McKay was one of the earliest in the group of gifted artists that established the friendly networks that became the Harlem Renaissance.

McKay had already built a notable reputation as a poet of the people in Jamaica, his birthplace. By 1922, ten years after coming to the United States to study agriculture, the powerful lilting works in *Harlem Shadows* solidified his leadership in the Harlem Renaissance.

Sharing a world view similar to that held by Du Bois, McKay's active support of black nationalism and freedom is deeply rooted in his poetry. British Prime Minister Winston Churchill climaxed his entreaties to the U.S. Congress for military support during WWII by reading "If We Must Die," a poem born from McKay's disdain for the heightened number of lynchings and mob attacks in America during the "Red Summer" of 1919.

McKay's life reflects the fragility of the Harlem Renaissance. One of its most widely reprinted authors with a broad network of black and white admirers, his career ended as abruptly as the Renaissance itself with the 1929 stock market crash. In the last years of his life, he became a devout Catholic and was trying, unsuccessfully, to find a publisher for his *Selected Poems.*

MAGGIE LENA WALKER

MAGGIE LENA WALKER is remembered as the first female bank president in the United States, a position she assumed after founding the Saint Luke Penny Savings Bank in 1903. She should also be remembered as a woman who was committed to justice and economic independence for the African American community.

Maggie Lena Walker showed African Americans how to establish an economically independent community by example. She diversified the Independent Order of St. Luke into banking, the free press, real estate, hotel, and retail grocery industries. She further created educational opportunities for African American women and encouraged cooperative networks.

Walker dreamed of an African American community that thrived with economic independence. The stimulation of viable black businesses and home ownership through bank loans and judicious saving was critical to making her dream a reality. Walker formed the *St. Luke Herald* to address her business goals and to bring to the forefront other issues relevant to African Americans. The following year she

established Saint Luke Penny Savings Bank with a strong belief that enough pennies could be saved to build up the black community. She later founded civic organizations and made a commitment to serving on the executive committee of the National Association of Colored Women.

Walker was born July 15, 1867, in Richmond, Virginia, to former slave Elizabeth Draper and an absentee father of Irish descent, Eccles Cuthbert, who worked as a reporter for the *New York Herald.* Stepfather William Mitchell, who was employed as a butler in the same household for which Walker's mother cooked, assumed the paternal role for Walker.

Walker learned the meaning of hard work after Mitchell became the fatal victim of a robbery. Walker had to help her mother in the family laundry business and babysit for her brother.

While attending school, Walker became a member of the Grand United Order of St. Luke, a mutual aid society (a cooperative insurance society) providing health and burial benefits to African American Civil War veterans. After volunteering at a lower level, she would come to play a vital role in the development of that organization. But first, following graduation at the head of her class in 1883, she adhered to the female tradition of becoming a teacher while working part-time for the Women's Union as an insurance agent and taking night classes in accounting and business management.

Three years later, she married Armstead Walker, who worked in his father's lucrative construction firm. They settled into a family life that added three sons and an adopted daughter to their household.

By 1899, Walker became executive secretary and treasurer of St. Luke's mutual aid society,

which she restructured for better debt management while foregoing two-thirds of her meager salary. The organization experienced phenomenal growth under her leadership. She began diversifying the company with an independent newspaper, a bank, a real estate division, a hotel, and a grocery store.

From her wheelchair, after a slip on her front steps severely damaged nerves and tendons in her knees in 1907, she accomplished more than most people achieve walking gingerly through life. After decades of unprecedented growth, she led St. Luke into new, roomier Richmond headquarters in 1924. She later orchestrated a merger with several African American banks in Richmond to form the Consolidated Bank and Trust Company, for which she became the board chairperson in 1929.

Walker proved to be just as influential in inching African Americans toward economic independence. She pursued that formidable goal through her day job and in her work with civic organizations, such as the National Association of Colored Women.

To further those ends, she helped organize and served as vice-president of the local chapter of the NAACP. She also cofounded the Negro Organization Society (which coordinated the actions of local community groups) and the Virginia Federation of Colored Women's Clubs, all while helping to finance a vocational girls school.

Walker worked to create business enterprises in the black community and provide employment for African Americans until her death in 1934. Her life stands as a legacy to cultural and economic renewal.

MARY MCLEOD BETHUNE

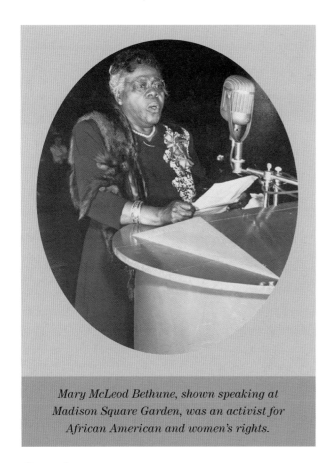

Mary McLeod Bethune, shown speaking at Madison Square Garden, was an activist for African American and women's rights.

M ARY McLEOD BETHUNE was a beacon of hope to generations of black youth and a tireless crusader for the African American cause. She helped shape the formation of the Civil Rights Movement, was a friend and advisor to the Roosevelt administration, and facilitated the distribution of federal dollars into black education and vocational training. Bethune founded scores of schools and organizations, most notably Bethune-Cookman College and the National Council of Negro Women. She was also one of the top social activists of the New Deal years.

Bethune was born in 1875, near Mayesville, South Carolina, the fifteenth of 17 children. Bethune attended Scotia Seminary in North Carolina and what became the Moody Bible Institute in Chicago. By 1895, after failing to get a job as a missionary in Africa, she moved first to Georgia and then to Florida to teach.

Believing that education was the primary route to equality for blacks, Bethune founded the Daytona Educational and Industrial Institute for young black women with just five students and $1.50. By using her charisma and strong belief in the project to raise money, she molded the facility into what is now Bethune-Cookman College.

Mary McLeod Bethune spent 60 years fighting to free African Americans and women from the political, economic, and social black hole into which they were relegated by racism and sexism. She championed humanitarian values throughout her life.

But the big, dark-skinned woman with the implacable will didn't stop there. In 1924, she became president of the National Association of Colored Women. Bethune had a brilliant vision of black women taking an active role in public affairs at a national level. By 1935, she had established the National Council of Negro Women (NCNW), an umbrella organization that grew to include 22 national groups with a strong lobbying presence in Washington.

The next year, Bethune took the helm of the Division of Negro Affairs for the National Youth Administration (NYA), which was an agency geared to helping young people get jobs during the Great Depression and the war effort. Bethune worked to achieve equal benefits for blacks and whites, lobbying for money for black college students and fighting to get African Americans in decision-making positions in the NYA and in other social organizations. Her efforts finally made it possible for blacks to get

pilot training and defense department jobs. In many ways her career as an educator and civic leader and that of Booker T. Washington can be twinned. But whereas he often used private philanthropic monies to promote personal and political ends, she strove to use her numerous contacts to broaden African American access to resources and opportunities.

In 1936, the pioneer formed the Federal Council of Negro Affairs, known as the Black Cabinet, which facilitated two precedent-setting national black conferences. Poor health forced Bethune to cut back her activities in the 1940s, and she began writing newspaper columns for the *Chicago Defender* and the *Pittsburgh Courier.* She died in 1955. In 1974, a statue was built in her honor in Washington, D.C.; it was the first in the capital to portray either a woman or an African American.

Bethune listens as First Lady Eleanor Roosevelt calls for federal antilynching legislation in 1939.

ROBERT S. ABBOTT

Robert S. Abbott founded the *Chicago Defender* in 1905. It would later become the most successful, influential, and widely circulated black weekly newspaper in the country. Abbott started the paper with just 25 cents and no staff, but the paper's success made him one of Chicago's first black millionaires.

A LEGENDARY FIGURE in the annals of American journalism, Robert Sengstacke Abbott founded the *Chicago Defender* in 1905. In its heyday, it was the most successful and influential black newspaper in the United States.

Abbott was born on November 24, 1870, to former slaves in St. Simon's Island, Georgia. But it was his stepfather, John Sengstacke, who aroused young Robert's passion to secure equal rights for African Americans. Abbott was so impressed with his stepfather that he later took Sengstacke as his middle name.

Abbott earned his law degree in 1898 from Chicago Kent College of Law and, for a few years, he practiced in Gary, Indiana, and Topeka, Kansas. But he returned to Chicago with the dream of publishing what he called "The World's Greatest Weekly, the *Chicago Defender.*"

Though Abbott reportedly had only a total of 25 cents to undertake this great endeavor, he was not deterred by his lack of resources. Financial support and articles written by friends kept his newspaper going—but Abbott was a one-man

Following in the tradition of legendary black newspapers, including Freedom's Journal, The North Star, The Guardian, New York Age, *and the* Pittsburgh Courier, *Robert Abbott helped the* Chicago Defender *become the most influential and widely circulated black weekly newspaper in the country.*

army. Working out of his small apartment, he peddled the *Defender* from door to door and through barbershops, churches, bars, and poolrooms in Chicago's African American community.

Although the city had a number of black papers at the time, none matched the strong political and social stance Abbott took in the *Defender*. From the beginning, he intended the paper to be an important voice against racial oppression and injustice. That voice spurred a circulation growth that reached 230,000 only ten years after the paper started.

The *Defender* was distributed throughout the South by Pullman porters on the railway cars.

So intense were Abbott's angry articles against lynching and oppression in the South that many historians credit him as a primary cause of the great migration of blacks from the South to the North during the 1920s and 1930s.

Abbott wanted the paper to speak for and provide advice to the black community. As such, the *Defender* voiced the concerns and outrage blacks felt—those opinions would never have seen print elsewhere.

The bloody Chicago Race Riot of July 1919 started when a group of whites stoned and drowned a young black man who swam beyond an imaginary point in Lake Michigan that blacks were not allowed to cross. There was much loss of life.

Two years earlier, the *Defender* had pointed out that the pent-up anger of blacks over jobs, housing, and politics would eventually lead to just such an explosive situation. The *Defender* gave exhaustive coverage to the five days of rioting. Afterward, Abbott was named a member of the Chicago Commission on Race Relations, which in 1922 published the frequently cited report "The Negro in Chicago." This report examined the causes of the 1919 riots and the great migration of blacks to Chicago.

One of Abbott's important legacies was started in 1929, when he created the Bud Billiken "Back-to-School" Parade to reward *Defender* newspaper boys and to promote education among black children.

Abbott died of Bright's disease on February 29, 1940. At the time, the *Chicago Defender* was the most widely circulated black weekly in the country.

MADAM C. J. WALKER

Using advertising and implementing a mail-order business helped Madam C. J. Walker transform door-to-door sales of her hair restorer into a beauty products empire.

AFTER 38 YEARS of a humble life in which she and her daughter lived virtually hand-to-mouth, Madam C. J. Walker perfected a hair-care formula. It was so popular with African Americans of the early 20th century that she became this country's first black female millionaire and a pioneer in the cosmetics industry. Though she became one of the most famous African Americans of her time, she enjoyed her business success for only 14 years before her death.

Born Sarah Breedlove in Delta, Louisiana, on December 23, 1867, Walker's parents were poor farmers and former slaves. They lived in a run-down shack on a plantation near the banks of the Mississippi River. The family slept on the dirt floor. Walker helped her parents and five siblings until she was orphaned at age seven. She then went to Mississippi, where she lived with an older sister.

At the age of 14, Walker married to escape the cruelties of her sister's husband. Her husband died when she was 20, leaving her to raise her two-year-old daughter, A'Lelia. For the next 18 years, Walker worked as a washerwoman in St. Louis. Determined to make life better for her daughter, she saved her small earnings and sent A'Lelia to Knoxville College. This was one of her proudest accomplishments.

When Walker found herself going bald, she began experimenting with medicines and secret ingredients to try to nurse her hair back to health. In 1905, she developed a formula, with sulphur as a main ingredient, that not only stopped her hair loss but enabled her hair to grow back quickly.

Walker always said the formula came to her in a dream after she prayed to God to save her hair. Some ingredients in the recipe that she envisioned were grown in Africa, so Walker sent for them. She prepared the concoction and, after applying it, found her hair growing back faster than it had fallen out. Walker then began selling this pomade preparation, which she called a "miracle hair grower," to friends and neighbors.

In order to expand her business, Walker moved to Denver in 1905. She continued to sell her product to local black women. Then, she decided to put the last $1.50 she had to her name into buying the necessary chemicals to manufacture the pomade in jars. Walker was now a businessperson, not a laborer.

Newspaperman Charles Joseph Walker, whom she had known in St. Louis, joined her in Denver, and they married. He brought his expertise in advertising to the operation. Now known as Madam C. J. Walker, she put ads in black publications and began the profitable mail-order arm of her business.

After personally showing her styling methods door-to-door throughout the South and East, she opened beauty schools and trained agents. These agents started their own businesses selling her growing line of products.

The success of her hair-care treatment system rested in the versatility of styling it offered African American women who wanted different hairstyles. The Walker System was an international success: Walker had sales agents in Central America, Panama, Costa Rica, Jamaica, and Haiti. Just before her death in 1919, she had hoped to travel to Europe to train more agents.

Some historians dispute whether Walker or Annie Turnbo Malone became the first black female millionaire. There is no doubt, however, that Walker ran a better business operation. Madam Walker and her daughter gave thousands of black women an opportunity to become entrepreneurs in their organization.

Walker's accomplishments paved the way for today's businesswomen. Just as important, she used her wealth and influence to help others by making large contributions to the NAACP's antilynching fund, the YMCA and YWCA, historic preservation projects, black churches, and black schools and colleges.

Madam Walker died May 25, 1919, at her New York estate, Villa Lewaro.

During her lifetime, Madam C. J. Walker built a multimillion-dollar business, opened cosmetic colleges in Pittsburgh and New York, and constructed a plant in Indianapolis.

JACK JOHNSON

IN THE EARLY 20TH CENTURY, when race relations were at one of the lowest points in history and lynchings and race riots occurred with regularity, John Arthur "Jack" Johnson became boxing's first black heavyweight champion of the world.

In 1908, Johnson won the title with a vicious beating of Canadian Tommy Burns. For 13 rounds, Johnson kept up a running conversation with Burns, even as he physically dismantled him. Though bloodied, Burns would not quit. Mercifully, police entered the ring in the 14th round to stop the fight.

The new champion became an instant hero to most of black America and a despised foe for much of white America, whose boasts of superiority over blacks in all areas were shattered.

Fanning the flames of hatred for Johnson was the fact that he was an arrogant figure in the ring and out—he swaggered, wore flashy clothes and jewelry, had six cars and a large entourage, and displayed a penchant for openly romancing and often marrying white women.

As a result, the boxing community came up with a succession of "great white hopes" to try and dethrone this "uppity" black fighter. Though controversial, Johnson was also one of the greatest boxers in history. He fought professionally from 1897 to 1928 and boxed in exhibitions as late as 1945. In those 48 years in the ring, he fought 114 bouts and was knocked out only three times. So outraged were whites that a law was passed to prevent the public showing of newsreels of his fights.

Born on March 31, 1878, in Galveston, Texas, Johnson quit school after fifth grade and worked a variety of odd jobs, including longshoring on the city's docks, which helped build his muscle strength. Despite his parents' objections, he began training as a boxer. After several amateur events, Johnson turned professional in 1897 at the age of 19, when he stood over 6 feet tall and weighed 180 pounds.

By 1901, Johnson was the best black boxer in Texas and began successfully boxing across the country. After winning the "Negro" heavyweight championship in 1903, he demanded to fight Jim Jeffries, the reigning white champion. Jeffries decided to retire rather than demean himself by fighting a black man, though he later did fight Johnson.

Tommy Burns won the vacated title, and financial considerations led him to fight Johnson. When Johnson humiliated Burns, Jeffries was lured out of retirement as the major white hope to defeat him. Johnson's 15th-round knockout of Jeffries in 1910 lead to several deadly race riots around the country. Laws were quickly passed to prevent the distribution and public viewing of Johnson's fights.

Johnson was convicted in 1913 of violating the Mann Act for transporting his girlfriend, later his wife, across state lines for unlawful purposes. He was sentenced to a year in jail. He and his wife fled to Canada, then to France.

Johnson defended his title until 1915, when he lost it in a 26th-round knockout by Jess Willard. Controversy surrounds the outcome; there is speculation that Johnson threw the fight hoping the government would drop charges against him. He fought exhibitions around the world and reveled in his flamboyant lifestyle until June 10, 1946, when he died in a car crash.

In addition to boxing, this colorful figure also appeared in circuses, carnivals, and in special exhibitions demonstrating his strength

Johnson enters the ring in 1931 at the age of 53, in the first of a series of boxing exhibitions he held throughout the country.

ANDREW "RUBE" FOSTER

Rube Foster ranks alongside Charlie Comiskey and Connie Mack as one of the titans of early 20th-century baseball.

ANDREW "RUBE" FOSTER was a gifted, influential athlete and entrepreneur who dominated every aspect of baseball from pitching to managing to ownership; he founded the first lasting black baseball league in 1920. The Negro National League (NNL) consolidated independent African American teams and established an organized season and championship.

The burly right-hander was born September 17, 1879, in Calvert, Texas. At 18, Foster was already a successful pitcher on the black baseball circuit; he was known for his mean screwball. In 1902, Foster pitched for Frank Leland's Chicago Union Giants, winning 51 games. The next year, the 6′4″, 200-pound star player had a 54–1 record with the Cuban X-Giants. Foster got his nickname, "Rube," around this time by beating white pitching great Rube Waddell of the American League's Philadelphia Athletics in an exhibition contest.

Foster continued to dominate the African American circuit in 1904, switching to the Philadelphia Giants and beating his former X-Giant teammates in two playoff games. A keen observer with an innate ability to lead, he began managing the Chicago-based Union Giants in 1907, leading them to a 110–10 record.

Four years later, Foster co-organized the Chicago American Giants. One of the best black teams in history, the American Giants were victorious in all but one championship series from 1910 through 1922. On Foster's teams, where all players were taught to bunt, the winning strategy usually included good pitching, an offense trained in the running game, and a sound defense.

At the height of the Jim Crow era, African American baseball teams were independent, and they traveled to any city or town where there was an opposing team and a chance for lucrative earnings. Teams were forced to depend on white booking agents who controlled sporting events, but Foster understood that no matter how great their talent, they needed to control the economics. In 1920, Foster organized the best black teams in the Midwest to form the Negro National League. This fledgling entity stabilized team rosters and maximized team revenues, and the teams thrilled African American fans.

While president and treasurer of the NNL, Foster retained control of the American Giants, who won the league's first three championships. In 1923, white booking agent Nat Strong formed the Eastern Colored League (ECL). For a while the two leagues feuded. Finally, the owners in both leagues agreed to a system based on the major leagues, including split schedules.

The best teams of each league met for a black World Series.

Foster, known as a stern disciplinarian with an eye for new talent, was an innovative baseball strategist. He used his vast experience and managerial skills to keep the NNL running smoothly and successfully. Mental illness forced him out of leadership in 1926. Foster died on December 9, 1930, in a state asylum in Kankakee, Illinois, and the NNL folded shortly thereafter. By then other black baseball leagues had formed. The Rube Foster era had laid the foundation for the modern Negro Leagues, where baseball greats Jackie Robinson and Hank Aaron began their careers.

In 1933, the NNL was revived by Pittsburgh, Pennsylvania, "numbers" king Gus Greenlee and several other African American owners. The league survived the Great Depression, backed by the wealth of Greenlee and other alleged gangsters. The NNL's East-West All Star games, played annually in Chicago, became a major black social event. Fifty-one years after Foster's death, he was voted into the National Baseball Hall of Fame.

Among the many teams Foster pitched for in the first decade of the century was the Royal Pongiana club.

W. C. HANDY

Handy, "The Father of the Blues," worked to introduce African American music to a wider audience. He was an accomplished musician, composer, publisher, and promoter.

WILLIAM CHRISTOPHER Handy's father was a former slave and Methodist minister who discouraged his son's interest in music. He allowed Handy to pursue it only if he didn't get involved in what his parents called "that low-down" music—ragtime and blues. But Handy was a teenager; he wanted to do what teens of any era want to do—swing with the rhythms of the day.

Handy was born November 16, 1873, in Florence, Alabama. In high school, he studied organ and trained in formal music theory to satisfy his parents, but on the side he played cornet in a local brass band and sang with church groups and minstrel troupes.

By age 18, he was an outstanding trumpet player. Two years later, his quartet enjoyed acclaim after appearing at the Chicago Columbian Exposition of 1893. Buoyed by that success, Handy's band toured the United States, Mexico, and Cuba, playing ragtime and minstrel music, including the marches of John Philip Sousa and the songs of Stephen Foster.

Traveling through the South, Handy became enamored of the rich musical heritage perpetuated by itinerant black blues singers playing on homemade guitars.

In Memphis in 1909, a political jingle he wrote in a bluesy fashion for a mayoral candidate (the infamous "Boss" Crump) enjoyed widespread popularity. Stimulated by that success, Handy started composing blues songs and collecting black folk music, which he published in blues form. This folk music was dramatically different from traditional black spirituals and work songs. The most famous of these pieces is "St. Louis Blues," which Handy had published in 1914.

He moved to New York to make his first recordings in 1918. Soon, his highly successful publishing company led the field in introducing the music of African American songwriters to the general public. This led to the "race records" marketing craze of the 1920s. Handy's songs became national hits and moneymakers.

Because of his formal training, Handy was able to capture in written form what was until then orally handed-down folk music of blacks in the South. His success in the commercial marketplace allowed him to promote this music nationally and eventually worldwide. If not for Handy, the blues may have remained virtually unknown or stayed in regional obscurity.

Handy lost his sight following World War I, then he regained partial sight. In 1943, he fell from a subway platform and became totally blind. He suffered a stroke in 1955, which left him wheelchair-bound, and he died March 28, 1958, of pneumonia.

Handy was survived by his second wife, Louise, whom he had married at the age of 80, the same year that Handy was portrayed in the movie *St. Louis Blues* by Nat "King" Cole.

Handy transcribes music at his piano. Thanks to his tireless efforts to put black folk music into writing, blues music thrived.

MARCUS GARVEY

MARCUS MOSIAH GARVEY was born in 1887 in St. Ann's Bay, Jamaica. His father, Marcus, was a stonemason and a descendant of the Maroon tribesmen, who 200 years earlier had organized slave revolts and created autonomous societies. The social consciousness of his ancestors must have been passed on to Garvey, who by the age of 20 had organized a printers' strike for higher wages. He was fired but went on to earn a reputation as a radical, a spokesperson for the poor and dispossessed, and an organizer and speaker for the working classes.

In 1910, Garvey left Jamaica for Costa Rica, where an uncle got him a job on a sugarcane plantation. That didn't last. He settled in an area where West Indians lived and started a newspaper, *La Nacion/The Nation,* which organized immigrants. Despite harassment from local authorities, he traveled to other Latin American nations. Two years later, he visited Europe and worked on the docks in England. Then he traveled to France, Germany, Italy, and Austria, writing for many newspapers.

It was not until 1914, when he returned to Jamaica, that Garvey's most important role would materialize. He founded the Universal Negro Improvement Association (UNIA), which he modeled after Booker T. Washington's Tuskegee Institute. It soon became one of the largest independent black organizations the world had seen. Its message of racial pride and self-reliance struck a chord among blacks worldwide.

Inspired by Washington's *Up From Slavery,* Garvey left Jamaica in 1916 for the United States. He began a lecture tour to organize chapters of the UNIA. In 1918, he started *Negro World,* a newspaper that reached 50,000

Garvey, in 1922, wearing his uniform as president of the Republic of Africa. He was perhaps the foremost proponent of the "Back to Africa" movement popular among many African Americans in the early part of the 20th century.

readers and was the first to publish many writers of the Harlem Renaissance.

Garvey was successful, acquiring restaurants, hotels, and the Black Star Line—the steamship company he procured to link people of African descent worldwide. He bought three ships, naming them after black leaders, including the *Booker T. Washington.* He also organized the African Orthodox Church.

In 1920, he campaigned for $2 million and collected $137,000 in just a few months to organize the first International Convention of the UNIA. It attracted tens of thousands of followers who marched through Harlem honoring their philosopher/prophet. According to historian Lerone Bennett, Jr., Garvey sold stock to his followers and admirers under an arrangement that barred white purchasers. He created the red, black, and green UNIA flag, which

would later represent black liberation. During this same period, he unsuccessfully appealed to the League of Nations to turn over German-held African nations to independent black rule.

Garvey had enemies, including J. Edgar Hoover, and, ironically, W.E.B. Du Bois. Du Bois was an integrationist who did not support a separate black state and repatriation. Du Bois was also opposed to Garvey's association with the Klu Klux Klan, his criticism of "mulatto" leadership, and his belief in black racial purity.

In 1923, when his steamship company went bankrupt, Garvey was convicted of mail fraud. He went to jail for two years. His sentence was commuted by President Calvin Coolidge before Garvey was deported to Jamaica. Garvey died in London at age 53 without setting foot in Africa.

A poster advertises a meeting where Marcus Garvey was the featured speaker.

CARTER G. WOODSON

Woodson had a late start in education. He was self-taught until he was 20, when he finally attended high school. He then went on to study at the University of Chicago and at Harvard University.

CARTER G. WOODSON did more for the scholarly study of black Americans than any other historian. He opened the long-neglected field of black studies to scholars and popularized the subject in schools and colleges.

Ironically, studying was something Woodson had to put off for quite a while. Born December 19, 1875, in New Canton, Virginia, he was the oldest of nine children of former slaves. Woodson could not attend school because his parents needed him to work in the coal mines.

Unable to attend high school full-time until he was 20, the self-taught young man made up for lost time by graduating in less than two years. Carter then studied at Berea College in Kentucky and, after earning a teaching certificate, taught in West Virginia high schools.

Through periodic visits and correspondence courses, Woodson received a bachelor's degree from the University of Chicago in 1908.

Meanwhile, from 1903 to 1906, he was a school supervisor in the Philippines and then spent 1906 and 1907 studying and traveling in Asia, North Africa, and Europe. In 1912, Woodson received a Ph.D. in history from Harvard.

Woodson explained his commitment to the study of African American history by contrasting Native Americans and Jews. Native Americans, he argued, had no recorded past and, after centuries of white expansion, had virtually disappeared as a people. Centuries of travail, however, had not destroyed the Jewish people, whose sense of their place in history had contributed to their very survival. A people without a sense of their past are doomed to perish. In 1915, along with several other associates, Woodson formed the Association for the Study of Negro Life and History (ASNLH) in Chicago to encourage scholars to engage in the intensive study of black history. Previously, the field had been denigrated by white historians who accepted the traditionally biased perceptions of black involvement in domestic and world affairs.

The ASNLH was primarily committed to historical research; training African American historians; publishing texts about African American life and history; collecting valuable or rare materials on the history of the race; and promoting that history through schools, churches, and fraternal groups.

From 1916 until his death in 1950, Woodson edited the *Journal of Negro History,* one of the premier historical publica-

tions in America during its time. From 1919 to 1920, Woodson was dean of the school of liberal arts and head of the graduate faculty at Howard University. From 1920 to 1922, he was dean at West Virginia State College. While there, Woodson founded Associated Publishers, which produced accurate, scholarly books on black life and culture. He also wrote *Negro in Our History,* one of the earliest African American history textbooks.

In 1926, this stern and demanding academician founded Negro History Week to focus attention on black contributions to civilization. The week was observed nationally and expanded into Black History Month in 1976 by proclamation of President Gerald Ford as part of the nation's bicentennial. Woodson was writing a six-volume *Encyclopaedia Africana* at the time of his death. He died of a heart attack on April 3, 1950.

Eleanor Holmes Norton, in 2001, stands in front of images of Carter G. Woodson and the Carter G. Woodson House. The house has been chosen as one of the 11 most endangered historic places by the National Trust for Historic Preservation.

OSCAR MICHEAUX

Micheaux was admitted into the Screen Directors Guild posthumously. His 1918 movie, Birthright, *is generally considered to be the first full-length film made by an African American.*

OSCAR MICHEAUX may not have been the most gifted filmmaker in history, but he was as good a huckster as any Hollywood producer. One of the first and most determined of African American filmmakers, he independently wrote, produced, directed, and distributed some 48 silent and sound feature films in the 30-year period between 1918 and 1948.

Micheaux's films were mostly melodramas, Westerns, and crime films, but these all-black productions were far more advanced than most Hollywood movies in portraying African Americans as anything other than subservient. Despite his affinity for genre movies, Micheaux attempted to address serious issues in a few of his films. *Within Our Gates* contains a sequence in which a character is lynched. *God's Stepchildren* concerns a light-skinned black who tries to pass for white. Whenever he

attempted this type of controversial material, however, he experienced problems with local censors.

Whether following the conventions of familiar genres or dealing with serious issues, Micheaux's movies did what movies are supposed to do—entertain. Millions of blacks frequented his films in the segregated movie theaters of the day. White audiences even saw his movies at midnight showings.

Micheaux was born January 2, 1884, in rural Cairo, Illinois, one of 13 children of former slave parents. He left home at 17 to become a Pullman porter and, after working the Chicago-to-Portland route, became enchanted with life out West. In 1904, Micheaux purchased a homestead in South Dakota and by all accounts became a successful farmer.

To spread the word to city-dwelling blacks back East about the opportunities waiting in the West, Micheaux began writing novels based on his own experiences. To sell his books, he took to barnstorming through black communities in the South and West on promotional tours. He held meetings in churches, schools, and homes and sold directly to that clientele.

In 1918, a black independent film company sought to buy the film rights to his novel *The Homesteader,* but Micheaux insisted that he be allowed to direct. When they refused, he refused. He raised funds from the same people he sold his books to in order to make the film himself. A moviemaking career was born.

Micheaux's filmmaking style was resourceful, to say the least. Always operating on shoestring budgets, he shot scenes only once, leaving in whatever miscues happened to be caught on camera, using mirrors to enhance whatever natural lighting happened to be available, and

making do with existing buildings instead of constructing sets. These quickie features were generally finished in six weeks. Micheaux, a hefty six-footer, would storm from town to town, stirring up demand for his current movie and raising funds to make the next.

In 1931, Micheaux released *The Exile,* the first all-sound film produced by a black movie company, and in 1948, his movie *The Betrayal* became the first African American–made film to premiere on Broadway. *Body and Soul* (1925) is considered by some critics to be his best picture, which featured the screen debut of a young Paul Robeson.

Micheaux died April 1, 1951, while, appropriately enough, on a promotional tour.

A promotional poster for Micheaux's movie Underworld, *a crime drama. In addition to crime dramas, Micheaux's repertoire included melodramas and Westerns.*

LOUIS ARMSTRONG

Louis Armstrong was an internationally known jazz singer and trumpet player and an improvisational genius. His innovations and technical mastery changed the course of music and influenced many other artists.

LOUIS ARMSTRONG was the father of the popular jazz swing movement of the early 1920s. His talent for improvisation, his technical prowess, and his feel for the music made him the principal model for jazz musicians of his time—and for many artists who remain popular today. Armstrong is frequently cited as one of the greatest artists of the 20th century.

Armstrong was born in 1901 in the impoverished Storyville neighborhood in New Orleans. Raised partly by his grandmother and later by his mother, Armstrong grew up listening to blues and ragtime played at popular neighborhood hangouts. He started singing tenor with a barbershop quartet as a teenager, then learned the bugle while in a reform school for delinquency. Armstrong had never touched a horn before the music teacher at school handed him an alto horn in practice one day. Eventually, he moved up to the cornet and became bandleader at the Home for Colored Waifs.

When Armstrong was released from reform school, he began sitting in with local bands and later replaced legendary New Orleans cornet player Joe Oliver as leader of the city's most popular jazz band. From age 18 to 22, he performed in clubs and on riverboats before moving to Chicago in 1922. There he played as sec-ond cornet in Oliver's Creole Jazz Band, a group that heavily influenced the Windy City's jazz musicians. In 1924, he moved to New York and joined Fletcher Henderson and His Black Swan Troubadours. From the beginning, other musicians were beginning to recognize and imitate Armstrong's innovative style.

Armstrong returned to Chicago in 1925 and began a series of recordings with his ensembles the Hot Fives and the Hot Sevens, which revolutionized the way jazz music was performed. During this time, he switched from the cornet to the trumpet because of its brighter tone. One songs in that series, "Heebie Jeebies," was his first recording as a scat singer,

The legendary Louis Armstrong popularized scat singing, perfected "swing" jazz, and created the first stop-time solo breaks during performances.

Armstrong was known the world over as "Satchmo," short for "satchelmouth." His white handkerchief, used for wiping his profusely perspiring brow, became his trademark.

allegedly because he dropped the sheet music. Armstrong also perfected the "swing" style of jazz, where notes are placed a fraction before or behind the beat, and the stop-time solo break, where the music stops for the featured player, then picks up again. His gravelly voice became a trademark that is still imitated today.

Armstrong went back to New York in 1929 and became a prolific performer on stage and on screen. He was one of the first African Americans to have a sponsored radio show, and he often appeared in feature films. But some critics feel his commercial success robbed his music of the flair it once had, and most experts consider Armstrong a pop singer after the mid-1930s.

Later, the government sponsored numerous international tours for Armstrong, who became a goodwill ambassador for American music. He suffered a heart attack in 1959, and increasing health problems caused him to curtail his performances.

Armstrong died July 6, 1971, in New York City.

BESSIE SMITH

At the height of her career in the 1920s, the Empress of the Blues was earning more than $2,000 a week, truly a queenly sum. Smith inherited the position of First Lady of the Blues from the legendary "Ma" Rainey and turned it over to her successor, Billie Holiday.

THE TURN OF THE 20TH CENTURY was a turning point for American culture: It marked the birth of two musicians who would create jazz and blues—Louis Armstrong and Bessie Smith. They are considered the father and mother of 20th-century blues. Two decades later, Armstrong would perform on Smith's recordings.

Historians say Smith, a tall, heavyset woman, became a professional singer in her teens by being discovered by older blues singer Gertrude "Ma" Rainey. Rainey was so impressed with Smith that she hired her to be part of her Rabbit Foot Minstrel Troupe. Some say it was to teach her; others say it was to prevent a younger and very talented Smith from taking over Rainey's musical throne.

A record company scout spotted Smith during a minstrel performance in Philadelphia and immediately signed her to a contract. This led to Smith cutting 159 songs in the 1920s and early 1930s, including "Downhearted Blues." Smith's phenomenal music was enhanced by her legendary producer, John Hammond, who also discovered her successor—Billie Holiday.

Blues singer Bessie Smith was an incredible interpreter of the music of the working class and of women. Her musical contributions included the addition of improvisation as well as the African American experience into musical history.

At the height of Smith's brilliant career, the Harlem Renaissance was all the rage. White critics began labeling blues and jazz recordings "race records," a not-so-subtle way of simultaneously disparaging and marketing black culture. Smith was earning about $2,000 a week—a phenomenal sum at that time.

On records as well as in tents, theaters, dance halls, cabarets, and juke joints, Smith sang her blues. This personal authenticity was later found in singers Billie Holiday and Judy Garland. Fans and critics were enchanted by the power and passion of Smith's delivery. Her words were wellsprings of solace and hope. Like a spiritualist, she helped her patients cope with grief and disappointment. And like many healers, she internalized a lot of the pain. Her genius set the stage for performers such as Billie Holiday and Janis Joplin.

Onstage, she was invincible, improbable, impregnable. Offstage, she tried to remain humble. This, of course, was her vulnerable side—a side with whom lovers and booze often found a familiar friend. Blues queens, like other African American women in the 1920s, searched for independence. This quest often manifested itself in the appearance of promiscuity, violence, and arrogance, partly because of the racial and sexual constraints society placed on women like Smith. She did not just sing the blues, she lived it. Her last appearance was at Harlem's Apollo Theater. Her fee had dropped to $250.

Smith died shortly after a huge truck pushed her car off the road somewhere between Memphis and Huntsville. In 1937, singer Bessie Smith, the Empress of the Blues, hit her last note.

Bessie Smith's performances were heartfelt— Smith didn't just sing the blues, she lived them.

Athlete, actor, activist, academician, orator, singer, lawyer, and linguist, Paul Robeson was a true Renaissance man. He was so gifted that he was celebrated throughout the world.

PAUL ROBESON was born April 9, 1898, in Princeton, New Jersey, the son of a minister father, who was a runaway slave, and school teacher mother, who died when Paul was six. After graduating high school with honors in 1915, he won an academic scholarship to prestigious Rutgers University. Though the only black student there, he was extremely popular.

Robeson received national attention for his athletic abilities at Rutgers. As an all-around athlete, he earned 12 varsity letters in football, track, baseball, and basketball; he was twice named a football All-American. He excelled just as well in his studies. Robeson won Rutgers' major oratorical contests four years in a row, and he earned Phi Beta Kappa (the nation's highest scholastic honor) in his junior year. In 1919, Robeson graduated as valedictorian of his class.

After deciding not to become a full-time professional athlete, Robeson entered Columbia University to obtain a law degree, which he did in 1923. He played pro football on weekends to support himself and his wife, Eslanda. She was a fellow Columbia student and a chemist who was the first African American to work at New York's Presbyterian Hospital.

After graduation, Robeson briefly worked at a prestigious law firm. He soon quit because of the lack of opportunity for blacks in the legal profession at the time and because of discriminatory practices. Robeson drifted into stage acting, having appeared in amateur productions in college. He met dramatist Eugene O'Neill in 1924 and was quickly signed as lead in O'Neill's *All God's Chillun Got Wings* and *The Emperor Jones.* Robeson's booming baritone and acting skills garnered instant acclaim.

Beginning in 1925, he gave immensely successful concerts of gospel spirituals and folk songs across the country. In 1927, Robeson opened in London in the musical *Show Boat* and sang

Robeson, speaking on the same program with Henry A. Wallace, in 1947. Robeson supported progressive causes, including Wallace's run for president on the Progressive Party ticket in 1948.

"Ol' Man River." That song has become an American classic forever associated with Robeson's deep tones.

With his star steadily rising, Robeson continued giving concerts to capacity crowds and starring in such plays as *John Henry* and *The Hairy Ape.* In 1943, when he starred as Othello with an all-white cast, the production set a record for the longest Broadway run of a Shakespeare play. Some consider it one of the most memorable events in the history of the theater. He also performed the play in London to acclaim.

By 1945, Robeson had become the most famous black man in America. He appeared in a dozen movies, including *King Solomon's Mines, Proud Valley, Sanders of the River, The Song of Freedom,* and the film versions of *Show Boat* and *The Emperor Jones.* In most of these movies, Robeson played black characters with dignity, in contrast to the stereotypical African American roles of Hollywood films of that day.

Robeson was a staunch opponent of racism and spent much of his time and energy fighting for equality for blacks in America. His frequent international concert tours colored his world view. He learned more than 20 languages, including Russian, and began to study his African heritage and its culture. Robeson and his family visited the Soviet Union in 1934. After being received warmly, they decided to remain there for several years.

Robeson became a supporter of progressive causes around the globe, including the rights of oppressed Jews, of anti-Fascist forces in Spain, and of African nations against European colonial powers. The more he studied ideas of universal fellowship and world peace, the more he spoke out in the United States and abroad on the plight of blacks in America. Robeson met with President Harry Truman to urge him to do something about the lynchings of blacks in the South. His increasingly vocal opposition drew the ire of some people, who labeled him "un-American."

In 1950, as the Cold War with the Soviet Union heated up, the State Department withdrew Robeson's passport because of alleged communist affiliations. Robeson vowed that he had never been a member of the Communist Party but would not sign an oath disavowing communism. This brought the great entertainer's singing and acting career to an end. Both blacks and whites in America turned their

backs on him. He was not allowed to travel abroad for eight years.

The Supreme Court restored his passport in 1958 after declaring the oath he was asked to sign unconstitutional. With his passport returned, Robeson left the country and toured until 1963. Poor health forced him back to America and into retirement. Robeson died January 23, 1976, at age 77.

Robeson in costume for a rehearsal for the play Othello *at the Shakespeare Memorial Theatre in Stratford-upon-Avon, Warwickshire, in 1959. This was a year after the Supreme Court restored his passport.* Othello *was Robeson's return to English theatre after a 23-year absence.*

Paul Robeson, with Mary Ure (Desdemona), in the 1959 production of Othello *at Stratford-upon-Avon.*

Robeson, with Lena Horne, at the Big Three Unity for Colonial Freedom rally, under the auspices of the Council on African Affairs. Robeson was chair of the Council.

When Locke became a Rhodes scholar, it dramatically dampened the arguments of many white American academians who believed that blacks were intellectually inferior.

DR. ALAIN LOCKE came from a family where education was a tradition. In 1907, he had the distinction of becoming the first African American Rhodes scholar, earning the academic world's highest honor. He remained the only black recipient of the scholarship during his lifetime.

It's not difficult to imagine Locke's achievement, considering the intellectual genes he inherited, in addition to the environment in which he grew. With teachers throughout his family tree, it is not surprising that he became a widely respected educator and intellectual.

Born September 13, 1885, in Philadelphia, Locke contracted rheumatic fever as a child, which left him with permanent heart damage.

He adjusted to the limitations by burying himself in books and the arts.

Locke graduated second in his high school class, then studied at the Philadelphia School of Pedagogy. He finished first in his class. After entering Harvard University, he completed the four-year program in only three years. He graduated Phi Beta Kappa and magna cum laude in 1907.

As a Rhodes scholar, Locke spent three years studying philosophy at Oxford, where he founded the African Union Society. After attending the University of Berlin from 1910 to 1911, he returned to the United States and received a Ph.D. in philosophy from Harvard in 1918.

Locke began teaching at Howard University in 1912, remaining on staff there for more than 40 years until his retirement in 1953 as head of Howard's philosophy department. During Locke's tenure, he reformed the university's liberal arts program, and his stature as an education reformer became respected nationwide. He also advocated the creation of an African Studies Program, but that was not implemented until 1954.

In 1925, Locke edited an anthology called *The New Negro,* which contained social essays, fiction, poetry, and dramatic and music criticism of the day. His reputation brought him to the attention of white cultural institutions and patrons and, through them, Locke was able to boost the careers of such literary luminaries as Langston Hughes and Zora Neale Hurston.

Between 1936 and 1942, Locke edited the "Bronze Booklets" series, which detailed cultural and scholarly achievements and progressive views of black life. For two decades, he reviewed and wrote about black literature and art. His numerous essays on black culture and its dramatic upsurge during the Harlem Renaissance led to Locke's recognition as the foremost authority in the field. In addition to his many other accomplishments, he was a respected collector of African art.

Locke died on June 9, 1954, in New York, of a recurring heart problem.

Because of his academic success, Locke became a symbol of intellectual achievement among African Americans.

LANGSTON HUGHES

The young Hughes was nicknamed the "bus boy poet" by critic Vachel Lindsay.

LANGSTON HUGHES wrote poetry from childhood on. His devastatingly observant yet sorrowful examinations of African American life in Harlem—and the black experience in general—are considered among the most powerful writings of the 20th century. One of Hughes's most famous poems, "I, Too, Sing America," is a powerful plea to the country to recognize and accept blacks on the basis of their myriad contributions. A mentor to a generation of writers, Hughes was one of the most important voices of the Harlem Renaissance of the 1920s and of the Civil Rights Movement of the 1960s.

> *Happiness lives nowhere,*
> *Some old fool said,*
> *If not within oneself.*

That line, from Hughes's poem "I Thought It Was Tangiers I Wanted," speaks volumes about the life of a man whose travels took him to some of the world's most exotic places, including Mexico, Spain, and Africa. Born in February 1902, Hughes had already lived in seven cities in the United States and Mexico by the time he was 12. The handsome writer had been class poet in grammar school, and he continued to write throughout his life. For several years after school, he traveled, teaching and working as a domestic. Then, in 1924, writer and critic Vachel Lindsay "discovered" Hughes and dubbed him the "bus boy poet."

Langston Hughes was a poet with the genius to set his mellifluous voice to music. A prolific novelist and playwright, Hughes used verse to illustrate black urban life and attack social injustice.

In 1926, Hughes published his first book of poetry, *The Weary Blues,* followed by several volumes remarkable for the musical nature of his language. In later works, Hughes sometimes gave directions for musical accompaniment to his verses, making him one of the earliest writers to combine the two forms of artistry.

One of Hughes's plays, *Mulatto* (1935), had a successful run on Broadway in New York. In the 1940s, Hughes created Jesse B. Simple, a fictional character in his *Chicago Defender* column, who represented the lives and racial consciousness of the black working class.

In all, Hughes published more than ten volumes of poetry, more than 60 dramas, scores of operas, anthologies of other black writers, and two autobiographies. During the 1930s, Hughes took aim at civil rights and economic issues.

Ten years later, he took his genius for observation and his talent for relating to the working class to several universities. He taught at Atlanta University, then he was appointed poet-in-residence at the University of Chicago's Laboratory School. In the 1960s, Hughes turned out an incredible amount of material, including *Ask Your Mama: 12 Moods for Jazz* (1961) and his last volume of poetry, *The Panther and the Lash* (1967).

Hughes, considered by many to be the "poet laureate of Harlem," died of congestive heart failure in New York in March 1967.

On June 23, 1926, Langston Hughes published The Negro Artist and the Racial Mountain, *the principle manifesto of the young writers, artists, and performers known as the Harlem Renaissance.*

ZORA NEALE HURSTON

CRITICS AND READERS alike marvel at the woman they've come to know as Zora Neale Hurston. A writer, anthropologist, and eccentric personality who reigned during the 1920s and 1930s, Hurston created a stir just about every time she appeared in public.

Hurston's writing career began when her short story "Drenched in Light" was published in Opportunity *magazine in December 1924.*

Hurston created a vast body of writings—plays, essays, novels, short stories, and anthropological studies—that both titillated and taunted the working and upper classes of blacks and whites.

Always outspoken, flamboyant, and colorful, Hurston never backed down from anyone—friend or foe. She spoke her mind, and she wrote with the same ferocious clarity. In doing so, she created a legion of fans who have spanned generations. But during her lifetime, Hurston stepped on many toes, and some people exacted sweet revenge on her. She said that being misunderstood was the price she paid for daring to be great. And great she was.

Her sterling masterpiece, *Their Eyes Were Watching God,* thrust her into dominance as a major player in the Harlem Renaissance. Ironically, after decades of celebrity, she died unnoticed in Florida from a long illness and was buried in a pauper's grave.

Hurston was born January 7, 1891, in the all-black town of Eatonville, Florida. Her parents and neighbors gave her the kind of support that was not always available to African Americans coping with racial discrimination and few economic opportunities. The world she knew broke apart, however, when her mother died in 1904. Her father then sent her to boarding school.

Hurston wandered from job to job until she found a position as a maid and wardrobe assistant in a traveling Gilbert and Sullivan theater company. During this period, she was bitten by the showbiz bug, but she finished high school at Morgan Academy in Baltimore. She went to Howard University and then earned a graduate degree in anthropology from Barnard College.

With the help of literary lions Charles S. Johnson and Dr. Alain Locke, Hurston began her career by publishing short stories in *Opportunity* magazine. She also collaborated with Langston Hughes and Wallace Thurman as editor of *Fire!* magazine. Four years later, Hurston cowrote *Mule Bone* with Hughes. A comedy about African American life, the play was never performed during her lifetime because Hurston and Hughes had a falling out.

Meanwhile, after developing her skills as an anthropologist, she wrote her second volume of folk-lore, *Tell My Horse,* published in 1938. It was largely ignored at the time because of taboos associated with the subject, but it still provides one of the most comprehensive looks at voodoo in Jamaica and Haiti.

During the 1940s and 1950s, Hurston suffered a quiet period because the naturalism of Richard Wright's novels and the feminist-naturalism of Ann Petry's work supplanted her popular folk voice. Even in this "quiet" period, though, she published her autobiography, *Dust Tracks on a Road* (1942); another novel, *Seraph on the Suwanee* (1948); and several articles.

Modern audiences might have ignored Hurston's work had it not been for writer Alice Walker's revival of her material in the 1970s.

Much of the controversy over Hurston's fictional work centers on her rejection of the prevailing notion that black culture is inferior and immoral. Additionally, Hurston rejected the belief that women should be subservient to men.

Hurston died poor and alone in 1960.

Clinton Derricks-Carroll and Harriet D. Foy during a March 2002 dress rehearsal of Hurston's Polk County. *The typescript was rediscovered at the Library of Congress, and the play was put on at the Arena Stage in Washington, D.C.*

JOSEPHINE BAKER

VITAL. EXUBERANT. FLAMBOYANT. Sensual. All these words fail to adequately describe Josephine Baker, the internationally famous singer, comedian, and dancer known not only for her almost nonexistent costumes in Paris revues but also for her battles against racism. In a 1975 interview, Baker said she was never a great artist, but she was a woman who believed in art and the idea of international brotherhood so much that she put everything she had into them.

Despite living in France, Baker was dedicated to helping the American Civil Rights Movement. In 1963, she returned to America for the historic March on Washington, D.C.

Baker was born Freda Josephine MacDonald on June 3, 1906, in St. Louis. Her family was so poor she had to leave school briefly at the age of eight to help support them. Baker was first married at age 13 to Willie Baker, then she joined a band and traveling show. While still in her teens, she became a chorus girl in *Shuffle Along* at Radio City Music Hall at age 16, performed on Broadway in 1924, then joined *La Revue Nègre* in 1925, which brought *le jazz hot* to Paris—the city she would call home for the rest of her life.

It was in Paris that Baker's sensuality and rhythm made her a star. She first performed wearing only a pink flamingo feather, then she joined *Les Folies Bergère* to dance topless wearing a string of fake bananas. The smooth-skinned chanteuse took Paris by storm, walking her pet leopard Chiquita, who wore a diamond collar, down the Champs-Elysées. The painter Picasso waxed rhapsodic about her "smile to end all smiles," and poet Langston Hughes collected her pictures and newspaper clippings.

Baker began singing professionally in 1930 and went on to star in films and open her own nightclub in Paris. She became a French citizen in 1937, but World War II sent the woman dubbed "*La Perle Noir*" (The Black Pearl) by her fans down quite a different career path.

Some say Baker entertained more U.S. and Allied soldiers on the front lines in North Africa than Bob Hope, though she received no recognition for it in America. She also volunteered as an ambulance driver for the French Resistance. After Germany occupied France, Baker did underground intelligence work and was rewarded by the French Government with the Legion of Honor.

She returned to the stage after the war but devoted much of her energy to raising what she called her "Rainbow Tribe," a group of 12 orphaned children of different nationalities. Baker called it an "experiment in brotherhood," and she moved the children into Les Milandes, a 15th-century chateau. Baker retired in 1956 to raise the kids full time, but financial problems forced her to return to the stage in *Paris Mes Amours,* a musical based partly on her own life.

Baker said in 1951 that her greatest desire was to see her people happier in America. She refused to perform in segregated venues and, in 1963, flew in for the historic March on Washington. Later that year she performed at a civil rights benefit at Carnegie Hall.

Baker, who had said she wanted to die at the end of a dance, died in Paris in April 1975 after performances celebrating the 50th anniversary of her arrival in that city.

Flamboyant chanteuse and vaudeville star Josephine Baker, who took Paris by storm in the 1925 American production of La Revue Nègre, *smiles at one of the pet leopards she used to take along on her strolls down the Champs-Elysées.*

A. PHILIP RANDOLPH

Randolph was an unceasing agitator for the rights of the black working class. His work helped integrate the military and labor unions.

A. Philip Randolph, far left, leads the picketers outside the Convention Hall before the opening of the Democratic National Convention in Philadelphia in 1948. Randolph was also chair of the League for Non-Violent Civil Disobedience Against Military Segregation.

ASA PHILIP RANDOLPH fought a lifelong battle to provide fair employment opportunities for African Americans. His work as a trade unionist and organizer directly resulted in the establishment of the first successful black labor union, the desegregation of the armed forces, and the end of employment discrimination by companies and government bureaus involved in the defense industry.

Randolph pioneered the use of mass, nonviolent, direction-action protests to win gains from the federal government that benefited African Americans. His methods were replicated in the Civil Rights Movement, of which Randolph served as senior statesman.

He was born April 15, 1889, in Crescent City, Florida, to middle-class parents. Randolph moved to New York City in 1911 because he was unable to find decent work in his native Florida. That experience had an indelible effect on him, marking the beginning of his struggle to secure the rights of the black working class. Almost immediately, Randolph became involved in union efforts and socialist politics in New York. He also attended the City College of New York, taking classes in political science, economics, philosophy, and history. In 1912, he founded an employment agency and attempted to organize black workers.

In 1917, following America's entry into World War I, Randolph and friend Chandler Owen founded the first black socialist paper, *The Messenger* (later called *The Black Worker*), which called for increased hiring of African Americans in the war industry and armed forces. Randolph also helped organize the Socialist Party's first all-black political club in New York City.

Eventually, he relinquished his formal ties to the party, but he continued to consider himself a Democratic Socialist. Randolph was also president of the National Negro Congress, but he left that organization because it was dominated by communists.

His growing reputation as a labor organizer brought Randolph to the attention of the black porters, who took care of passengers on Pullman sleeping car trains. Being a Pullman porter was a plum job for blacks, but the porters were still besieged with poor working conditions, including low pay and long hours.

In 1925, Randolph was hired as an organizer and founded the Brotherhood of Sleeping Car

A. Philip Randolph received an honorary degree from Harvard Business School in 1971. Randolph is standing with Harvard Business School Dean Lawrence E. Fouraker.

A. PHILIP RANDOLPH

Porters. The Pullman Company had crushed earlier efforts by the porters to organize. Randolph fought the Pullman Company for 12 years, but in 1937, the company signed a major labor contract with the Brotherhood. Randolph had forged the first successful black trade union, which he took into the American Federation of Labor (AFL), despite the discrimination in its own ranks.

Randolph's success with Pullman launched his ascension as a national black leader. Following the certification of the Brotherhood as a bargaining agent, he returned to his fight for black inclusion in the military and the defense industry. He threatened to lead a massive march on Washington, D.C., in 1941 and bring an invasion of thousands of blacks to the White House lawn.

Fearing that Randolph was successfully mobilizing the forces needed to make the march a reality, President Franklin Roosevelt issued an executive order banning discrimination by companies with defense contracts. For the first time, the federal government said racial discrimination was wrong and committed itself to fair employment practices.

The success of that effort gave Randolph leverage to lay down another threat. He proposed that blacks boycott the draft. The potential of this confrontation may have influenced President Harry Truman to issue an executive order in 1948 to ban segregation in the military. Though Randolph didn't follow through with either threat, the results revealed the power of mass demonstrations.

Randolph spent the 1950s pursuing civil rights activities, particularly in the field of labor. After the AFL merged with the Congress of Industrial Organizations (CIO) in 1955, Randolph became the only black member of the organization's

BAYARD RUSTIN

A young student from the City College of New York strolled through the door of A. Philip Randolph's office wanting to know if the tales of this black leader were true. The 27-year-old was Bayard Rustin. Rustin would later become an extraordinary leader by harnessing the power of the masses, something Randolph talked to him about that first day.

Within two years of the meeting, Rustin had departed the Young Communist League and began walking in the footsteps of Randolph. After mentoring him in the use of nonviolent protest, Randolph continued to call upon Rustin's exceptional abilities as a political organizer over the next four decades.

They were a force even presidents could not surmount. The threat of a mass march on Washington organized by Rustin and Randolph compelled President Franklin Roosevelt to sign a 1941 executive order opening jobs in defense industries to African Americans. In 1948, they orchestrated the same threat to achieve an executive order from President Harry Truman to desegregate the military.

Upon gaining those commitments, Randolph called off both marches, thus antagonizing the young, impatient Rustin. But whether they worked together or parted ways, Randolph's striking model for peaceful mass action was not lost on Rustin. Joining with others to form the Congress of Racial Equality (CORE) in 1942 and the 1955–56

Montgomery Bus Boycott, the precursor to the Southern Christian Leadership Conference (SCLC), Rustin's skilled actions hit their mark in the struggle against segregation.

With Randolph's adroit counsel, Rustin also supported liberation efforts around the globe and in the United States. Still, it was in 1963 that Rustin demonstrated his preeminence in the Civil Rights Movement by finally delivering his mass March on Washington, where 200,000 participants formed the largest protest of its time.

Rustin publicly denounced A. Philip Randolph after Randolph canceled the 1948 March on Washington, which was largely organized by Rustin. Achieving their desegregation goals with just the threat of a march was not enough for the young militant. But after two and a half years of reflection, Rustin reconnected with Randolph.

In part, Rustin was so effective because he avoided the spotlight, preferring to work in the shadows of Randolph and Dr. King. His extraordinary ability to harness the power of numbers for landmark actions during the Civil Rights Movement helped redefine the laws of the United States. His commitment to human liberation extended across many continents from Africa to India. It covered many races and ethnicities from Japanese American detainees during WWII to Southeast Asian refugees after the Vietnam War to Haitians escaping oppression. He was also a staunch supporter of Israel. Rustin died in 1987.

Executive Council. In 1960, he used that platform to establish the Negro American Labor Council to attack segregation in the AFL-CIO.

The culmination of his career came when Randolph, at the age of 74, served as director and chairman of the 1963 March on Washington, D.C., for Jobs and Freedom. The next year, President Lyndon Johnson presented him with the Presidential Medal of Freedom, the nation's highest civilian honor.

Randolph remained involved in his activities as a vice president of the AFL-CIO until 1968, focusing on ending discrimination in unions. He also attacked black separatism on college campuses. His criticism of the union often landed him in hot water with union brass. By the end of his labor career, Randolph's agitation had transformed the labor movement and laid the groundwork for the modern civil rights era.

Randolph died May 16, 1979, at the age of 90.

EDWARD "DUKE" ELLINGTON

Duke's songs will live forever. His memorable classics include "Take the A Train" and "Satin Doll."

Edward "Duke" Ellington was a common man who rose to royalty. His legacy of composing more than 1,000 songs spanning several musical forms has earned him a place in history as one of America's greatest composers.

NO ONE PLAYED LIKE HIM. No one arranged music like him. No one loved life like him. And no one, absolutely no one, wrote songs like him. He was one of a kind. Though he was born at the turn of the century, Edward Kennedy Ellington enriched millions worldwide, earning him an eternal place among royalty. Long live the Duke!

His dad, James Edward, was a well-heeled butler and caterer who lived like a king despite his meager means. His mother, Daisy, had the confidence of a queen, even though the family lived in segregated Washington, D.C., where separate was never equal.

After hearing a terrific pianist named Harvey Brooks in Philadelphia during a summer trip with his parents, Edward decided the musician's life was for him. It was around this time that the well-mannered, fancy-dressing, popular piano-playing boy got his royal nickname—Duke.

By the time he was 22, Duke was already a successful pianist and bandleader. He married Edna Thompson, a pianist who schooled him in piano and music theory when they were both still in high school. They had a son, Mercer, in 1919, who followed in his dad's footsteps.

Duke's big break came in the 1920s when he auditioned for Harlem's Cotton Club. During the Cotton Club era, the flamboyant Duke Ellington Orchestra made nationwide radio broadcasts from the club and recorded "Black and Tan Fantasy." The Duke Ellington Orchestra soon became the first black musicians featured at Carnegie Hall and among the first prominently featured in major motion pictures. Duke's band became a magnet for the most talented musicians in the country. Chicago bassist Ernest Outlaw talked about how there was no one else who did what Ellington did, that he was "beyond category." He was always looking to do something different and unique.

Historian Dempsey Travis said: "Duke's creative abilities reached into classical, gospel, and even African areas of music, in addition to the jazz that he popularized." Travis was interviewed on jazz station WNUA-FM in Chicago, where he discussed his book, *The Duke Ellington Primer.* "No other American

Ellington is shown with his band during the 1930s. His band was one of the first black bands to be featured prominently in major motion pictures.

EDWARD "DUKE" ELLINGTON

composer had the depth and the production of Duke, which is why he is without question America's greatest composer."

Inspired by his fellow musicians and the high life he lived off the bandstand, Duke wrote more than 1,000 compositions. These include "It Don't Mean a Thing if It Ain't Got That Swing," "Satin Doll," "Sophisticated Lady," and his trademark tune written in collaboration with Billy Strayhorn, "Take the A Train."

Duke, as a person and as a composer, responded to the times. The Civil Rights Movement did not escape his perceptive eye. His contribution, while less vocal than others, was nevertheless very significant. In 1963, he wrote an ambitious show called *My People.* He dedicated it to the immense contributions of many African Americans. The show received rave reviews when it played in Chicago that same year.

Two years later, the Pulitzer committee recommended that Ellington receive the famous prize, which is an honor given only to the most accomplished people. The selection board made the unusual decision to ignore the committee's recommendation. Many felt racial bias was the motivation behind the board's decision. Ellington was hurt that he didn't receive the Pulitzer. He mused, "Fate is being very kind to me. Fate doesn't want me to be too famous, too young." He was 66 years old.

That same year, Ellington opened San Francisco's Grace Cathedral with the first of three sets of religious music that he called the Sacred Concerts. They consisted of both vocal and instrumental music composed for performance in large churches, synagogues, cathedrals, and mosques.

As happened to many musicians at the time, Ellington's manager put his name on all of Ellington's musical creations. The manager received half the royalties on all of Ellington's works, yet he never wrote one note.

In 1967, Billy Strayhorn, Duke's friend and collaborator for almost three decades, died. The death of his best friend moved Ellington in ways few could predict. Later that year, he recorded *And His Mother Called Him Bill,* which featured only Strayhorn tunes. "Sweet Pea" Strayhorn's death inspired Duke in other ways, too. Ellington composed, recorded, and toured at a hectic pace. In 1968, the National Academy of Recording Arts and Sciences finally honored him at age 69 with not one but two Grammy awards.

The Duke Ellington Orchestra continued to play its exciting brand of jazz, classical, African, spiritual, and ballet music. Ellington wrote the ballet *The River* for Alvin Ailey's dance company. Meanwhile, the orchestra performed before Queen Elizabeth of England and President Richard Nixon, who gave Duke the Presidential Medal of Freedom, the highest honor a civilian can receive.

Duke Ellington, a chain smoker all his life, died of lung cancer in 1974. Yet, he lives on in the thousands of songs he left behind. Grammy Award–winning composer and musician Wynton Marsalis hails Duke Ellington as "America's greatest composer."

THOMAS DORSEY

Personal tragedy led Dorsey to write "Take My Hand, Precious Lord."

ORIGINALLY A BLUES MUSICIAN of some renown, Thomas Andrew Dorsey eventually worked exclusively within a religious setting and elevated gospel music into a nationally recognized art form. Dorsey wrote more than 1,000 songs—dozens of which have become classics—as one of the genre's most prolific composers.

Born July 1, 1899, in Villa Rica, Georgia, Thomas, the oldest child in the Dorsey family, was raised in a religious household. He played piano during the revival services of his father, a traveling Baptist preacher.

But as a youth, he was strongly influenced by blues pianists around Atlanta. To help support his family, Thomas began playing blues piano in area saloons at the tender age of 11 under the stage name "Georgia Tom." In 1916, he moved to Chicago to study at the Chicago College of Composition and Arranging and earned a reputation in the city's blues and jazz club circuit.

In the early 1920s, Dorsey performed with several jazz groups, including the Whispering Serenaders. His own Wildcats Jazz Band toured with popular blues singer Ma Rainey until 1928. Dorsey had several of his blues compositions, notably "Riverside Blues," recorded by such major jazz musicians as Joseph "King" Oliver. Dorsey also toured with legendary blues guitarist Tampa Red, with whom he composed and recorded several songs, including "Tight Like That" and "Terrible Operation Blues." But, sticking to his upbringing in sacred music, Dorsey continued to write religious compositions. In 1921, his song "Someday, Somewhere" was included in the National Baptist Convention's Gospel Pearls Collection.

In the late 1920s, Dorsey turned his focus exclusively toward gospel, combining the spirituality of his lyrics with blues melodies and rhythms, which were not initially accepted in area churches because of their secular sound.

In 1931, Dorsey experienced a personal tragedy when he lost his wife and daughter in childbirth. That experience led him to write "Take My Hand, Precious Lord," which has become a gospel standard and is Dorsey's most famous work.

That same year, Dorsey formed the world's first gospel choir at Ebenezer Church in Chicago and opened the first publishing company dedicated exclusively to the sale of gospel music. In 1932, he became the lifelong choir director of Chicago's Pilgrim Baptist Church and, along with gospel legend Sallie Martin, founded the National Convention of Gospel Choirs and Choruses to train gospel vocal groups and soloists. Dorsey presided over that organization for 40 years and, during the same period, toured the country extensively with gospel caravans as both a performer and a lecturer.

He remained active in promoting gospel music around the country until his death in Chicago on January 23, 1993, at the age of 93.

Dorsey made it big on the blues and jazz circuits; he was the cool cat known as "Georgia Tom."

WALTER F. WHITE

Despite receiving a strong black vote in his presidential election, Franklin Roosevelt did not show an equally strong commitment to African Americans. The "Deal" for them was anything but new. Walter White decided to get racial issues into the Oval Office through Eleanor Roosevelt. His persistence established a lasting friendship with the first lady and gave him access to the president when necessary.

WALTER FRANCIS WHITE was born in Atlanta on July 1, 1893. At the age of 13, during an Atlanta race riot, White and his father sat inside with guns drawn as a mob threatened to invade their home. A decade later, in 1916, the city's school board was moving to limit public education for blacks to sixth grade, while white students could proceed to high school. That same year, White graduated from Atlanta University and was appointed secretary of a newly formed NAACP branch in Atlanta. The branch fought the school board on the public education issue, causing the board to eventually back down.

White's actions caught the attention of James Weldon Johnson, then field secretary for the NAACP. Johnson was influential in getting White a position in 1918 as assistant executive secretary of the organization. At the time, the NAACP had dedicated itself to the passage of the antilynching law. Congressional advocates of the bill needed hard figures to support their position, but there were no computer data banks during that era. Everything had to be collected by hand.

White's blue eyes, blonde hair, light complexion, and Southern upbringing made him the logical person to secrete himself in rural work camps of the Deep South to gather the necessary information. Year after year, White volunteered to eat and sleep with men who sometimes murdered African Americans for fun. The danger of just walking those lands was palpable. Slavery may have ended, but that did not deter the tradition of white citizens stopping any black person or, for that matter, any stranger on the road and questioning where they belonged. A hint of suspicion in this back country often led to the victim's fatal disappearance.

Even though he was almost lynched himself on one occasion, White always returned home with both a tally of lynchings for the year and vivid details about the murders of African Americans in the South. In 1929, White published his highly regarded book *Rope and Faggot*, a major indictment of lynching in America.

As compelling as this information was to some people, it was never enough to force the passage of the antilynching bill. White's efforts, however, did turn national attention to the atrocities perpetrated in the South and helped open the doors of the White House and U.S. legislature to the NAACP.

In addition to the antilynching campaign, White organized the defense for innocent blacks involved in the 1919 Chicago Race Riot and other high-profile legal cases. After Johnson became the NAACP's first black secretary in 1920, White worked with him for a decade. The organization flourished, and White became an invaluable administrator.

White succeeded Johnson in 1931. Under his leadership as executive secretary, the NAACP greatly increased its number of local branches, eased the transition from white to black executive leadership, and created a legal division that won key court battles. Legal successes, such as the landmark school integration decision *Brown* v. *Board of Education* expedited civil rights advancements by removing the legal basis for segregation. White's NAACP also helped end all-white election primaries, restrictive housing practices, and legally sanctioned public discrimination.

A heart attack forced a leave of absence in 1949 and tempered White's activities after he returned to work in 1950. Just as he was beginning to feel normal, White was felled by a fatal heart attack in 1955. White's assistant, Roy Wilkins, succeeded him.

White's light skin and blue eyes allowed him to pass for white while gathering information in the South about the atrocities happening to blacks.

ROBERT JOHNSON

DID ROBERT JOHNSON make a deal with the devil—his life for genius on the guitar? The trade supposedly took place at midnight on a southern crossroad and even sparked the movie *Crossroads,* which was loosely based on the event. Of course, that story is fiction.

Stories about Johnson range from pure speculation to the limited perspectives of family and friends. A full account may never surface because Johnson was a traveling bluesman whose notoriety during the 1930s was marginal, certainly not enough for news outlets to document his life as an incredible blues guitarist and songwriter.

What is known is that he was born out of wedlock to Julia Major Dodds and Noah Johnson on May 8, 1911, in Hazelhurst, Mississippi. The bluesman believed his father was Charles Dodd, his mother's husband, who, because of an acquaintance's vendetta, fled to Memphis, Tennessee, before Johnson was conceived. Dodd changed his last name to Spencer to throw off the lynch-minded, the same name that was given to Robert.

Johnson and his mother joined Charles Spencer's Memphis household about two years later. Spencer's children, who Johnson believed were his half-siblings, were already there with Spencer's mistress and her children. Johnson's mother left him in Memphis, and he was treated like a full member of the family. When he was somewhere between seven and nine years old, Johnson rejoined his mother and her second husband, Willie Willis, in Robinsonville, Mississippi.

In Robinsonville, Johnson developed into a delta bluesman much to his stepfather's dismay. He started his musical career using a one-string

Johnson lived a short life, about 27 years, but his passion and genius has inspired many of the biggest rock stars in modern history.

harp followed by a harmonica. A few years passed before playing the guitar interested him. He apparently began shadowing the two best musicians in town, Willie Brown and Son House, yet this failed to improve his ability. Brown and House did not hear much guitar talent coming from him, so they advised him to stick with the harmonica.

Johnson ignored their advice. He had learned about his true paternity, so he changed his name and went to Hazelhurst to search for his father. While he never found Noah Johnson, he did meet Ike Zinermon (or Zinnerman), a bluesman working juke joints, who mentored him on the guitar. When Brown and House next saw Johnson, he could play any song requested

after hearing it only once. It was a mystery to them how Johnson had become so accomplished; hence, the story of Johnson trading his soul to the devil.

Ironically, Johnson would meet his end near the crossing of Highways 82 and 49E, alternately called "Three Forks," "Three Points," or "Three Corners." His demise began when he cast considerable attention on one young lady, who may have been the roadhouse owner's companion or wife. No one knows for sure if the joint's owner sought poisonous retribution. Johnson, not suspecting trouble, accepted an open bottle of whiskey that was supposedly laced with strychnine. He drank the whiskey, fell ill while performing, and died a few days later on August 16, 1938.

Johnson's music lives on today in the form of 29 songs recorded in 42 takes in 1936 and 1937. Columbia Records issued the songs in 1961 largely due to the influence of fan John Hammond. Some songs are piano-based boogie with Johnson's guitar carrying both the bass and lead notes. Keith Richards, himself a legendary guitarist, said this about Johnson's abilities: "When I first heard [him], I was hearing two guitars, and it took me a long time to realize he was actually doing it all by himself."

The compilation was reissued twice in the 1990s after Johnson's music had become deep-rooted in contemporary music. Decades after his death, his music continues to inspire Richards and other rock 'n' roll superstars such as Bob Dylan, Jimi Hendrix, Eric Clapton, as well as the members of the Rolling Stones, Red Hot Chili Peppers, and more. Many of these stars have joined Johnson in The Rock and Roll Hall of Fame and Museum. Johnson was one of the first inducted in 1986.

ERNEST EVERETT JUST

Ernest E. Just became the first to win the NAACP's renowned Spingarn Medal. In 1916, he was only the second African American to earn a Ph.D. in biological sciences.

ERNEST EVERETT JUST revolutionized the world's view of cell fertilization and development. His discoveries in marine biology laid the foundation for ongoing genetic and medical advances.

Just was born August 14, 1883, in Charleston, South Carolina. His single mother was busy working, teaching, and organizing, so Just cared for his siblings while earning an education and toiling in the area's phosphate fields.

Scholarships became Just's ticket to an education, beginning at the Kimball Academy in Meriden, New Hampshire. He graduated in three years before enrolling at Dartmouth College. He graduated magna cum laude and Phi Beta Kappa in 1907 with honors in botany, history, sociology, and zoology. Just then taught English at Howard University.

Starting in 1909, Just's summer vacations were reserved for his first love—science. He pursued graduate credit as a research assistant to Frank

R. Lillie, director of the marine biology laboratory in Woods Hole, Massachusetts, and head of the zoology department at the University of Chicago. Just discovered that the outer ectoplasm rather than an inner membrane inhibited sperm from fertilizing eggs. He made strides at Howard as head professor of the new zoology department.

Just completed his Ph.D. in zoology with Lillie at the University of Chicago in 1916. He returned to Woods Hole to advance research in artificial parthenogenesis—cell development chemically induced without the aid of sperm. Such reproduction suggested that genetic material existed in eggs, which contradicted theories that eggs were merely incubators for the genes in sperm.

Just continued with his experiments at Woods Hole until 1928, when he could no longer bear racial snubs. His research shifted to facilities overseas. Working at Naples Zoological Station in Italy fulfilled a dream. He later became the first American invited to the Kaiser Wilhelm Institute for Biology in Germany.

Strife at home, at Howard University, and racist Fascism pushed Just to the Sorbonne in France by 1938, where he worked until Germans soldiers entered Paris in 1940. He was briefly imprisoned by Hitler's forces, but the U.S. State Department rescued him. He returned to Washington, D.C., but Just died of cancer in 1941. His work in advanced cellular biology can be found in his 50 published works, including *The Biology of the Cell Surface.*

PERCY LAVON JULIAN

Percy Lavon Julian was a trailblazer in chemistry who used ingenuity to pioneer products with global impact. Though best known for creating synthetic cortisone at a cost affordable to arthritis sufferers, he was far from a one-hit wonder.

Julian was born in 1899 to Alabama parents who stressed education. His two brothers became physicians, while his three sisters each received master's degrees. Julian's work enjoyed the most recognition of all. After graduating valedictorian from DePauw University in Indiana in 1920 and earning a master's degree from Harvard University in 1923, he was locked out of teaching positions in white colleges. Julian taught at black universities for a few years before obtaining a fellowship for doctoral studies in Vienna. There he embarked on groundbreaking soybean research to synthesize physostigmine, a drug used for treating glaucoma.

Julian successfully completed that synthesis in the United States at DePauw before becoming the first African American director of research at Glidden Company, a leading chemical manufacturer headquartered in Chicago. As chief chemist at Glidden, he created such lifesaving products as flame-retardant aero-foam, lower-cost cortisone, and 64 other patented inventions from soy.

In 1950, the City of Chicago named Julian Chicagoan of the Year, yet just a few months later his home was set on fire by an arsonist. A year later, dynamite exploded outside his children's bedroom window. Despite the scientific discoveries Julian had made that were improving lives, there were people who could not accept a black family's success. Julian was undeterred.

After establishing Julian Laboratories in 1954, he discovered that wild yams in Mexico were more effective than soybeans for some of his products. With labs in two countries, his total number of patents increased to more than 100, and lives around the globe were made better for it. Julian continued researching hormones until his death in 1975.

KATHERINE DUNHAM

Dunham earned a Ph.D. in anthropology from Northwestern University after studying the origins of dance in Jamaica, Martinique, Trinidad, and Haiti.

CHOREOGRAPHER KATHERINE Dunham popularized Afro-Caribbean dance throughout the world and elevated black dance into a serious, accepted art form. Dunham was so serious about learning and establishing this medium as "art" that she majored in anthropology in college—all the way through the doctoral level—to study the original African and West Indian dance forms in their native environments.

Dunham herself was a mini-United Nations of mixed African, American Indian, French-Canadian, and Madagascan heritage. She was born June 22, 1909, in Chicago. She exhibited an early interest in athletics and music, which merged into her natural talent for dance.

At the age of 15, Dunham organized a cabaret party to raise funds for her church. At 21, she had started a dance school, which folded from lack of funding. But she soon joined the Negro Dance Group, where she learned ballet and mime and was allowed to teach her pupils what she knew of African tribal dance.

After Dunham trained 150 young dancers for a program at the 1934 Chicago Century of Progress Exhibition, she received a Rosenwald Foundation grant through Northwestern University to visit Jamaica, Martinique, Trinidad, and Haiti to study the origins of the countries' peoples and their dances. She later received a Guggenheim Fellowship to continue her studies and eventually received a B.A. and an M.A. from the University of Chicago and a Ph.D. in anthropology from Northwestern University. Her studies led her to develop a new technique called "dance-isolation," which involves mov-ing one part of the body while all the other parts remain motionless.

Dunham's first ballet, *L'Ag'Ya,* based on a fighting dance from Martinique, was accepted by the Federal Theater Project of the Works Progress Administration. It was performed with success in Chicago in 1939. A year later, Dunham established her first ensemble, the Katherine Dunham Dance Company, which opened at New York's Windsor Theater with Dunham's own work *Tropics* and *Le Jazz Hot.* The per-formance was a huge success.

Shortly after, the Dunham Dance Company was asked to take part in the all-black musical *Cabin in the Sky,* with Dunham playing the role of Georgia Brown. The production had a long run, after which Dunham appeared in *Stormy Weather* and choreographed *Pardon My Sarong* and *Windy City.*

In 1943, she was guest artist for the San Francisco Symphony Orchestra and then again for the Los Angeles Symphony Orchestra in 1945. Over the next 20 years, Dunham and her dance troupe visited almost every country in the world.

Dunham gave her last dance performance at the Apollo Theater in 1965. Afterward, she established the Performing Arts Training Center, now called the Katherine Dunham Center for the Performing Arts, at Southern Illinois University. She passed away on May 21, 2006.

After studying native dance in Africa and the West Indies, Dunham developed a new technique called "dance-isolation," which involved moving one part of the body while other parts remained motionless.

WILLIAM GRANT STILL

WHILE MUCH HAS BEEN written about African American musical contributions to jazz, blues, and rock, little has been penned about black classical composers. Perhaps the least known of the important artists of the Harlem Renaissance, Dr. William Grant Still was the first African American classical composer to have his symphonic work *Afro-American Symphony* performed by a major American orchestra.

Still was born in Woodville, Mississippi, on May 11, 1895. Both of his parents were musicians, and his father was the town's bandmaster. He received his early musical training at home, and he later attended the Oberlin College Conservatory of Music.

Afro-American Symphony premiered in 1931 with the Rochester Philharmonic under Dr. Howard Hanson. To this day, it remains a classic in its repertoire and has since been performed by other major orchestras throughout the world.

Yet another first, Still's opera *Troubled Island,* based on a libretto by Langston Hughes, was the first African American opera to be performed by a major company. Laszlo Halasz conducted the piece for The New York City Opera in 1949 in honor of the company's fifth anniversary. *Troubled Island* is based on the life of Haitian leader Jean-Jacques Dessalines, who ruled the world's first black independent nation from 1804 to 1806. The libretto deals with the subject of black liberation and is above the usual operatic standard, in part because of Still's technical prowess and the passion of noted poet Hughes, who fashioned the work from a successful play. Reviewers for the *New York Herald Tribune* praised Still for having a flair for opera music, although they criticized him for not fully developing his ideas.

In 1955, Still became the first African American to conduct a major orchestra in the Deep South when he led the New Orleans Symphony Orchestra. He was also the first black to conduct a major American orchestra, performing his original work with the Los Angeles Philharmonic. He died in 1978.

Still's work can be divided into three creative periods. The first was his experimental period (1920–1929), which some say was perhaps his most exciting period. The second period

Still had a number of firsts as an African American composer: He wrote the first symphony and opera to be performed by a major American orchestra and opera company, respectively. He was also the first African American to conduct a major orchestra in the South.

(1930–1939), perhaps his most popular and prolific was his African American period with many of his works carrying a black theme. During this time he wrote "And They Lynched Him on a Tree," the *Sahdji* ballet, *Troubled Island,* and *Afro-American Symphony.* The third period (1940–1978) was a combination of the first two, with some interesting twists. This is when he composed his opera *Highway No. 1 U.S.A.* and his "Poem for Orchestra," which was commissioned by the Cleveland Orchestra.

With today's rising pride in African American music, interest in black classical composers such as Still is skyrocketing. In the 1970s, Sister Elise, of the Catholic Order of the Sisters of the Blessed Sacrament, cofounded two black opera companies: Opera/South and Opera Ebony. Opera/South performed Still's *Highway No. 1 U.S.A.* and "A Bayou Legend." In 1971, classical singer Natalie Hinderas recorded *Natalie Hinderas Plays Music by Black Composers* on Desto Records and featured Still's compositions. Still has been dubbed the "Dean of Black Classical Composers," and his work remains as not only a reference point for some of the more contemporary African Americans in this genre but also a body of work that accurately reflected the times and Still's unique vision of the world.

Still goes over his "Suite for Violin" with Louis Kaufman, who featured the work in one of his recitals in 1944.

CHARLES HOUSTON

CHARLES HAMILTON HOUSTON ranks with the turn-of-the-century giants W.E.B. Du Bois, Booker T. Washington, and Marcus Garvey, as well as with the titans of the Civil Rights Movement: Martin Luther King, Jr., Malcolm X, Thurgood Marshall, and A. Philip Randolph. He was a brilliant lawyer. His successful appearances before the U.S. Supreme Court on matters of racial discrimination laid the groundwork for the landmark *Brown* v. *Board of Education* case, which ended racial segregation in public schools. Because the *Brown* case led to further court decisions outlawing various other forms of discrimination and to legislation enacting civil rights laws, it can be said that Houston had a major impact on dismantling legally sanctioned racism in America.

Born September 3, 1895, in Washington, D.C., Houston showed his brilliance early when he graduated from high school at the age of 15. He then graduated from Amherst College four years later as a Phi Beta Kappa and one of six class valedictorians.

Houston earned his law degree from Harvard University in 1922, graduating cum laude and in the top five percent of his class. He became the first black student selected as editor of the *Harvard Law Review* and, in 1923, the first African American awarded a doctorate of judicial science degree from Harvard. That same year, he received a one-year fellowship to study civil law at the University of Madrid.

Houston was admitted to the D.C. bar in 1924. From 1924 to 1950, he had a private practice with his father, William, who was a graduate of Howard University's law school. During those years, however, there were various interruptions in Houston's practice.

While teaching at Howard University, Houston was appointed vice dean in 1929 to run the university's three-year day program and the law school library. His most notable accomplishments there were helping the law school receive accreditation from legal sanctioning bodies and significantly improving the curriculum.

In 1934, Houston took a leave of absence from Howard. The NAACP retained him as special counsel to direct a campaign against discrimination in public education and transportation. This work would establish the strategy of the NAACP to end all legal segregation. His assistant special counsel was Thurgood Marshall, who would go on successfully to argue the *Brown* case in 1954.

This brilliant legal strategist was one of the most gifted constitutional lawyers the black community, or any community, has ever produced. Working primarily on behalf of the NAACP, Houston's victories before the Supreme Court helped end legal discrimination in America.

In two of Houston's early Supreme Court cases, in 1935 and 1938, the court overturned death sentences of black defendants who had been convicted by juries from which blacks had been excluded because of race. In 1938, Houston also won his argument in *Missouri ex rel. Gaines* v. *Canada.* The Supreme Court ruled that the state of Missouri could not bar blacks from entering the state university law school without providing a separate but equal law school for blacks.

The *Missouri* case was a major victory for the NAACP and the "equalization strategy" employed by Houston. It forced the Supreme Court to take a hard look at the good-faith efforts of states to provide equal accommodations under the "separate but equal" policy.

In this case, Missouri had been willing to provide scholarships for African Americans willing to go to other states to study law. However, the Supreme Court saw that as a way for Missouri to duck the expense of maintaining its own state law school for black students.

In the 1940s, as a member of the NAACP's National Legal Committee and as general counsel of the Association of Colored Railway Trainmen and Locomotive Firemen and of the International Association of Railroad Employees, Houston argued two successful cases before the Supreme Court that outlawed racial discrimination in union bargaining representation.

When Houston passed away in April 1950 from a heart ailment at the age of 55, five Supreme Court justices attended his funeral. He was respected in legal circles for his ability as a constitutional lawyer and for the brilliance of his attacks on discrimination.

BILLIE HOLIDAY

Jazz singer Billie Holiday was forced to darken her face early in her career to play the Fox Theater in Detroit. The management felt she was too light-skinned to play with Count Basie's black band.

BILLIE HOLIDAY, the legendary jazz singer with the small voice and innovative phrasing, influenced and inspired generations of musicians. She had an uncanny ability to infuse raw emotion into what might otherwise have been ordinary songs. Despite the tragedy of a life shortened by abuse and drug addiction, Holiday was a pioneer in the cultural war on racism.

Born Eleanora Fagan in Baltimore, Maryland, on April 7, 1915, Holiday's life was tough from the beginning. Her father, Clarence Holiday, played guitar with Fletcher Henderson. But her father abandoned the family early, and Holiday was left in the care of relatives who abused her. Holiday had little schooling and did menial work before moving to New York in 1928 to join her mother. The cinnamon-colored woman with the expressive face was jailed briefly for prostitution before embarking on her musical career.

Holiday started out singing at small clubs in Brooklyn and Harlem before being discovered in 1933 by talent scout and producer John Hammond. Her first recording was a novelty tune called "Your Mother's Son-in-Law." Hammond arranged for Holiday to record with Benny Goodman. In 1935, he set up regular recording sessions with studio bands, including some of the finest musicians of the day, such as pianist Teddy Wilson and tenor sax magician Lester Young.

Holiday and Young were musical soul mates. She nicknamed him "Prez," and he dubbed her "Lady Day." From 1935 to 1942 she did some of her greatest work, including "God Bless the Child" and "Fine and Mellow."

During this time, Holiday was among those challenging racial segregation in music. For several months in 1938, she sang with Artie Shaw's white big band. This made the singer one of the first black artists to be featured with a white orchestra.

The next year, Holiday began singing at Cafe Society, an interracial nightclub in New York City's Greenwich Village. It was there that Holiday first performed the antilynching ballad "Strange Fruit," a song with such viscerally horrific images of black people hanging from trees that some whites walked out of performances. Her record label, Columbia, refused to record the tune.

By the end of the 1940s, Holiday was so popular that she got a chance to make a movie, *New Orleans,* with her idol, Louis Armstrong. But she was disgusted at having to play a maid. The woman known for her innate ability to embellish her vocal instrument by using shifts in rhythm, such as singing behind the beat, became addicted to heroin in the early 1940s.

She was jailed on drug charges in 1947, and her personal problems began seriously affecting her ability to perform. Holiday had a series of relationships with abusive men and began drinking heavily, which coarsened her distinctive voice.

Holiday's final, glorious collaboration with Lester Young, Coleman Hawkins, Roy Eldridge, and others on the 1957 television special *The Sound of Jazz* included a legendary version of "Fine and Mellow." It recalled some of Holiday's best work. In 1959, Holiday collapsed and was taken to New York City's Metropolitan Hospital, where she died July 17, while under arrest for narcotics possession.

Holiday's influence on music was great. Frank Sinatra acknowledged patterning his singing style after her. In 1958, he called Holiday "the most important influence on American popular singing in the last 20 years."

Holiday first sang "Strange Fruit," an antilynching ballad, at Cafe Society, an interracial nightclub in Greenwich Village. Her record label, Columbia, refused to record the haunting tune.

JESSE OWENS

Track-and-field specialist James Cleveland "Jesse" Owens ran like the wind—legend has it he was across the finish line before you could see him take off.

JESSE OWENS won four gold medals for America in the 1936 Olympic Games in Berlin. His long jump record stood for 25 years, and, for a time, Owens held or shared the world record for every sprint event recognized by the International Amateur Athletic Federation.

Owens was born September 12, 1913, to a father who was an illiterate Alabama field laborer. His athletic gift came to light early when he consistently outran the local boys, though the frail Owens suffered from malnutrition.

An amazed and sympathetic coach, Charles Riley, took Owens under his wing. Riley worked him out for 45 minutes a day before school, and Owens held several jobs after classes. Riley's efforts paid off: As a high school senior, Owens tied the world record in the 100-yard dash and won three events in the 1933 National Interscholastic Championships in Chicago. It was the first of several astonishing track meets that would put Owens in the record books.

The next record came on May 25, 1935, when, as a student at Ohio State University, Owens participated in a Big Ten Conference track meet at the University of Michigan. The 21-year-old tied the world record for the 100-yard dash and set new world records for the 220-yard dash, the 220-yard low hurdles, and the broad jump (as the long jump was called at that time).

His crowning moment was yet to come. At the 1936 Olympic Games in Berlin, Owens won four gold medals and, before the eyes of the world, dashed Adolf Hitler's boasts of Aryan superiority. Not only did Owens win the gold, but he tied the Olympic record for the 100-meter dash and set new Olympic records for the 200-meter run and the long jump.

The coup de grâce came when Owens ran the final leg of the 400-meter relay race, in which the American team broke a world record. Hitler was so disgusted that he refused to shake Owens's hand, despite personally congratulating other Olympic winners.

Unfortunately, though Owens was celebrated on his return to America, he was not embraced. Promised endorsements never materialized. Penniless, he hired himself out to race against horses and motorcycles. He couldn't afford to finish college and finally landed a job as a city playground worker.

It wasn't until 1955 that America began to recognize Owens's accomplishments. The government sent him abroad as an Ambassador of Sports, and he gave speeches on patriotism and fair play. He was also named secretary of the Illinois State Athletic Commission.

Following his death on March 31, 1980, in Arizona, Jesse Owens was posthumously awarded the Congressional Medal of Honor in 1990 and also appeared on a commemorative postage stamp.

VONETTA FLOWERS

At the 2002 Winter Olympics, Vonetta Flowers proved what thinking outside the box can yield—a gold medal. She is the first African American to win gold in the Winter Olympics. She accomplished all of this with teammate Jill Bakken in the first women's bobsled competition in the games.

Flowers was born October 29, 1973, in Birmingham, Alabama. While on the University of Alabama track and field team, she was named an NCAA All-American on seven occasions.

As an assistant track coach at her alma mater, Flowers still envisioned summer gold in her future when her husband, Johnny, noticed a sign for bobsled teams posted in the athletes' hotel during the 2000 Summer Olympics. She didn't make it through the trials for the Summer games, so she and her husband found themselves with time on their hands. Without any prior experience, they jokingly decided to try out for the Winter games. An injury precluded Johnny from becoming a part of the team, but Flowers made it.

Flowers's track speed provided the fast start her team needed to maintain competitive top-ten finishes during the World Cup bobsled season that preceded the 2002 Olympics. The crowning moment for Flowers and her teammate was so appreciated that German competitors lifted the duo on their shoulders in celebration of their history-making win.

JOE LOUIS

After being told that an upcoming opponent was "quick," the legendary Brown Bomber coined the phrase, "He can run, but he can't hide."

JOE LOUIS BARROW, the son of Alabama sharecroppers, was born in 1914 at the beginning of World War I. By World War II, he was known as the "Brown Bomber." He would go on to become perhaps the greatest prizefighter this country has ever known.

Louis, his siblings, and his mother moved from the Deep South to Detroit when Joe was 12. His mother had visions of him becoming a great violinist, but after a family friend (who was a 1932 Golden Gloves champion) invited Louis to the gym to work out as his sparring partner, Louis's violin days were over. Louis accepted the offer—and landed a right punch that almost knocked his friend out of the ring.

In 1935, after a sensational string of early victories, Louis finally faced a major opponent—

former world heavyweight champion Primo Carnera. To many, Carnera represented the Fascist ambitions of Italian dictator Benito Mussolini, who was on the verge of invading Ethiopia, the world's oldest independent black nation. Louis was an African American who symbolized the free world and also the pride of the African people. On the night of the fight, Yankee Stadium was filled with a record crowd of mostly blacks and Italians. By the sixth round, the gigantic Italian stallion had been soundly defeated.

In June 1936, Louis faced an opponent who was seen as a symbol of Aryan supremacy: Max Schmeling, the former German heavyweight champion. It was a great fight. In the twelfth round, Schmeling knocked out the Brown Bomber.

Louis came back in 1937 to recapture the title from James J. Braddock with an eighth-round knockout. In 1938, he faced Schmeling for a

Joe Louis, a heavyweight boxing champion during the Depression and World War II, emerged when all Americans needed a hero. He was the first crossover hero, beloved by both blacks and whites. That he opened up professional sports to other African Americans made him immortal.

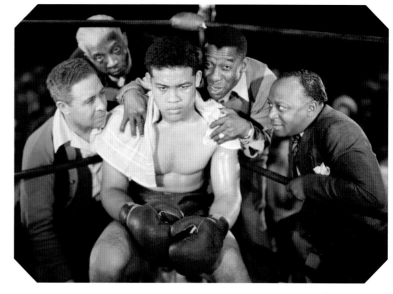

Louis, shown here in a publicity photo, was a methodical fighter. His quick, two-fisted attack style was virtually inescapable.

rematch that received international attention. In what some have described as the most anticipated fight of the 20th century, Louis avenged himself and his race with a stunning first-round knockout after two minutes and four seconds. Louis's victory delighted millions of black radio listeners and raised the morale of other Americans who needed a lift during the bleakest of the Depression years. In Harlem alone, tens of thousands of people celebrated in the streets, yelling, "Joe Louis is the first American to KO a Nazi." Malcolm X described Louis's prominence this way: "Every Negro boy old enough to walk wanted to be the next Brown Bomber."

Louis went on to defend his title a record 25 times. In doing so, he became America's first African American hero, destroying the myth of racial inferiority as soundly as he defeated his opponents in the ring.

He died April 12, 1981, in Las Vegas. The former army sergeant was buried at Arlington National Cemetery.

JACOB LAWRENCE

JACOB LAWRENCE was an African American painter and educator who became famous for using vivid blocks of color and a highly formalized style to create dramatic images of African American historical figures and neighborhoods. Lawrence, admired for narrative series such as "Migration of the American Negro," used art to explore his cultural heritage and to educate others about the realities of black life.

Jacob Lawrence is one of the few African American artists who have sustained mainstream recognition.

Just before Lawrence died in June 2000, *The New York Times* art critic Michael Kimmelman wrote that he couldn't think of another American artist whose works were so true, modest, and filled with love—even the pieces that tell tragic stories. Howard University art historian Scott Baker lauds Lawrence for his originality and for never compromising his style in a quest for mainstream recognition.

Lawrence was born in September 1917, in Atlantic City, New Jersey, the eldest of three children. His railroad cook father left the family in 1924. The children spent a brief time in foster homes before joining their mother in Harlem when Lawrence was 13. The teen started to get into trouble, so his mother enrolled him in an after-school arts and crafts program at the Utopia Children's Center. There he met his mentor, artist Charles Alston. Lawrence dropped out of school at age 17 to work in a printing shop, but he also took Alston's classes at the Harlem Art Workshops. The budding artist supplemented his education by walking 60 blocks from his home to the Metropolitan Museum of Art, where he examined the works of the early Italian Renaissance painters.

Writers such as Langston Hughes, Richard Wright, and Ralph Ellison met Lawrence at Alston's studio. The connections he made there helped him get his first federal art project grant. When he was 19, Lawrence produced paintings about life in Harlem during the Great Depression. The works, in somber colors on brown paper, depict scenes of abject poverty, police intimidation, and racial exploitation. Lawrence once remarked that his work depicts events from the many "Harlems" that exist throughout America. The artist said he wanted to show people the happiness and the tragedies that exist in low-income neighborhoods of color.

In 1937, Lawrence began work on a series on Toussaint L'Ouverture, the Haitian revolutionary, and he followed that narrative with a series on the lives of Frederick Douglass and Harriet Tubman. Next, Lawrence completed his landmark series of 60 paintings on the "Migration of the American Negro," which chronicles the journey of Southern blacks to the North in the wake of World War I. Lawrence said these works illustrated the fact that despite the efforts of blacks to improve their social conditions, African Americans encountered similar problems in both the northern and southern parts of the country.

At a time when other black artists were finding it difficult to get shown, Lawrence was exhibiting regularly at the Downtown Gallery in New York City and also at the Whitney Museum of American Art. He began his teaching career at Black Mountain College in North Carolina, later moved to the Pratt Institute, and retired from the University of Washington in Seattle in 1986 as professor emeritus. When he died at home on June 9, 2000, Lawrence was working on paintings for a new exhibition at the Manhattan gallery DC Moore. He was one of the first black artists to garner sustained mainstream recognition in the United States.

Lawrence painted "The Libraries Are Appreciated" in 1943. His series of paintings on the migration of blacks in America garnered much respect.

MARIAN ANDERSON

Despite Anderson's love of classical music, her passion was jazz. She was an avid collector of jazz records, and she played jazz piano.

KNOWN AS THE "baby contralto" when she sang in Philadelphia churches as a child, Marian Anderson became one of the 20th century's most celebrated singers, with a nearly three-octave voice that ranged from low D to high C. She was the first African American to solo with New York's Metropolitan Opera, and she retired in 1965 after a farewell concert at Carnegie Hall.

Anderson made history twice. In February 1939, the world-famous contralto was refused permission by the Daughters of the American Revolution to sing in Constitution Hall in Washington, D.C., because of her color. A resulting nationwide protest caused First Lady Eleanor Roosevelt to resign from the group and arrange for Anderson to give a free Easter morning concert on the steps of the Lincoln Memorial. An estimated 75,000 people, including government officials, Supreme Court judges, and everyday citizens, attended. She eventually sang at Constitution Hall, but not until 1953.

Anderson made history again in 1955 when she was invited to become the first African American soloist to perform at the Metropolitan Opera House in New York City. Langston Hughes called Anderson's performance as Ulrica in the Verdi opera *Un Ballo in Maschera,* "a precedent-shattering moment in American musical history." *The New York Times* deemed the breakthrough so important to the issue of race relations in America that it ran a front-page story on Anderson's debut the next morning.

Anderson was born in Philadelphia on February 27, 1902, with what she called a compulsion to make music. She ran errands for neighbors to earn enough money to buy a violin from a pawn shop and later persuaded her father to buy a piano, which she and her sisters taught themselves to play.

But what she did most was sing. In fact, Anderson often missed her classwork because she was singing at nearby schools and at churches. In 1919, she began studying with the famous music teacher Giuseppe Boghetti. Her church paid for the first year of instruction, but Boghetti was so enamored of her talent that he spent years tutoring her for free.

In 1925, Anderson bested 300 other young singers in a competition to win a contract for concert tours. This led to her appearance with the New York Philharmonic Orchestra. From 1933 to 1935, she toured Europe on fellowships and sang for royalty in England, Sweden, Norway, and Denmark. It was during this extended excursion that the famous opera singer Arturo Toscanini called one of Anderson's concerts something you hear only once every 100 years.

Three years after her return to America, Anderson was considered one of the country's leading contraltos. Her recordings were national hits, and her concerts were sellouts. By 1941, she was one of America's highest-paid concert artists and, in 1978, she received the John F. Kennedy Center for the Performing Arts Award for her "lifetime achievements in the arts." Anderson died in 1993.

In 1939, Anderson sang at an Easter morning concert on the steps of the Lincoln Memorial after being denied permission to sing at Constitution Hall by the Daughters of the American Revolution.

MAHALIA JACKSON

The powerful contralto of Mahalia Jackson carried gospel music to new realms on radio, into the sphere of international popular music, and across color barriers.

MAHALIA JACKSON produced an inventive contralto style by fusing traditional Baptist hymns with jazz and a rousing sanctified gospel beat that was so uplifting she became the first gospel superstar. After rebounding from mediocre responses to several of her early records, the entertainment industry quickly rolled out the red carpet for the "Queen of Gospel Song" when "Move On Up a Little Higher," composed by W. Herbert Brewster, sold more than two million copies. It became clear in 1948 that a legend was in the making.

On October 16, 1911, Jackson became the newest inhabitant of John and Charity Jackson's three-room home in the impoverished Water Street neighborhood in New Orleans. Money may have been lacking, but music was plentiful in a city known for melodious innovations.

Jackson learned to sing gospel about the same time that she added talking and walking to her physical repertoire. At age four, she performed in the children's choir at Mount Moriah Baptist Church. Following her mother's death, four-year-old Mahalia and her brother joined aunts who adhered to a strict religious upbringing. Somehow, over the course of her childhood, Jackson still became influenced by contemporary jazz and blues, in addition to the foot-stomping spontaneity of sanctified gospel. When Jackson blended that musical gumbo, she served the world gospel with enough spice and passion to start a fresh tradition that lit up congregations from New Orleans to her new home in Chicago.

Family finances caused Jackson to quit the eighth grade and get a job as a domestic in New Orleans. By 1928, she was living with an aunt in Chicago, where her choral pleasures were resumed at Greater Salem Baptist Church. There she teamed with Louise Barry Lenon and the three Johnson brothers to form the professional Johnson Gospel Singers. Soon Jackson caught the attention of Thomas A. Dorsey, who helped launch her solo career.

At one point in 1932, before her fame was at its height, she went to a Professor DuBois for a music lesson. She was instructed to stop hollering and to enunciate her words so white folks could understand them—it was her last lesson. Studs Terkel, however, had no problem recognizing Jackson's talent when he booked her as a regular on his radio show. Nor did the French Academy have any difficulty appreciating Jackson's recording of "I Can Put My Trust in Jesus." An award from that academy led to a successful European tour and more hit records worldwide. She also shared her unique vocal style on *Ed Sullivan's Toast of the Town.*

In 1954, Jackson's rising star won her the first gospel radio show in the nation. A few years later, she became the first gospel performer in the Newport Jazz Festival. She also appeared in several films, such as *Imitation of Life* in 1959, and performed at the 1961 inauguration of President John F. Kennedy.

Despite overtures, Jackson refused numerous offers to sing in Las Vegas. She would not sing religious songs amidst gambling and vice. She did, however, visit churches on Chicago's South Side, where she often sang for free.

Throughout the late 1950s and '60s, Jackson often responded to calls for support from Martin Luther King, Jr. Jackson's voice could be heard during numerous civil rights demonstrations, including the historic Montgomery bus boycott and the 1963 March on Washington, D.C.

Jackson suffered a series of heart attacks that slowed the pace of her career. Months before her fatal heart attack on January 27, 1972, she stirred the crowd at a final concert in Germany.

Mahalia Jackson, the "Queen of Gospel Song," was sometimes criticized for her jazzy and rousing gospel renditions, but those are the very qualities that made her music so loved around the globe.

DOROTHY IRENE HEIGHT

President Bill Clinton applauds Dorothy Height after presenting her with the Presidential Medal of Freedom, the nation's highest civilian honor, during a ceremony on August 8, 1994.

SOCIAL ACTIVIST Dorothy Height, the spearhead behind the Black Family Reunion Movement, spent decades trumpeting the fight for African American civil rights, women's issues, and economic well-being for people worldwide. Her work with groups such as the Young Women's Christian Association (YWCA), Delta Sigma Theta Sorority, Inc. (DST), and the National Council of Negro Women (NCNW) made her a leader in the battle for equality and human rights.

Height was born March 24, 1912, in Richmond, Virginia. Her family moved to the small mining town of Rankin, Pennsylvania, where Height was a tall, straight-A student who excelled in athletics. She was active in the YWCA as a teenager and was involved with the organization most of her life. She went to New York University for college, earning both her bachelor's and master's degrees in four years. She also studied at Columbia University and the New York School of Social Work.

Height's youth club activities took her to several Christian youth conferences in the United States, Holland, and England. She also helped Eleanor Roosevelt plan a 1938 World Youth Congress in New York. At the same time, Height worked for New York's Welfare Department and was asked to examine the unrest following the 1935 riots in Harlem. During this period, Height met Mary McLeod Bethune, a magnetic civil rights activist and the founder of NCNW, an umbrella group for women's rights organizations. Height began volunteering for the group to help in its mission.

Height began her long career with the YWCA in 1938, running a lodging home for black women in Harlem, then later in Washington, D.C. This powerful speaker ran training programs for YWCA volunteers and developed programs for interracial education. She eventually helped desegregate the YWCA and later directed its Center for Racial Justice.

In 1939, Height began her tenure with DST, guiding the national black sorority toward a greater commitment to activism. She was national president from 1947 to 1956, during which time she established the group's first international chapter in Haiti and organized bookmobiles for African American communities in the South.

Height then took on one of her most powerful positions—president of NCNW. The council's goals included uniting black women of all classes and stressing interracial cooperation. During Height's tenure, the NCNW has helped women open businesses, sponsored job training, and run voter registration programs. She continues to guide its fight for equal rights for women of color worldwide. Since 1986, the council has sponsored annual celebrations nationwide called Black Family Reunions. These reunions are an attempt to renew the concept of the extended black family and thereby to improve social conditions.

Height, the recipient of numerous awards and honorary degrees, continues to be a firebrand in the struggle to improve the lives of blacks and women.

During the 1990 visit of South African Ambassador Dr. Pete Koornhof (left) to the United States, pressure escalated in his country to end apartheid. Here, Height and Jesse Jackson join him in singing "We Shall Overcome."

RICHARD WRIGHT

Wright, in 1945 at his typewriter in New York just after his autobiography, Black Boy, *was published. Wright worked determinedly to win economic rights for all blacks.*

AN IMPORTANT WRITER of the 20th century, Richard Wright was one of the first and most forceful authors to call attention to the consequences of racial exploitation of blacks. His existential writings explored the recurring theme of how African Americans live in a country where structural racism denies their very humanity.

Wright's most compelling argument was made in his 1940 novel *Native Son,* the raw and powerful story of Bigger Thomas, a young black man in Chicago who accidentally kills a white girl. Thomas then learns the depths of hostility that the white world harbors against blacks.

Native Son was an international best-seller that quickly sold more than 300,000 copies; it was translated into six languages and became a Book-of-the-Month Club selection. Wright also turned the work into a powerful Broadway play, starring Canada Lee and staged by Orson

Welles. In 1941, he won the Spingarn Medal, the NAACP's highest honor, for his novel. The book earned him fame and encouraged him to pursue a lifelong writing career.

Wright was born in Roxie, near Natchez, Mississippi, on September 4, 1908, and he grew up in poverty in orphanages and with various family members. His dismal childhood gave him a dark outlook on life.

He had trouble adjusting to Southern racism and Jim Crow segregation. He determined that if he was to survive, he had to go north to live. Wright moved to Memphis in 1925, and two years later, he moved to Chicago, where he worked odd jobs until being accepted into the Federal Writers Project during the Great Depression.

Wright came to the public's attention with *Uncle Tom's Children,* a collection of short stories released in 1938 that won the author a Guggenheim Fellowship. In those stories and other works, especially the brilliant essay "The Ethics of Living Jim Crow," Wright explored the often violent racial tensions in the rural South. With *Native Son,* he shifted locales to the big northern ghettos, where the same tensions culminated with similar results.

In 1945, Wright published his autobiography, *Black Boy,* which has become an American classic. Also chosen as a Book-of-the-Month Club selection, *Black Boy* was translated into six languages and outsold *Native Son.* The story is about Wright's early childhood in the South and his young adulthood in Chicago. The book examines the painful workings of the racist social order.

After the success of *Black Boy,* Wright left America, disturbed by the country's

racism and having found more freedom in his travels abroad. His first novel after moving to France was *The Outsider,* a story about Cross Damon, who searches for a new identity and a new approach to life in the Communist Party. In his creative and esoteric way, Wright explored the possibility of escaping unwanted but traditional burdens while also exploring the dark recesses of a man disconnected from his fellow beings. *The Outsider* led some critics to call Wright the first American existentialist.

Wright lived the rest of his life in Paris, where he died of a heart attack on November 28, 1960, at the age of 52.

Wright in front of movie posters for the Argentine film Sangre Negra, *based on his novel* Native Son. *Wright starred in the film. The movie was set in Chicago.*

CHARLES RICHARD DREW

Drew's outstanding work with blood revolutionized medical surgery and saved countless lives. He found a way to separate plasma from whole blood, which allowed for longer blood storage. He was given the NAACP's Spingarn Medal in 1944 for his efforts.

DR. CHARLES RICHARD DREW not only revolutionized the medical profession by developing a way to store blood and plasma, he also created the world's first blood bank. But Drew had another priority—crusading to change the way African Americans, especially as physicians, were viewed and treated by whites.

Born the eldest of five children on June 3, 1904, Drew lived in the racially mixed Foggy Bottom neighborhood of Washington, D.C. The area was an enclave where blacks rarely had to deal with the federally sanctioned Jim Crow laws.

Drew was an exceptional student and athlete at Dunbar High School. He decided to become a doctor after his sister died of tuberculosis in 1920. After graduating from Amherst College in Massachusetts, Drew taught for two years, then he went to McGill University in Montreal, Canada, for medical school.

While Drew served his medical internship at the Royal Victoria Hospital in Montreal, he saved an elderly man who needed a blood transfusion in order to have his leg amputated. During that time, many people died because doctors had to match the blood type before a transfusion could take place. Drew's research changed all that.

In 1935, Drew taught and practiced at Freedmen's Hospital at Howard University, where he invented a way to separate plasma from whole blood, making it possible to store blood for a week instead of just two days. More research turned up a bigger revelation: Transfusions could be performed with plasma alone, negating the need for blood typing since plasma contains no red blood cells. In 1938, Drew got a fellowship in blood research at New York City's Columbia Presbyterian Hospital and ran its first blood bank.

In 1940, Drew became the first African American to earn an advanced doctorate of science degree, and he invented a technique for long-term plasma storage. He set up the world's first blood bank in Britain that same year, as part of the country's World War II effort. As America prepared to enter the war, Drew was appointed medical director of the American Red Cross's National Blood Bank program. But the U.S. War Department issued an edict forbidding the armed forces to mix black and white blood, even while admitting in a memo-

randum that their decision was based on "reasons not biologically convincing, but which are commonly recognized as psychologically important in America." A furious Drew called a press conference, asking, "How have we, in this age and hour, allowed once again to creep into our hearts the dark myths and wretched superstitions of the past? Will we ever share a common brotherhood?" Drew resigned his post.

In April 1941, Drew was certified as a surgeon by the American Board of Surgery. He then returned to Howard University as a full professor. Two of his students became the first Howard graduates to qualify for the American Board of Surgery, and Drew continued pushing his students to seek internships and residencies in white establishments. His efforts greatly increased the number of blacks getting jobs outside the African American medical community.

Drew was appointed chief of staff at Freedman's Hospital in 1944 and was awarded the Spingarn Medal by the NAACP. In 1947, he began an unsuccessful crusade against the American Medical Association (AMA) for a policy that effectively kept blacks from joining. The AMA didn't change its policy until 1968. (In 1996, the AMA elected its first African American president, Dr. Lonnie R. Bristow.) Drew was later named consultant to the surgeon general of the U.S. Army.

By 1950, despite an international reputation, Drew remained poor, since black medical researchers made far less money than private practitioners of any race. He died the morning of April 1, 1950, when he fell asleep while driving to a medical conference at Tuskegee. Drew, despite a blood transfusion at the hospital, died of internal injuries. He was 45.

TUSKEGEE AIRMEN

THE INCREDIBLE STORY of African American aviators in World War II began on a lone Alabama runway at Tuskegee Army Air Field on March 21, 1941, with the activation and construction of a segregated airfield for the 99th Pursuit Squadron. On March 7, 1942, five pilots stood on the runway at graduation exercises, poised to take their place in aviation history. First Lady Eleanor Roosevelt took a flight with black pilot Dr. Charles Alfred Anderson to show her support for the program.

This airfield came at a time when African Americans were shackled by legal white supremacy in the South and racial exclusion in the North. Any act of so-called disrespect could result in injury or death. Learning how to fly, to many whites and a few blacks, was one such act.

African Americans had routinely been excluded from piloting in the Army Air Force. Equally frustrating were the persistent myths that blacks were incompetent to fly. Yet, there were more than 100 black pilots at the time and at least two black flight schools. The history of black pioneers in aviation, including Eugene Bullard and Bessie Coleman, had begun in France 20 years earlier.

Under Major Benjamin Davis, Jr., the Tuskegee Airmen had their first taste of combat against the fortified island of Pantelleria. The successful attack on the island and subsequent triumphs in the European and African theaters should have proven blacks were invaluable in battle, but it did not.

The success of the Tuskegee Airmen in engaging the Nazi Air Force during World War II contributed to the desegregation of the American military by executive order of President Harry Truman in 1948. Lena Horne is shown here with the Airmen in a publicity photo.

The 99th Squadron of Airmen originally reported to the 33rd Fighter Group under the command of Colonel William W. Momyer in Great Britain. When Major Davis was recalled to Washington, D.C., in 1943, to assume command of the 332nd Fighter Group, he learned that Momyer had reported the 99th as a failure: "They have failed to display the aggression and daring for combat that are necessary to a first class fighting organization." Major Davis answered the allegations with the facts of his squadron's performance—facts later substantiated in a study ordered by the Army Chief of Staff. With their reputation cleared, the Pentagon activated three more squadrons of Airmen

and, along with the 99th, assigned them to the 332nd Fighter command of Major Davis.

Of the original 926 pilots who graduated from Tuskegee, 450 were sent overseas for combat assignments. They flew 1,578 missions, earned more than 900 medals, and never lost a bomber that they escorted. Captain Luke Weathers scored two victories in one day. Piloting a P-51, Lieutenant Clarence Lester, whose bomber formation en route to targets in Germany was attacked by 30 or more ME-109 and FW-190 enemy planes, engaged the enemy and destroyed three of their fighters. The Tuskegee Airmen clearly demonstrated that African American fighter pilots could be as good as their white counterparts.

On July 26, 1948, President Harry Truman issued two executive orders desegregating the military, thanks in part to the efforts of the brave black Tuskegee Airmen.

For years, black aviators had to leave the United States to find militaries receptive to their piloting skills. Two civilian flight schools were formed by some early African American pioneers in aviation, but the American military still withheld the opportunity to commission black pilots. Persistent lobbying by civil rights activists finally changed that situation with the opening of the Tuskegee Army Air Force School in 1941.

MABEL STAUPERS

DESPITE THE FACT that almost one million blacks served in the military in World War II, America had a whites-only policy for nurses. That policy did not change until seven months before the Japanese surrendered. An African American activist named Mabel Staupers is credited with changing this Jim Crow policy.

Staupers was born in 1890 in Barbados, British West Indies, and came to the United States with her family in 1903. In 1917, she received her R.N. from Freedmen's Hospital in Washington, D.C., and just three years later, she became the superintendent of the Booker T. Washington Sanitorium in New York City. Staupers also served as a consultant on nursing to U.S. Surgeon General James C. Magee in 1941, before she was elected president of the National Association of Colored Graduate Nurses (NACGN) in 1949.

The NACGN encouraged its members to enroll in the American Red Cross, which, at the time, was acting as a medical-staff procurement agency for the military, finding doctors and nurses to serve in the military. While the Red Cross said yes to black women, the military said no.

In 1941, even after the attack on Pearl Harbor, both the Army and Navy Nurse Corps declared they would not accept black nurses. The Army Nurse Corps later reluctantly reversed their Jim Crow policy after it was leaked to the press. In 1941, the Army Nurse Corps accepted 56 African American nurses. According to Dr. Darlene Clark Hine, Staupers's biographer and an expert on the plight of black nurses, these women were only to serve in segregated hospitals or wards, tending to only African American soldiers.

Staupers's voice was tireless in its call for the entrance of black nurses into the American military and then for equal treatment for African American nurses once they were recruited. Staupers even petitioned First Lady Eleanor Roosevelt in 1944 to protest the humiliation of black army nurses overseas. The nurses were not allowed to assist American soldiers; they could only treat enemy captives.

Staupers's group was so outraged that they kicked off a huge media campaign to stop this apartheid among military nurses. While their campaign publicly embarrassed a military that was being challenged on segregation on other fronts, two things occurred that helped the plight of black nurses. First, white nurses went off to war, opening incredible opportunities at home. Also, the Cadet Nurse Corps was created to provide education grants to nurses, so many black women were finally able to afford nursing school. By 1943, the army raised its quota of African American nurses to 160.

Meanwhile, the handful of black nurses that were allowed in the military were often subjected to harsh treatment. Black army nurses stationed in England, for example, were forced to care for German prisoners of war. Only white nurses were allowed to treat the U.S. soldiers.

Staupers met with Eleanor Roosevelt in 1944 to protest the humiliation of black army nurses. She told the first lady that she hoped black nurses wouldn't be used just to nurse the enemy but would also be used to nurse American soldiers who were fighting the war. Her sharp words struck a chord with Mrs. Roosevelt. The restriction was eventually lifted.

Staupers published her autobiography, *No Time for Prejudice,* in 1951. That same year she was awarded the prestigious NAACP Spingarn Medal for her courageous efforts to integrate nurses into the military.

Staupers died of pneumonia October 1, 1989, at her home in Washington, D.C. She was 99 years old.

Staupers wrote about her tireless work on behalf of black nurses in her autobiography, No Time for Prejudice, *which was published in 1951.*

JOHN H. JOHNSON

Johnson began his career as a 19-year-old, $25-a-week office worker for Supreme Liberty Life Insurance Company. He later bought the company. Johnson made his fortune as publisher of black-oriented magazines. While his company has produced as many as five publications at one time, its major successes remain EBONY and JET magazines.

BY SHEER STRENGTH of will and determination, John Harold Johnson rose from the poverty he experienced as a child in rural Arkansas to become one of the wealthiest black men in the nation. He founded and ran the Johnson Publishing Company empire, which for decades was by far the largest black-owned business in American history.

From 1945 until his death in 2005, Johnson published *EBONY* magazine, a lifestyle and general interest publication for African Americans that has a circulation of over one million and is the crown jewel of his business. Johnson's second gold mine is *JET,* a pocket-size weekly magazine that has provided news to the black community since 1951.

Johnson was born January 19, 1918, in Arkansas City, Arkansas, which had no public high school for blacks. After going through eighth grade twice, his mother brought him to Chicago in 1933 to continue his education.

John H. Johnson was a publishing magnate for more than 50 years, with *EBONY* and *JET* magazines helping make him one of the richest black men in America. A member of numerous halls of fame, he also sat on the boards of major American corporations and institutions.

The ridicule he suffered at school because of his tattered clothes intensified Johnson's efforts to succeed. In addition to being an honor student, he pushed himself to become student council president and editor of the school newspaper. His hard work earned him a scholarship to the University of Chicago.

In 1936, Harry Pace, president of Supreme Liberty Life Insurance Company, then the largest black-owned business in America, met Johnson at an Urban League dinner. Pace gave him a job so he could afford the remaining expenses for college and day-to-day life. Johnson attended the University of Chicago but dropped out to work full-time as Pace's personal assistant. Johnson, however, was not a man to leave work undone. He entered Northwestern University in 1938 and resumed two more years of study at the university's School of Commerce.

One of Johnson's responsibilities at Supreme Liberty Life Insurance Company was to brief Pace on news events of interest to blacks. This task gave Johnson the idea of developing a magazine to deliver similar information to the black community at large.

When no one would back his concept, he borrowed $500, using his mother's furniture as collateral. With the money, he paid for a mailing to 20,000 of Supreme Insurance's clients seeking prepaid subscriptions to his newly proposed magazine. The mailing produced 3,000 responses with $2 each, enough for Johnson to publish his first issue of *Negro Digest* in November 1942.

To overcome industry resistance to broader distribution of a magazine devoted to an African American audience, Johnson encouraged fellow insurance employees to request the magazine from newsstands. Then, to totally eliminate assumptions about low market demand, he reimbursed coworkers for news-

Johnson, his wife (second from right), and Louis J. Borremans (right), Counsel General of Belgium, congratulate Edith Sampson (second from left) on her appointment to the United Nations.

stand purchases. His plan worked. By the middle of 1943, the magazine had a usual circulation of 50,000. Its demand was significantly enhanced by an October column written by First Lady Eleanor Roosevelt. The column was titled "If I Were a Negro."

In November 1945, Johnson was able to launch *EBONY*, which provides positive role models and stories of black success. The magazine immediately sold out its initial 25,000 copies, marking a new period of growth to approximately nine million readers. Large advertisers were slow in coming, but they did finally arrive in 1947. Zenith Radio was the first major account.

In 1951, Johnson scored another big hit with the weekly *JET* magazine, which revived the old news digest approach. Other facets of Johnson's business conglomerate included the spin-off magazine *EM: Ebony Man* and Fashion Fair Cosmetics, which is worth about $30 million and was developed to fill a void in the beauty industry with fashion shows and cosmetics for blacks. Johnson also owned radio stations, an insurance company, extensive real estate, a mail-order firm, and a nationally syndicated TV show. He published several other magazines, which have had lives of varying lengths. His personal wealth gave Johnson a net worth of $150 million by 1990.

Through the years, Johnson Publishing Company has fostered African American racial identity and pride in the many accomplishments of black people. It has also promoted

freedom and independence among the global community of Africans.

For his achievements and business breakthroughs, Johnson received the prestigious Spingarn Medal in 1966 from the NAACP. Many more honors have been bestowed since that time, including Magazine Publisher of the Year by the Magazine Publishers of America in 1972 and the 1994 Center for Communication's Award. One of the most illustrious tributes was the presentation of the Presidential Medal of Freedom in 1996.

Johnson, in 1963, with Stewart Udall (center), United States Interior Secretary, as he presents Kenya's Prime Minister Jomo Kenyatta (right) with a signed portrait of President Lyndon Johnson.

Johnson ran his private empire as chairman of the board until his death, although day-to-day operations have been handled by his daughter, President and Chief Executive Officer Linda Johnson Rice, since 1989. Together with Rice's mother, Eunice, who is secretary-treasurer of the company and producer-director of the *EBONY* Fashion Fair show, they run this highly successful family enterprise.

S. B. FULLER

John H. Johnson became one of the greatest black entrepreneurs offering products to a growing African American market. Preceding Johnson by a decade, S. B. Fuller took a different course of action. He believed direct sales was the best way to capitalize on market opportunities regardless of race.

Fuller was first exposed to selling this way during his childhood when he sold soap door-to-door after school in Memphis, Tennessee. Decades later, in 1935, he borrowed $25, using his car as collateral, to launch his own business. People needed soap even during the Depression. So with his meager start-up capital, he bought a quantity of the product to market door-to-door in Chicago with the help of his wife, Lestine, a top salesperson in her own right.

From this inauspicious beginning, Fuller later purchased his soap supplier, Boyer International Laboratories, which also manufactured cosmetics under the Jean Nadal brand. At its peak, Fuller Products was a somewhat diversified manufacturing company with annual sales in excess of ten million dollars.

Unfortunately those revenues were gradually decimated by a boycott started in the late 1950s after the southern White Citizen's Council discovered the popular Jean Nadal company was owned by an African American. Then Fuller's silence about the adverse impact of discrimination on black businesses during his induction into the National Association of Manufacturers brought further wrath from black nationalist leaders in 1963. The company could not recover from the second boycott. Fuller declared bankruptcy. The restructured firm limped on, but it was unable to regain its previous glory.

The kindness Fuller extended to people throughout Chicago came back to him manifold in the 1980s. John H. Johnson honored his mentor's seventieth birthday with $70,000 in proceeds from a prestigious dinner tribute and $50,000 worth of stock certificates. Almost 2,000 people attended that celebration; a similar event was held for his eightieth birthday. Fuller died in 1988.

ADAM CLAYTON POWELL, JR.

During a 1966 press conference, Powell called for $7 billion to fund the federal Anti-Poverty Program, more than four times the amount requested by President Lyndon Johnson.

TEN YEARS BEFORE the Civil Rights Movement was at full steam, Congressman Adam Clayton Powell, Jr., was a strong voice in government, advocating the abolition of segregation and employment discrimination. He led the people of Harlem in a movement that opened jobs, brought better housing conditions, and put food in their stomachs.

When Powell went to the House of Representatives in 1945, he became the first black congressperson from the northeastern United States and only the fourth black representative in the 20th century. Powell quickly pushed 60 pieces of major legislation through Congress that benefited poor and middle-class Americans, including the Title 1 Educational Act, Head Start, Manpower Development and Training Act, and National Defense Education Act. His practice of attaching the Powell Amendment, which denied federal funds from appropriation bills passed by the House to any institution practicing discrimination, caused one member to punch him during a committee session. His legislative insistence opened the doors of opportunity to African Americans in education, government, and the private sector.

Powell was born on November 29, 1908, in New Haven, Connecticut, but he went to New York when his father was offered the pastorship of the Abyssinian Baptist Church in Harlem. Though Powell adored Harlem's nightlife, he promised his parents he'd enter the ministry.

He graduated from Colgate University in 1930, then received his master's degree in religious education from Columbia University in 1932. He took over Abyssinian when his father retired in 1937. Powell used his pulpit to address political and social issues. He also wrote articles for the *New York Post* and was a columnist in Harlem's *Amsterdam News* newspaper.

In 1941, Powell was elected to New York's city council. Then, in 1944, he decided to take his fight national by running for Congress—and winning—term after term. The House seniority rule was not always upheld for Powell, but it was finally maintained in 1961 when Powell became the chairperson of the powerful House Committee on Education and Labor.

He was an uncompromising, defiant agitator who took congressional colleagues to task for racist attitudes and disparaging remarks, and this endeared Powell his constituency that reelected him to Congress for 25 years. However, Powell's brash nature and flamboyance fostered enemies who used the fallout from a defamation lawsuit to strip Powell of his chairmanship and expel him from Congress.

The defamation lawsuit came about when Powell tried to deflect attention from his legal battle against tax evasion charges. He publicly attacked the Mafia and New York Police Department for their role in illegal gambling in Harlem. During a radio interview, Powell referred to Mrs. Esther James as a "bag woman" in those activities. James sued Powell for libel, who refused to participate in the legal action. He was cited for contempt of court after failing to pay her damage awards. Powell's tax evasion charges, though, ended favorably.

Those situations, however, were enough to get the ball rolling on his ouster from Congress. But Powell urged Harlemites to "Keep the faith, Baby," and he easily won the special election to fill his own vacancy. The Supreme Court declared unconstitutional Congress's failure to seat him. Stripped of his seniority and influence, Powell only occasionally showed up. By the late '60s, many Harlemites began to view Powell as an absentee congressperson, inattentive to his district. In 1970, he was defeated for renomination by Charlie Rangel. Powell retired to Bimini and died in a Miami hospital on April 4, 1972.

Powell (left) and Malcolm X talk at the Siloam Presbyterian Church in Brooklyn just before the March 16, 1964, boycott of the New York City public schools.

BESSIE COLEMAN

SOARING SKYWARD, FAR beyond the dusty cotton fields of her home state of Texas, Bessie Coleman has secured a place in history as the first licensed female African American pilot.

Coleman was born on January 26, 1892, to sharecroppers George and Susan Coleman in Atlanta, a small town in Texas. As a young girl, her family purchased land in Waxahachie, Texas, hoping to build a better life. In 1901, Coleman's father tried unsuccessfully to coax his wife and family away from the racism blanketing Waxahachie and Texas in general. He thought Native American territory in Oklahoma was where he, with a mixed heritage of African American and Cherokee, could truly live free.

Coleman, the tenth born, grew up quickly after her father left. She tended three younger siblings, helped in the cotton fields, and excelled in her eight years of school. In the evenings, the family read about things that seemed impossible to achieve in Waxahachie. In 1915, Coleman followed her brothers Walter (a Pullman porter) and John north to bustling Chicago.

Coleman became a manicurist on the South Side of Chicago, and for a while, that seemed to be as big as her dreams would get. That is until Walter and John returned from World War I and teased her with stories about female pilots in France. Flying sounded like freedom to Coleman, so she reacted to their challenge by applying to aviation schools.

Probably blinded by racial and gender stereotypes in America, the schools refused to admit Coleman, so France appeared to be the next best choice. Coleman learned French and crossed the Atlantic with financial backing from Robert Abbot, founder of the *Chicago Defender* newspaper, and Jesse Binga, founder of Binga State Bank.

She breezed through L'École d'aviation des frères Caudron and was licensed on June 15, 1921. After three months of training, the first African American aviatrix returned to fanfare in New York City. Unfortunately, the only pilot jobs open to blacks at the time were air shows, which required advanced training. So Coleman went to Germany, where she received the first flying license ever granted to a woman.

"Queen Bess" returned to the States, this time ready to barnstorm. With support from Abbott and his newspaper, Coleman mounted her first air show, looping over Curtiss Field in New York on September 3, 1922. More intense aerial stunts and lectures pulled her across America, where she drew integrated audiences along the way. She purchased her own JN4 army plane, but it crashed on her first flight. Coleman recovered from injuries sustained during the crash, but she found herself in a down period, without a manager and in need of a new plane.

Appearances picked up in 1925 after she joined the Theater Owners Booking Association. Then, in 1926, Coleman's dream of establishing an American flying school seemed about to materialize. She had gained financing for another JN4, but problems arose during the mechanic's flight from Dallas to Jacksonville, Florida, where she lived. The mechanical issues persisted during her test flight on April 30, 1926. With the mechanic at the helm, Coleman sat in the backseat unbuckled. A small woman, she needed freedom to lean out and check the airfield below for a parachute jump the next day. The controls jammed while the plane was airborne, causing it to roll and spill her to the ground. She died upon impact; the mechanic died in the crash.

Though loved by many during her aviation career, Coleman received even more accolades after her death. Three funerals were held in her honor as her body rolled by train through Jacksonville, Orlando, and Chicago. In 1929, an aviation school was established in her name, and the Bessie Coleman U.S. postage stamp premiered in 1995. In 1990, Chicago Mayor Richard Daley named a portion of a street after her by O'Hare Airport. She was inducted into the Texas Aviation Hall of Fame in 2000.

Bessie Coleman raced skyward to become the first African American female pilot. She entertained thousands of people with gravity-defying stunts in "roaring twenties" air shows around the country.

SEPTIMA POINSETTE CLARK

SEPTIMA POINSETTE CLARK, often referred to as the "queen mother of the Civil Rights Movement," was instrumental in breaking down voter and teacher discrimination in the United States. She refused to compromise citizenship to discrimination and pushed America closer to its founding promise of equality for all, including on the educational front.

Clark was born May 3, 1898, the second of eight children to Peter and Victoria Poinsette in Charleston, South Carolina. Education was valued in the Clark household, and all children attended school at least through eighth grade. Clark was enrolled in a private school as well as the town's public school for blacks. To earn tuition, she became a maid and babysitter. She earned her high school diploma from Avery Normal School in 1916.

Clark worked in a bakery until her teaching career got underway on Johns Island in the Gullah territory off the coast of South Carolina.

Clark not only taught children on the island, but adults also sought her assistance.

Clark furthered her education after marrying sailor Nerie Clark in 1919. His navy allowance helped pay for tuition at North Carolina's A&T College. Meanwhile, she worked at her high school alma mater, Avery Normal School. She was also busy lobbying for more African American teachers and principals in Charleston's black public schools. Although she didn't earn a degree at A&T, she would later take extension courses from Benedict College in Columbia, South Carolina, earning her degree in 1942. She received a master's degree from Hampton Institute in Virginia in 1946.

In Columbia, Clark turned to community activism. She became a member of organizations that focused on community health, education, and employment opportunities. In 1945, Clark worked with NAACP attorney Thurgood Marshall to fight, and win, the court battle for

Clark knew education was one key to freedom and voting was another. She brought both forces together in Citizenship Schools that taught southern blacks how to pass voter registration requirements.

equal salaries for black teachers, who received about half the pay of white teachers at the time.

Clark was ousted from the South Carolina school system in 1954 because of her NAACP membership. This freed Clark to direct and teach at the Highlander Folk School in Tennessee. Highlander became sacred ground in the Civil Rights Movement with its leadership workshops and its part in creating Citizenship Schools for blacks who were prevented from voting because of literacy requirements.

Clark opened Citizenship Schools across the South, and her efforts doubled in 1961 when the literacy program transferred to the SCLC. By 1970, Clark had helped more than 100,000 African Americans become voters.

Clark's accomplishments were heralded during the 1970s with the Race Relations Award from the National Education Association and the Living Legacy Award from President Jimmy Carter. Her memoir earned the American Book Award prior to her death on December 15, 1987.

JULIEANNA L. RICHARDSON

Julieanna L. Richardson founded and is executive director of what may become the most extensive video collection of African American history makers in the world. The nonprofit organization HistoryMakers was established in 1999 to capture the stories of African Americans who participated in significant events.

Richardson was born in Pittsburgh, Pennsylvania, on June 10, 1954. Her father, a professional golfer, faced discrimination, which sparked Richardson to public service. While studying the arts, specifically the Harlem Renaissance, at Brandeis University, she was inspired to interview Butterfly McQueen, the first black Oscar-winner, and Lee (Leigh) Whipper, the first black member of the Actors Equity Association. Those interviews infused life into the Harlem Renaissance for Richardson.

After completing law school at Harvard University and establishing the Chicago Cable Commission for Chicago's city government, Richardson founded Shop Chicago, an entrepreneurial cable TV venture, before HistoryMakers came to fruition. In just five years, HistoryMakers has archived 5,000 video stories, documenting the oral histories of such notable African Americans as civil rights leaders Andrew Young and the Rev. Jesse Jackson and social activists Dorothy Height and Dick Gregory.

The University of Illinois awarded HistoryMakers a million-dollar grant to explore technological innovations to make the interviews available to a wide audience. And it is reaching a huge audience; it is among the most frequently consulted African American Web sites.

JOHN HOPE FRANKLIN

John Hope Franklin, historian, educator, and prolific author, has spent his life teaching people about the contributions African Americans have made to history. Franklin's legacy makes it possible for blacks to understand their importance in building and maintaining the American dream.

ARGUABLY THE NATION'S greatest living historian, John Hope Franklin is proof that African Americans have always played an important role in interpreting their past. Franklin, who has been awarded more than 30 honorary degrees and has been a professor at many universities, uses his vast knowledge and clarion voice to trumpet the accomplishments and chronicle the struggle of blacks in helping to build this country.

Born January 2, 1915, in Rentiesville, Ohio, the son of Mollie and Buck Franklin, Franklin graduated magna cum laude from Fisk University in Nashville, a legendary haven for scores of America's best and brightest blacks. He then enrolled in Harvard University, receiving a master's degree in 1936. The dark-skinned, slim man returned to Fisk to teach for a year, but he went back to Harvard for his Ph.D. in 1941.

Believing in education as a path to freedom and equality for blacks, Franklin launched a journey that included passing his knowledge on to students at several colleges and universities. In North Carolina, Franklin taught at St. Augustine's College while writing a dissertation on free blacks in that state. Franklin likes to tell the story of his summer researching the state archives. By tradition, librarians brought requested materials to visiting scholars at their desks, but no white librarian was willing to bring him material. Ironically, this meant Franklin was free to wander the stacks unencumbered. The result, his first landmark publication, *The Free Negro in North Carolina, 1790–1860,* was published in 1943.

Brooklyn College invited the brilliant young scholar to join its faculty in 1956. Eight years later, Franklin became a professor of history at the University of Chicago, the first major white university to tenure an African American scholar. Franklin chaired the history department there and was named the first John Matthews Manly Distinguished Service Professor of History.

In 1982, Franklin held the post of James B. Duke Professor of History at Duke University. He retired from that position in 1985 and accepted an appointment as professor of legal history at Duke University Law School, a position he held for seven years.

Franklin's achievements haven't been limited to teaching. In 1949, he was the first black to read a paper before the prestigious Southern Historical Association, and later he became its president. Franklin was also the first African American president of the American Historical Association, Phi Beta Kappa, and the Organization of American Historians. He was one of the social scientists who drew up the historical brief for the NAACP's legal argument for the plaintiff's case in the historic *Brown* v. *Board of Education* case.

A prolific author, Franklin's many books include *From Slavery to Freedom* (1947, seventh edition 1994), which is still the premier African American historical survey, and *A Southern Odyssey: Travelers in the Antebellum North* (1976). He also wrote the award-winning *George Washington Williams: A Biography,* which was published in 1985. Franklin's other honors are too numerous to list, including other professional offices, fellowships, and honorary doctorates.

A lifelong champion of civil rights, Franklin spoke against Judge Robert Bork's confirmation as a U.S. Supreme Court Justice before a Senate committee in 1987. At President Clinton's request, Franklin chaired a national conversation on race, where he held town hall meetings across the country. At the end of his tenure, he was awarded the Presidential Medal of Freedom. Duke University has dedicated the John Hope Franklin Center for Interdisciplinary and International Studies, honoring one of the nation's most distinguished scholars.

In the 1960s, Franklin became the first tenured African American scholar at a major white university when he became a history professor at the University of Chicago.

JACKIE ROBINSON

Jackie Robinson will long be remembered as the first black major-league baseball player and the first African American elected to the Baseball Hall of Fame.

JACK ROOSEVELT ROBINSON was born in Cairo, Georgia, in 1919, when many cities were erupting in race riots. World War I black soldiers were returning from segregated quarters in the military to increased discrimination at home.

Two decades later, Robinson, a top UCLA athlete, became the school's first four-letter man. He excelled in basketball, football, track, and baseball.

When World War II was starting, Robinson, swept up in the fervor, entered the army as a draftee applying for Officer Candidate School (OCS). He was turned down because he was black. Robinson, not one to take no for an answer, consulted with his friend and fellow draftee World Heavyweight Champion Joe Louis. Louis used his clout to get Robinson accepted into OCS. Robinson became a second lieutenant and spent the rest of the war fighting segregation at bases in Kansas and Texas instead of fighting enemies in Germany and Japan.

It was during this tumultuous time that Robinson became friends with Branch Rickey, president of the Brooklyn Dodgers. Rickey encouraged the young athlete to use his talents and energies to integrate major-league baseball. According to Rickey, Robinson could help him take a losing team to the winner's circle while breaking the "color line."

Rickey hated segregation as much as Robinson. Rickey had once seen a black college player turned away from a hotel. He got the player a cot in his room. Rickey never forgot seeing this player crying because he was denied a place to lay his weary head just because of the color of his skin. Rickey wanted to change things, and he saw a way to do just that with the talented, poised Jackie Robinson.

Robinson played shortstop with the Negro League Kansas City Monarchs, and he never lost sight of his ultimate dream, to play with Rickey's Brooklyn Dodgers. Finally, Rickey's scouts caught up with Robinson and invited him to come to New York.

Told of the immense difficulties he would face if he played with an all-white team, the ever-confident Robinson agreed anyway. He gave his word he would never be part of a racial incident, and he kept his promise despite a lifetime of standing up to bigotry. Robinson had to endure fans calling him ugly names. Players, even sportswriters, defamed him with catcalls and verbal abuse. But Robinson didn't fight back. He knew his actions could ruin the chances of other African American players. Besides, he had given Branch Rickey his word.

After a year with the Dodgers' top farm team, the Montreal Royals, Robinson displayed amazing skill, winning the hearts of many who saw this black wizard play ball. In his very first game, he hit a three-run homer. That year, the team won the Little World Series. After Robinson's last game in Montreal, the crowd stormed the field, recited Robinson's name repeatedly, hoisted him on their shoulders, and paraded him around the field.

In 1947, after officially joining the Dodgers, Robinson was named Rookie of the Year by *The Sporting News* magazine. He helped the Dodgers win a National League pennant. Robinson also led the league in stolen bases and hit .297. This was the beginning of a series of accolades he would garner in his brilliant ten-year career with the team. Ford Frick, who was president of the National League, gave Robinson a Silver Bat award for winning the National League batting title in 1949.

Robinson's all-around skills earned him election into the Baseball Hall of Fame in 1962, the first year he was eligible.

In 1949, the same year he captured the National League Most Valuable Player Award, two former teammates from the Negro leagues joined him on the All-Star Team—Roy Campanella and Don Newcombe. Robinson was still receiving threats on his life for playing a "white man's game," despite his great success. Robinson responded to a hate letter by hitting a home run in the next game he played.

JACKIE ROBINSON

In 1955, the Dodgers won the World Series—a feat that Robinson called "one of the greatest thrills in my life." In 1957, at age 39, he retired with a lifetime batting average of .311. And in 1962, Robinson became the first African American elected to Baseball's Hall of Fame.

Robinson went on to become both a civil rights activist and businessman. On the business end, he became vice president of a company called Chock Full O'Nuts. Now that other blacks had joined him in integrating baseball, he was free to actively fight discrimination. His activism caught the attention of Martin Luther King, Jr., and Jesse Jackson, both of whom consulted with him on a variety of social justice issues. Additionally, Robinson continued to be a staunch supporter of the NAACP. Robinson's quest for economic justice for African American entrepreneurs inspired him to reestablish the Freedom National Bank in Harlem in 1964, which was owned and operated by blacks.

Early in 1972, the Dodgers retired Robinson's number 42. Robinson died of a heart attack on October 24, 1972, in his Stamford, Connecticut, home just a few days after he threw out the first pitch at the 1972 World Series. The Reverend Jesse Jackson eulogized the trailblazing athlete at the funeral. Robinson's ideals

Jackie Robinson is pictured with Branch Rickey, the president of the Brooklyn Dodgers. Rickey encouraged Robinson to use his talents to break baseball's "color line."

and values are kept alive today through the Jackie Robinson Foundation, a nonprofit organization launched in 1973 by Rachel Robinson, his widow. The organization provides leadership development and education for underprivileged youths.

Major League Baseball dedicated the 1997 season to the 50th anniversary of Robinson's debut in the major leagues, with all players wearing "Breaking Barriers" arm patches.

Robinson's accomplishments have been celebrated with three U.S. postal stamps. He was on a 20-cent stamp as part of the Black Heritage series, which was issued in August 1982. The stamp pictured at right was issued in February 1999, and another 33-cent stamp was issued in July 2000.

ELLA JOSEPHINE BAKER

THERE IS HARDLY A MAJOR campaign or influential organization during the modern Civil Rights Movement in which Ella Baker did not take part. At pivotal times, when civil rights institutions were reaching into black communities across the country, Baker was there rousing folks to the cause. When nationwide training was needed to increase civil disobedience, she was there helping prepare warriors for the struggle.

The considerable influence of Ella Baker was felt throughout the modern Civil Rights Movement. She raised activism to new levels by inspiring public participation in the key civil rights organizations of the time: NAACP, SCLC, and SNCC.

Baker never coveted a formal leadership role. She preferred showing others the path she knew so well until they grew comfortable making their own way along it. She believed grassroots civil rights organizations had the greatest potential to go beyond small skirmishes and eventually effect social change.

The irrepressible Ella Josephine Baker was born December 13, 1903, to Blake and Georgianna Ross in Norfolk, Virginia. Baker's grandmother taught her to resist social oppression, telling stories of the tortures of slavery and giving tribute to those who revolted against bondage. Through the examples of her family and community, Baker was able to witness the power of a neighborhood acting together for the benefit of others.

Baker began challenging policies that she saw as unfair while in college at Shaw University in Raleigh. After graduating valedictorian in 1927, she took her activist spirit to New York City. There she joined the Young Negroes Cooperative League, which focused on black economic development via group efforts, such as buying in bulk to offer lower prices to its members. She left the League to join the literacy program under President Franklin Roosevelt's Works Progress Administration.

In New York, Baker worked with organizations striving for equality and justice for all Americans. She entered the struggle more directly in 1940 as field secretary for the National Association for the Advancement of Colored People (NAACP). Baker helped establish field offices around the nation and, in due course, had an extensive network of contacts and financial backers that would serve her well as the Civil Rights Movement grew.

Baker resigned from the NAACP and moved on to the Southern Christian Leadership Conference (SCLC) in 1957. Although she became acting director, the SCLC favored strong central leadership rather than local, grassroots politics. She left the SCLC and, two years later, took a job with the Young Women's Christian Association, a better fit for her. She was in her element, with grassroots, ad hoc, decentralized, and insurgent movements. It might be said that Baker was the "mother" of grassroots black activism in the 20th century.

Seeing enough vitality to light a fire under the slowing pace of the Civil Rights Movement, Baker organized a coordinating meeting for the many clusters of student activists across the South. More than 200 arrived at Shaw University, and they formed the Student Nonviolent Coordinating Committee (SNCC). Baker continued to offer these young women and men the sage counsel and training that fostered cohesive demonstrations during the 1960s. She also helped broaden the students' focus beyond lunch counters to desegregation of public transportation and to the exercise of black Americans' right to vote.

Baker offered strength and encouragement behind the scenes of the Freedom Summer voters' registration drive in Mississippi. She provided guidance as SNCC volunteers formed the Mississippi Freedom Democratic Party (MFDP) to threaten the all-white state delegation to the 1964 Democratic Convention. Until her death in 1986, Baker was a formidable force for self-determination in America.

Ella Baker encouraged the young energetic members of SNCC to keep pressure on the American public to end segregation. She advised them not to be slowed or diverted by more cautious civil rights organizations.

RALPH BUNCHE

Though active in global affairs, Bunche also involved himself domestically, speaking out against racial discrimination. He participated in the Selma and Montgomery, Alabama, civil rights marches in 1965.

BORN IN ABJECT POVERTY, Ralph Bunche rose to become one of the United States's greatest diplomats. His lifelong mission was to secure peace and to promote social justice throughout the world. In the process, he helped establish the United Nations, mediated an Arab-Israeli peace accord, and was the first African American to win the Nobel Peace Prize.

Bunche was born August 7, 1904; his father was a barber in a Detroit ghetto. His parents' poor lot in life worsened after his birth. The dismal conditions they lived in caused his father and his mother to die from tuberculosis and rheumatic fever, respectively, when he was only 12.

But Bunche had shown early scholarly promise in elementary school. After moving to Los Angeles with his grandmother, he graduated from high school as class valedictorian in 1922. In 1927, he graduated from the University of California at Los Angeles summa cum laude and Phi Beta Kappa, with a degree in international relations.

His studies earned Bunche a graduate spot at Harvard University, where he received a master's degree in government in 1928 and a Ph.D. in political science in 1934. He was the first African American to earn that doctorate at Harvard.

Bunche went on to study at Northwestern University, the London School of Economics, Capetown University, and throughout Africa. He also established the Political Science Department at Howard University in Washington, D.C. Between 1938 and 1940, he collaborated with Swedish sociologist Gunnar Myrdal on *An American Dilemma.* The book was a landmark study of race relations in the United States.

During World War II, Bunche became a specialist on African affairs within the State Department, making him the first African American to hold an important position in that government branch. Afterward, he helped draw up the charter for the United Nations and developed the framework for governing the defeated countries.

Bunche earned his stripes during the 1948 Arab-Israeli War, when he became the key mediator of the conflict after the original United Nations negotiator was assassinated. Bunche secured a truce between the countries in 1949 and won the Nobel Peace Prize for his effort. He dedicated the rest of his life to the United Nations, calling it the greatest peace effort in history.

A key United Nations member for two decades, Bunche rose to the post of undersecretary for special political affairs. The chief trouble-shooter for resolving global unrest, his most important accomplishments involved resolving the 1956 Suez crisis, helping to end the 1960 crisis in newly independent Zaire, and directing the 1964 peacekeeping expedition to Cyprus. Bunche also found time to march with Dr. Martin Luther King, Jr., on behalf of civil rights.

Ralph Bunche retired from the United Nations in 1970 and died in New York City on December 9, 1971.

Bunche reads his Nobel Peace Prize diploma, which honors his work negotiating an Arab-Israeli truce in 1949. He was a U.S. diplomat, working at the United Nations, when he received the prize.

GWENDOLYN BROOKS

The former poet laureate of the state of Illinois received numerous honors, including a Lifetime Achievement Award from the National Endowment for the Arts in 1989.

GWENDOLYN BROOKS was a Pulitzer Prize–winning poet who used her unique vision of the African American community to focus on the rigors of urban existence, empowerment, and the flavor of street life. A muse to the black experience and the former poet laureate of Illinois, she held more than 60 honorary degrees.

Gwendolyn Brooks started writing when she was only seven years old. Strongly influenced by writers ranging from e. e. cummings to Langston Hughes, her poetry has provided a voice for, and given a portrait of, the African American struggle.

Her writings include award-winning poetry for both adults and children, an autobiographical novel, and short stories. A humanitarian, Brooks used the royalties from her works to provide scholarships for aspiring black writers.

Brooks's poetry is praised for its technical brilliance and crafting; it includes the influences of colloquial speech, spirituals and blues, in addition to traditional rhyme and sonnet forms. She often wrote in free verse, and Brooks had such skill with language that her work is appreciated by the most highbrow of literary critics but is still accessible and enjoyable for the most ordinary of readers.

Brooks was born June 7, 1917, in Topeka, Kansas, the daughter of a teacher and a janitor who had once studied medicine. During her happy childhood on the streets of a south side Chicago neighborhood known as Bronzeville, Brooks learned early to appreciate education, literature, and music.

She attended predominantly white high schools and discovered that it was difficult for a quiet black girl to fit in. A shy and somewhat lonely child, Brooks displayed a penchant for concocting rhymes as early as age seven.

By age 11, Brooks was already keeping her poems in a notebook. She studied the poetry of T. S. Eliot, Shakespeare, Ezra Pound, Paul Laurence Dunbar, and Countee Cullen. She developed a love for alliteration and the music of language. At a very early age, she decided that her life's work would be poetry. By the age of 13, she had already been published in local newspapers and a national magazine. While in high school, Brooks sent poems to legendary black poets James Weldon Johnson and Langston Hughes. Hughes's enthusiasm for the writings of the 16-year-old sustained Brooks in her desire to succeed as a writer. In 1941, a modern poetry class at the South Side

Community Art Center in Chicago helped hone her talent in serious poetic technique. A 1943 award from the Midwestern Writer's Conference validated her efforts.

By 1945, Brooks published her first book of poetry, *A Street in Bronzeville,* which depicted the lives of poor and working-class blacks. The same year, she was chosen as one of America's Top Ten Women by *Mademoiselle* magazine. A review in *Poetry* at the time said her writing showed "a capacity to marry the special quality of her race with the best attainments of our contemporary poetry tradition."

Brooks received Guggenheim fellowships in 1946 and 1947, plus grants from the American Academy of Arts and Letters and the National Institute of Arts and Letters. Brooks became the first African American in the country to win a Pulitzer Prize, for her 1950 book *Annie Allen.* Some black critics accused her of writing the book for white approval. Several other books followed, including the 1953 novel *Maud Martha,* a semiautobiographical account of a black woman growing up in Chicago. The book describes black-white relations between the period of the Depression and World War II.

Gwendolyn Brooks was the first African American to win a Pulitzer Prize of any kind, which she did in 1950 for her book of poetry titled *Annie Allen.* Brooks's esteemed lifetime body of work and superb language skills led to her appointment as poet laureate for the state of Illinois.

GWENDOLYN BROOKS

Brooks changed the direction of her writing when the black empowerment movement began in the 1960s. Her 1960 collection of poems, titled *The Bean Eaters,* marked a transition and revealed her growing conscious-ness about the oppression of African Americans. Her 1968 book, *In the Mecca,* examines life in black tenements and includes odes to Malcolm X and Medgar Evers. *In the Mecca* was nominated for a National Book Award.

With *Riot,* in 1969, Brooks began publishing exclusively with black presses. Her previ-ous works had been published primarily by Harper's. In the early 1970s, *Aloneness, A Brookside Treasury, Jump Bad, Beckonings,*

and her autobiography, *Report From Part One,* were all published by Broadside Press, the Detroit-based company owned by Detroit Poet Laureate Dudley Randall. In 1987, Brooks herself published *Blacks,* an anthology of her published works from the beginning of her career.

Brooks was chosen as poetry consultant to the Library of Congress for 1985 and 1986, and she received a Lifetime Achievement Award from the National Endowment for the Arts in 1989. In 1990, she became the first scholar to hold the Gwendolyn Brooks Distinguished Chair in the English department at Chicago State University. Brooks died in 2000.

In 1950, Brooks won a Pulitzer Prize for her collection of poetry titled Annie Allen. *At the time, she was a 32-year-old housewife, the mother of a nine-year-old son, and a part-time secretary.*

RITA DOVE

The earthy poet Rita Dove has followed in Gwendolyn Brooks's renowned footsteps not only by expressing beautiful themes of African American life but by becom-ing, in 1987, the second African American poet to win the Pulitzer Prize. Dove, a prolific and award-winning author, was granted the high-est compliment in American verse. It came with her appointment as Poet Laureate of the United States and Consultant in Poetry to the Library of Congress. In 1993, Dove became the youngest and first African American to receive the two-year Poet Laureate appointment. She was chosen again in 1999 as Special Consultant in Poetry at the Library of Congress for a year.

Born in Akron, Ohio, on August 28, 1952, Rita Dove always excelled. She was one of the 100 most outstanding high school gradu-ates honored at the White House in 1970 as a Presidential Scholar. She went on to graduate summa cum laude, Phi Beta Kappa, and Phi Kappa Phi in 1973 from Miami University in Oxford, Ohio.

Following a stint as a Fulbright scholar at the Universitat Tubingen in Germany, she entered the University of Iowa Writers' Workshop, where she obtained a master of fine arts degree. There she met her husband, who was a German Fulbright fellow at the school. The two have one daughter.

She had renown from published works in magazine anthologies prior to the 1980 publica-tion of *The Yellow House on the Corner,* her first poetry collection. She received the Pulitzer Prize in 1987 for her poems of *Thomas and Beulah,* which were patterned after the lives of Dove's grandpar-ents. More recently, her collection of poems titled *On the Bus with Rosa Parks* was published.

Dove is presently commonwealth Professor of English at the University of Virginia in Charlottesville. She was Poet Laureate of the Commonwealth of Virginia from 2004 to 2006.

THURGOOD MARSHALL

Thurgood Marshall argued many cases before the U.S. Supreme Court while working with Charles Houston. Later, Marshall became the first African American Supreme Court justice.

Thurgood Marshall, America's first African American Supreme Court Justice, was also the most successful lawyer arguing cases before the high court.

THE MAN WHO WOULD ultimately grow up to become America's first African American Supreme Court justice was born in Baltimore in 1908. His father was a country club steward and Pullman car porter, and his mother was a teacher. The judge's name was Thurgood Marshall.

For 25 years prior to joining the high court, Marshall was "the most important advocate for America," said his colleague Justice William J. Brennan, referring to Marshall's 29 winning arguments before the Supreme Court—a record that remains unmatched by any lawyer, black or white.

Marshall's mother, who had considerable influence over him, traced her African roots to a 17th-century Congolese slave who caused so much trouble that his slave master finally set him free. Freedom was Thurgood Marshall's driving passion as well.

Marshall's paternal grandfather was a freeman who enlisted in the Union Army during the Civil War. He took the first name Thoroughgood in order to satisfy Army regulations that every soldier must have a first and a last name.

During the Depression, Marshall attended Lincoln University in Pennsylvania, where he met his wife, Vivian Burley. Marshall was a dedicated student prankster until settling into marriage with Burley. He graduated cum laude in 1930.

At Howard University Law School, he learned the benefit of applying the law to social engineering from his mentor, veteran litigator Charles Houston. After Marshall had established a private practice in Baltimore, Maryland, and Houston had begun the NAACP's legal campaign to desegregate schools, Marshall brought the Donald Murray case to Houston. Together, in 1935, the two lawyers were victorious in arguing for Murray's admission to the all-white law school at the University of Maryland.

As a consequence of the Murray case, many states began allocating more funds to graduate programs at black colleges in an effort to create some semblance of parity in education. Such meager public actions did not deter the NAACP from its mission to bury the "separate but equal" doctrine and open the doors of all schools to African Americans.

Thurgood Marshall, Charles Houston, and Donald Gaines Murray (left to right) are shown as they prepare the 1935 desegregation case against the University of Maryland.

During those early days as outside legal counsel for the NAACP, Marshall added all of $25 per year for stationery and postage and $5 per day for research and court appearances to the revenues of his practice. Marshall's larger role as special counsel for the NAACP in 1938 meant handling all cases related to constitutional rights. Marshall argued the subtleties of the Fourteenth Amendment, winning a clear majority of cases.

After Houston officially resigned in 1938, Marshall founded and headed the nonprofit NAACP Legal Defense and Education Fund. Marshall's success rate rose to 29 out of 32 major cases presented to the highest court in the land. He won the coveted NAACP Spingarn Medal in December 1946 for his distinguished service as a lawyer before the Supreme Court.

For the decade or so after Marshall took the helm, case after case dealing with segregation moved him closer to his goal of having the U.S. Supreme Court overturn the previous ruling

THURGOOD MARSHALL

Plessy v. *Ferguson,* which declared that separate but equal was constitutional.

On May 17, 1954, after Marshall presented his side, the Supreme Court handed down its epic decision in *Brown* v. *Board of Education.* The ruling stated that segregation in public schools was unconstitutional and that separate but equal has no place in American society. Jim Crow segregation was dead. Without a constitutional leg to stand on, *Plessy* v. *Ferguson* was eventually toppled by *Gayle* v. *Browder.*

But Marshall didn't just work for justice in the United States. During 1960, Marshall worked for three months to draft the constitution for the soon-to-be-independent republic of Kenya.

Marshall was also a proponent of women's rights. For example, Constance Baker Motley had been denied employment by other legal groups. Marshall hired her at the NAACP and

Lawyers George E. C. Hayes, Thurgood Marshall, and James M. Nabrit (left to right), on the Supreme Court steps in 1954. They argued for the abolition of segregation in public schools. The Court declared segregation unconstitutional that year.

DAISY BATES

Vandals, bombings, and economic reprisals: None of these could stop Daisy Bates and her husband, L. C. Bates, from continuing the NAACP's national assault on discriminatory practices in education and voting.

Born in segregated Arkansas around 1920, Daisy Bates (née Gaston) lived with discrimination in education and voting. The impact of that upbringing was so profound it sparked her unrelenting voice in the Arkansas Civil Rights Movement. In 1941, her marriage to L. C. Bates created a unison call for equal rights.

After Thurgood Marshall successfully argued the *Brown* v. *Board of Education* case before the Supreme Court, Bates used the considerable influence of their family newspaper, the *Arkansas State Press,* and her presidency of the state conference of the NAACP to move integration of the state's primary and secondary schools beyond

paper promises. She, along with accompanying international pressure, cast a global spotlight on the showdown between the Little Rock Nine and Arkansas Governor Orval Faubus in 1957.

On September 25, Faubus's armed state troopers and a crowd of rioting townsfolk blocked the Central High School entrance to nine black children. The situation lasted until it was brought under control by President Eisenhower, who sent in a thousand U.S. paratroopers from the 101st Airborne and federalized the Arkansas National Guard.

In 1962, Bates documented that event in her book, *The Long Shadow of Little Rock.* After recovering from a stroke in 1968, she headed the Mitchellville OEO Self-Help Project and reopened the *Arkansas State Press,* which had closed in 1959. After her husband's death, she turned the paper over to new owners. Bates died in 1999.

encouraged her career. She successfully argued the famous James Meredith case and was appointed to the federal court bench in New York by President Lyndon B. Johnson.

President John Kennedy named Thurgood Marshall to the U.S. Second Circuit Court of Appeals in September 1961 over the objections of Kennedy's brother Robert, who feared the appointment would upset southern politicos. At that time there were no blacks working in the courthouse, in either white or blue collar jobs.

During Marshall's four years of service on the appeals court, none of his more than 130 rulings were reversed by a higher court. With this stellar record, President Johnson, in 1965, named Marshall the first African American solicitor general of the Department of Justice, where he was victorious in 15 of the 19 cases he litigated for the Justice Department.

Two years later, President Johnson selected Marshall to sit on the Supreme Court. After enduring repeated Congressional hearings, he became the first African American to hold a high court seat. During his tenure on the bench, Marshall wrote the majority opinion on many cases upholding civil rights and constitutional democracy.

Marshall served with great distinction until his retirement on June 27, 1991. He was replaced on the bench by neo-conservative African American judge Clarence Thomas. This choice did not sit well with Marshall. Shortly before he died, in 1993, he warned against "picking the wrong Negro," adding, "there's no difference between a white snake and a black snake. They'll both bite...."

LITTLE ROCK NINE

ERNEST GREEN, Elizabeth Eckford, Jefferson Thomas, Terrence Roberts, Carlotta Walls Lanier, Minniejean Brown Trickey, Gloria Ray Karlmark, Thelma Mothershed-Wair, and Melba Pattillo Beals—people marked in history as the Little Rock Nine. At issue was the equalization of public education in America.

Central High in 1957 was one of the largest high schools in Arkansas, with enrollment at about 2,000 students. Some of the students' parents were resistant to the court-ordered integration. Hundreds of African American students were reduced to just nine, yet segregationists were loathe to share the school with even a few.

Little Rock Nine with Daisy Bates (top row, second from right). Many went on to distinguished careers. Ernest Green was appointed Assistant Secretary of Housing and Urban Affairs under President Jimmy Carter and is an executive with Lehman Brothers in Washington, D.C. Minniejean Brown Trickey served as Deputy Assistant Secretary for Workforce Diversity at the Department of the Interior during the Clinton administration. Terrence Roberts worked as a clinical psychologist and taught at UCLA and Antioch College. Gloria Ray Karlmark became a patent attorney and published an international magazine for the computer industry.

Meanwhile, the other eight students were escorted from the opposite side of the school. Armed guards refused to allow them on campus. The students left with two ministers walking in front and two guarding the rear.

Attorneys on both sides filed a flurry of requests in the lower courts. Waiting for the outcome put the Little Rock Nine back where they started—being tutored by Daisy Bates. This continued for three weeks. After one more mob-ridden attempt at desegregation, President Dwight Eisenhower nationalized the state guardsmen and deployed the 101st airborne troops. On September 25, 1957, with the military backing them, the nine black students were finally allowed into the school.

A few white students terrorized them whenever military bodyguards were not present. Minniejean Brown, fed up with the taunting, dumped chili on a tormenter. Brown received a suspension and was later expelled for returning another derogatory comment from a white student with an insult.

Arkansas Governor Orval Faubus responded to integration by warning that blood would run in the street if the African American students were not stopped. He even threatened to use the state's National Guard to help. These were surprising words since the Little Rock school board had agreed to comply with the Supreme Court's 1954 *Brown* v. *Board of Education* decision. Later clarification of the ruling stating that public school integration should occur with "all deliberate speed" left the issue open for debate about how quickly desegregation would take place. Parties on both sides, including the NAACP, litigated that specific point right up to the second day of school, September 4, 1957.

Word of impending trouble spread the day before the black students were to arrive, as whites outside the school grew to mob proportions. Daisy Bates, head of the state NAACP chapter, organized a biracial group of ministers to meet the black students while local police waited on alert. Elizabeth Eckford, who had no telephone, did not learn about the meeting place. Instead, she stepped off the public bus and into a mob that was calling for her lynching, among other obscenities. Though Eckford's face remained stoic, her knees were shaking.

A guard with a bayoneted rifle blocked Eckford from entering campus. She left through the horrifying mob, which swarmed and spit at her. Reporter Benjamin Fine and Grace Lorch, both white, intervened. With the mob close at hand, Lorch accompanied Eckford onto the first bus that arrived. News cameras captured it all.

Ernest Green become the school's first African American graduate. Carlotta Lanier and Jefferson Thomas followed in his footsteps. To stop that from happening, all Little Rock public schools were closed and an attempt was made to privatize them. The U.S. Supreme Court reopened the schools on August 12, 1959. By the time the schools reopened, many students attended private schools.

The situation in the U.S. school system remains far from perfect today. But, thanks in part to the bravery of the Little Rock Nine, a legal precedent was set: No state was above federal law.

MILES DAVIS III

THE MUSICAL GENIUS of Miles Dewey Davis III never faded during his lifetime. His creative brilliance pushed him to always search for the next great musical sound, cool and fusion jazz among them. He blended jazz with other musical genres in ways that had never been done before.

Davis was born to Cleota Henry and dentist Miles Davis II on May 26, 1926. The family lived in Alton, Illinois, until his father established a dental practice in an interracial section of East St. Louis, Illinois. Davis's musical development began when he received a trumpet from a neighbor, Dr. John Eubanks.

Davis loved jazz. Saxophonist Charlie "Bird" Parker, trumpeter Dizzy Gillespie, and bandleader Duke Ellington were his heroes. In 1944, when big band leader Billy Eckstine landed across the river in St. Louis, Missouri, with an ensemble that included Parker and Gillespie, 18-year-old Davis rushed to play with them during rehearsal.

Davis studied classical trumpet and piano at the Juilliard School of Music, but his "jazz lessons" entailed cruising around town with greats Dizzy Gillespie and Charlie Parker.

As soon as Davis arrived, Gillespie pulled him on stage to replace the trumpeter who had fallen ill. Davis was almost too mesmerized with these jazz masters, especially Parker, to play.

That incredible experience solidified Davis's decision to go to New York City, the heartbeat of jazz. His parents agreed to let him attend Manhattan's Juilliard School of Music, where he studied classical trumpet and piano.

Gillespie left Parker's band in 1945, so Davis took his spot and appeared on that year's Savoy record. Two years later, Davis cut a record on the same label with the Miles Davis All-Stars. Davis's experimentation with musician Gil Evans helped create a more lyrical, cooler jazz, and the *Birth of the Cool* album, recorded in 1949, proved to be groundbreaking.

In 1949, Davis tackled Europe. There, he experienced racial freedom and true love—with actress Juliette Greco. Leaving Greco hit him hard. On his return to America, he turned to heroin. He still performed in Manhattan clubs, but a racially laced drug arrest made news in 1950. In the absence of drug evidence, the charges were dropped, but few club owners booked the musician after that.

Prestige Records took a chance on Davis. But since he received only nominal pay, he resorted largely to a street life until he was able to kick his heroin addiction in 1954. Davis's creative zeal and career then hit new heights. Expressive orchestral sounds on *Sketches of Spain* yielded his first Grammy Award, and the album *Miles Davis in Person* hit the *Billboard* music charts—another first—in 1961.

Breakthrough compositions in the 1960s reflected growth in modern technology. Electric instruments fused jazz with contemporary funk and rock music and fueled Davis's popular-

Miles Davis enjoyed almost 50 years of ingenuity in jazz, entertaining audiences around the globe and making roughly 100 records during his lifetime.

ity. His *Bitches Brew* album ranked 35 on the *Billboard* charts in 1970.

An intense performance schedule plus drug addiction to manage pain from sickle cell anemia and disintegrating hip bones contributed to Davis's retreat by 1975. Actress Cicely Tyson got him medical attention, while sketching and painting helped ease his drug cravings.

Davis reemerged in 1980 with new ideas for fusing jazz with contemporary styles. Collaborating with talented musicians, such as Herbie Hancock and Joe Zawinul, brought the styles reverberating in Davis's mind to life.

Before his death on September 22, 1991, he took part in one more fusion involving jazz and rap. Rapper Eazy Mo Bee collaborated on Davis's last recording, *Doo-Bop*, which won him an eighth Grammy Award. He was inducted into the Rock and Roll Hall of Fame in 2006.

RALPH ELLISON

RALPH ELLISON, author of the landmark novel *Invisible Man*, was one of the most influential African American writers of the 20th century even though he only published one novel before his death at age 80. A contemporary of Harlem Renaissance poet Langston Hughes and author Richard Wright, Ellison intertwined his love of music and literature to create a language that helped convey vivid, visceral images of the political and social constraints on black life.

Ellison was born March 1, 1914, in Oklahoma City, Oklahoma. His father, who sold ice and coal, died in an accident when Ellison was three years old. His mother, a socialist who was arrested several times for violating segregation orders, supported the family by working as a domestic. The old magazines she brought home for her son helped ignite his interest in jazz and fashion. Ellison started playing the trumpet in high school, and he excelled in music.

In order to prevent him from going to an all-white Oklahoma college, local officials gave him a scholarship to Tuskegee Institute (now Tuskegee University) in Alabama. He dropped out when his scholarship ended in 1936, and he moved to New York to study sculpture and earn enough money to return to school in the fall. Instead, he met Hughes and Wright.

The self-styled Renaissance man studied white writers, including Ernest Hemingway and James Joyce, and wrote reviews and fiction for black magazines and Communist Party publications. In 1938, Ellison joined the Federal Writer's Project and began interviewing older African Americans, collecting black folklore and oral histories.

His early stories, "Slick Gonna Learn" (1939) and "The Birthmark" (1940), explored the trials

Ralph Ellison was a Renaissance man; not only was he a novelist and writer of essays and short stories, but he was also an accomplished photographer and jazz trumpeter.

and tribulations of black life. African American customs and language were the heart of several other Ellison stories, including "Flying Home" (1944). The next year, Ellison wrote a sentence: "I am an invisible man." It became the opening line of his 1952 book, which many critics have called one of the greatest novels ever. In 2000, a group of distinguished literary critics named *Invisible Man* the greatest American novel of the 20th century.

The premise of the book, the idea that American society deliberately ignores African Americans, introduced readers to a black reality. The novel is the story of an unnamed Southern black man's journey from innocence to experience as he searches for his place in the world. The rhythms of jazz echo in Ellison's words, and critics have called *Invisible Man* an

exploration of the African American psyche. It also won the prestigious National Book Award.

He followed the influential novel with two collections of his essays, speeches, and interviews about being African American and that experience—*Shadow and Act* (1964) and *Going to the Territory* (1987). Ellison lectured at many colleges and universities, including Rutgers, Yale, and New York University.

He also received several awards, including a 1985 National Medal of Arts for *Invisible Man* and for his teaching. A tragic fire in 1967 destroyed more than 300 pages of his long-awaited second novel, which was still unfinished when Ellison died of pancreatic cancer in April 1994.

After Ellison's death, *The Collected Essays of Ralph Ellison* (1995) and *Flying Home* (1996), a collection of short stories, were published. Ellison's literary executor, John Callahan, published an edited version of thousands of manuscript pages as the novel *Juneteenth* in 1999.

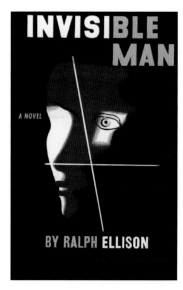

Invisible Man tells the story of a black man searching for his identity in a nation rife with prejudice.

CHUCK BERRY

Chuck Berry performs at his 75th birthday celebration at the Pageant Theater in St. Louis on October 18, 2001. Berry has been called "The Father of Rock and Roll."

ON HIS 75TH BIRTHDAY, guitar virtuoso Chuck Berry, the legendary singer-songwriter who is one of the earliest pioneers of rock and roll, was still doing his trademark "duck walk," hopping one-legged across the stage to the raucous cheers of his fans. Berry's hits from the 1950s to the 1970s evoke images of the sock hops and soda shops where teens of that generation hung out.

The visionary lyrics and hard-driving rhythms of this flashy performer influenced bands ranging from the Beach Boys to the Rolling Stones and made him one of the legends of a musical style that evolved out of an amalgamation of rhythm and blues and country and western. Berry was one of the first black musicians to garner wide popularity with white audiences.

Born October 18, 1926, Berry grew up in a lower-middle-class African American neighborhood in St. Louis, in a family that was fiercely proud of its black and Native American ancestry. His first taste of performing was singing gospel at Antioch Baptist Church. While growing up, he listened to the blues and to country music on the radio, including the music of Muddy Waters and T-Bone Walker. Berry learned to play guitar, piano, and saxophone in high school. He joined a trio in the 1950s, performing jazz, country, and rhythm and blues.

Berry met bluesman Waters, one of his idols, in Chicago, and he ended up being signed by Chess Records. His first hit was "Maybellene" in 1955. It was from his first recording session, and it stayed on the pop charts for 11 weeks. Berry followed "Maybellene" with more hits, including "Roll Over, Beethoven," the anthem "Rock-and-Roll Music," and, of course, "Johnny B. Goode," in 1958. The latter tune ended up among the pieces of music placed on a gold-plated copper record attached to the *Voyager I* satellite, which was sent into space so distant civilizations could sample the culture of 20th-century earth.

Berry continued recording and performing in the 1960s and '70s, landing his first number-one single with the novelty song "My Ding-a-Ling" in 1972. In 1984, Berry was awarded a Grammy for Lifetime Achievement, and he was inducted into the Rock and Roll Hall of Fame in 1986. In 2000, Berry was one of the honorees at the 23rd annual Kennedy Center Honors.

His music inspired artists from Elvis to the Beatles, and critics have called Berry the true father of modern rock and roll. Berry's shows combine precise diction with poetic lyrics that offer vivid descriptions of high school life, though he says the words to his newer songs reflect the life he lives now, along with that of the generation right behind him. His songs have been recorded by Buddy Holly and Linda Ronstadt, among others, and his music is in the repertoire of most rock and roll bands.

Berry has had a host of legal troubles, spending time in reform school for attempted burglary, then later in jail for illegally taking an underage girl across state lines, and still later for tax evasion.

But Berry says he isn't worried about his legacy, that he's just tried to do his best. He says the roar of the crowd keeps him going, along with the fact that he is still learning, and that makes life fun.

Chuck Berry in 1980. Age has not slowed the rocker; he still duck-walks across the stage at performances.

ROY WILKINS

Roy Wilkins steadfastly chipped away laws that impeded the full pursuit of rights owed all American citizens, thus guiding the nation to constitutional enlightenment.

IF ACTIONS ARE THE MEASURE of a human being, then Roy Wilkins clearly reached the greatest heights. At considerable risk to his own life, he shifted the pursuit of civil rights into the courtroom where racially biased Jim Crow laws were finally overturned.

Applying Wilkins's unrelenting yet gentlemanly style, the National Association for the Advancement of Colored People (NAACP) proceeded to lobby both the legislative and executive branches of the United States government to pass the 1957 and 1960 voting rights bills, following those with the 1964 Civil Rights Act.

Impressing politicians not only about the rightness of his cause but also by emphasizing how racial equality could help them put President Lyndon B. Johnson just a phone call away, he helped add enforcement teeth to the 1965 voting rights bill along with the 1966 and 1968 civil rights acts.

Roy Ottoway Wilkins was born on August 30, 1901, the first child of Mayfield and William Wilkins. He lived in a modest apartment in segregated St. Louis, Missouri, until his mother died from tuberculosis. His Aunt Elizabeth arrived on the scene to take care of the funeral arrangements for her sister. She then took four-year-old Roy, his sister, Armeda, and brother, Earl, to an integrated and more prosperous life with her and her husband, Sam Williams, in St. Paul, Minnesota.

The racism experienced by most African Americans did not fully hit Wilkins until the lynching of three black men by a reported 5,000 white citizens in Duluth, Minnesota, just up the Mississippi River from St. Paul. Two generations out of slavery, 18-year-old Wilkins made every effort to cope with his rage by denouncing the growing crime wave against fellow African Americans, first as a journalist and later through his efforts at the NAACP.

Following graduation from the University of Minnesota, he worked as a newspaper editor and reporter for the black-owned *Kansas City Call* in 1923. That position and his work as a social advocate for the Kansas City chapter of the NAACP gradually helped him forge a relationship with Walter White, then the assistant executive secretary at NAACP headquarters.

By the time White orchestrated Wilkins's relocation to New York in 1931, Wilkins had married the love of his life, Minnie Badeau. The couple found themselves blossoming in the richness and freedom of Harlem, a mecca of African American intelligentsia and culture.

As White's assistant, Wilkins soon envisioned the NAACP making a tangible impact on the daily lives of most African Americans; he slowly helped reprioritize resources, from lobbying for passage of a limited antilynching law to breaking down widespread Jim Crow laws in education and voting.

After White's death in 1955, Wilkins moved from acting head of the NAACP and editor of *Crisis* magazine to executive secretary. Throughout his 22-year reign, he always considered himself employed by his fellow blacks to secure full citizenship. If Dr. King was the ultimate outsider, bringing the struggle to the streets, Wilkins, ever measured in temperament and tone, was the ultimate insider. He lobbied legislators, litigated cases, and ensured the passage of landmark legislation.

Although the latter years of his work were tarnished by fractionalized disputes over the benefits of the Black Power Movement, Wilkins remained steadfastly opposed to any hint of racial separatism in the young militant movement. Until his retirement in 1977, he bore criticism of being out of step and selling out with characteristic dignity. In recent years, his contributions to the nation have been reevaluated, and his place in the pantheon of giants of the Civil Rights Movement is broadly acknowledged. Wilkins died September 8, 1981.

Roy Wilkins was the first African American leader that President Nixon met with after taking office in 1969.

ROSA PARKS

Rosa Parks's refusal to submit to white privilege kicked off a liberation struggle that named her the "Mother of the Civil Rights Movement."

SHE WAS BORN Rosa Louise McCauley in Tuskegee, Alabama, in 1913. For the next 42 years, she would live her life in obscurity until one fateful day in Montgomery, Alabama.

In December 1955, 42-year-old seamstress Rosa Parks joined the workers at the bus stop after a hard day at her tailoring job. It seemed like the bus would never come. When it finally arrived, all the seats in the back, where blacks were allowed to sit, were quickly taken. Parks sat down in the white section. The bus driver told her and several other African Americans to give up their seats to whites who got on after she did. Parks refused to move. The bus driver called the police, and Parks was arrested. She and her husband later lost their jobs.

Her refusal to give up her seat sparked a movement against segregation in Montgomery, which started with a 381-day bus boycott by African Americans. The leader of that boycott went on to become quite famous—a young black minister named Dr. Martin Luther King, Jr. So successful was the boycott that Dr. King was arrested and his life was threatened. Subsequently, King and his father, Martin Luther King, Sr., and other ministers, including the reverends Ralph Abernathy and Wyatt T. Walker, founded the Southern Christian Leadership Conference (SCLC). These events, kicked off by Parks's nonviolent passive resis-

tance, officially launched the Civil Rights Movement. On December 21, 1956, the boycott ended when the U.S. Supreme Court declared bus segregation unconstitutional.

Parks was not the first black woman to refuse to move to the back of a Montgomery bus. A year earlier, another black woman had been arrested for a similar "offense." But she was an unwed mother, and Montgomery's civil rights leadership feared she would not be an acceptable "role model" around which the community could rally.

Nor was this Parks's first attempt to fight discrimination. In the 1930s, Parks and her husband, Raymond, had worked courageously in a futile attempt to free the Scottsboro Boys, nine black men who were falsely accused of raping two white women. She knew she was putting her life at risk by working for this cause. During

Parks, accompanied by E. D. Nixon, former president of the Alabama NAACP, arrives at the Montgomery, Alabama, courthouse on March 19, 1956. She stood trial for refusing to yield her bus seat to a white man.

For more than 50 years, Rosa Parks has been a guiding symbol in the struggle for black equality. Here she is fingerprinted after her arrest.

the 1950s, Parks was the secretary of the Montgomery branch of the NAACP.

She and her husband moved to Detroit, where she lived until her death on October 24, 2005. For many years, she served as a staff assistant to Representative John Conyers. In 1994, Parks, then 81 years old, was attacked by a robber. With help from the community, the robber was caught and convicted, and he apologized.

In the mid-1990s, Parks wrote her autobiography *Rosa Parks: My Story,* then she authored *Quiet Strength,* an autobiography with Gregory Reed, which focuses on the faith and hope of a woman who changed a nation by starting the Civil Rights Movement. In her book, Parks recalls her outrage at being asked to stand up so a white man could sit: "After so many years of oppression and being a victim of mistreatment that my people had suffered, not giving up my seat—and whatever I had to face after not giving it up—was not important."

MARTIN LUTHER KING, JR.

Dr. Martin Luther King, Jr., was a prominent civil rights leader who remains the most outstanding symbol of that movement, a movement that led to voting rights for African Americans and an end to legal employment discrimination and segregation of public facilities. King won the Nobel Peace Prize in 1964, and his birthday is now a national holiday.

THE REVEREND DR. MARTIN Luther King, Jr., was the leading organizer of the Civil Rights Movement of the 1950s and 1960s, which led to desegregation of public places, the abolition of legal discrimination against African Americans in employment, and voting rights for blacks.

King's success was in elevating the issue of equality into a moral crusade. He appealed to the conscience of the nation and brought pressure on the federal government to pass legislation that remedied many of society's inequities.

This eloquent, stirring orator was able to convince people of goodwill that justice is inherent in the civil rights cause. He galvanized people of all colors, particularly massive numbers of blacks, into actions that were fraught with danger; indeed, these actions cost King his own life when he was assassinated April 4, 1968, at the age of 39.

King was born on January 15, 1929, in Atlanta, Georgia, into a family of ministers. At age 15, he was accepted into Morehouse College under a program for gifted students. He received his bachelor's degree in sociology at 19 years of age.

His educational accomplishments continued at Crozer Theological Seminary in Chester,

Pennsylvania. King graduated first in his class and was the first black student body president. He met and married Coretta Scott while attending Boston University, where he received his Ph.D. in systematic theology in 1955.

King holds a copy of his book, Why We Can't Wait, *which details the history of the civil rights struggle. The book was also a response to eight Alabama white clergy who denounced King's protest actions.*

King left higher education with more than a doctorate degree. Through studies of classic philosophers and modern activists, such as Mahatma Ghandi, King formulated a philosophy of nonviolence that played a guiding role in the rest of his life.

After college, he accepted the pastorship at Dexter Avenue Baptist Church in Montgomery, Alabama. In December 1955, a black seamstress named Rosa Parks was arrested in Montgomery for refusing to give up her seat on a bus to a white man. Park's courageous act sparked a bus boycott that gave rise to the Montgomery Improvement Association, through which King's national leadership evolved.

Though King's home was bombed during the Montgomery bus boycott, he remained undeterred. He continued to inspire local African Americans to walk, car pool, take taxis, and find transportation other than buses. The boycott forced the bus company to desegregate the following year. The Supreme Court declared the bus segregation law unconstitutional in December 1956. King's persuasive leadership brought renewed life to the nationwide struggle for social change.

King began traveling extensively and lecturing about peacefully seeking justice for blacks. He shared his *Pilgrimage to Nonviolence* more widely in his book discussing the Montgomery bus boycott, published in 1958. His philosophies on nonviolence were further expanded into fundamental actions for social change expressed in the famous *Letter from*

Pictured are (left to right) Roy Wilkins, King, and A. Philip Randolph at the Lincoln Memorial during the Freedom Pilgrimage rally on May 17, 1957.

MARTIN LUTHER KING, JR.

King, at the March on Washington, D.C., waves to the crowd after his "I Have a Dream" speech on August 28, 1963.

Birmingham Jail. It was written during King's period of confinement after defying a local city ordinance with a protest march on Good Friday in 1963.

When attack dogs, fire hoses, and clubs were used by local law enforcers against men, women, and children, who asked only to sit at the lunch counter of their choice or to vote for the candidate of their choice or to drink at the water fountain of their choice, America's image as the greatest bastion of human rights and individual freedom was shattered. This darker view of the country brought enormous global pressure to rectify the situation.

In a glorious show of unity in August 1963, King delivered his stirring "I Have a Dream" speech to the largest crowd of demonstrators seen in the nation's capitol up to that day. The Civil Rights Act was passed the following year.

Resistance to the federal law persisted, and following a bloody confrontation in Selma, Alabama, in 1965, King called on religious leaders of all denominations and differing factions of the Movement to join him in a second attempt to march 54 miles to Montgomery in support of black voting rights. By the end of the five-day protest, more than 20,000 people had walked into Alabama's capitol. President Lyndon Johnson maneuvered the Voting Rights Act of 1965 through Congress soon after the event.

It is ironic that the man in the forefront of elevating the nation's moral consciousness and promoting world peace would have his privacy invaded by the Federal Bureau of Investigation. Under the broad powers assumed for fighting Communism, the FBI countered progress toward civil rights with attempts to discredit the Movement and selected leaders through a paper titled "Racial Tensions and Civil Rights," as well as the infamous COINTELPRO (counterintelligence program) surveillance. King, a Nobel Peace Prize winner, was not exempt from this invasion of privacy. With the FBI watching, King persisted in advocating global freedom, peace (including an end to the controversial Vietnam War), and economic justice.

Building on his past successes, he began organizing a multiracial Poor People's Campaign to continue in Washington, D.C., until basic economic rights were secured. By the start of that action, demonstrators had to pitch camp without King, who had been fatally shot on the balcony of the Lorraine Hotel in Memphis in April 1968. James Earl Ray originally confessed to the murder. Prior to his death years later, Ray provided the details of a conspiracy. In 1999, a Memphis jury agreed that Lloyd Jowers and others, including government agencies, participated in a conspiracy related to King's assassination.

CORETTA SCOTT KING

Coretta Scott King became an icon for nonviolence, a beacon of hope for the Civil Rights Movement. Withstanding the threats on her life and a bomb exploding in her Montgomery, Alabama, home, she proudly demonstrated for freedom. Locked arm in arm with her husband, she showed determination and dignity.

Her commitment to freedom was apparent before she ever met Martin Luther King, Jr. During her college years in Ohio, for example, she objected to the de facto segregation of the North that placed limits on her social and educational options. She joined the Antioch chapter of the NAACP, along with a race relations committee and a civil liberties committee to help shape a different future. After marrying King, she added caring for a family and performing the duties of a minister's wife to her lifetime commitments.

Coretta King was born in Marion, Alabama, in 1927. She was aptly prepared to face the challenges of the mission to achieve social justice. Since her husband's death, their mission continues through Mrs. King's formation of The King Center and other activities of national interest. She and her family protested apartheid in South Africa. She was in the forefront of interracial coalitions striving for full employment and international delegations of women discussing Soviet Union–United States relations.

She ensured that the high social standards to which her husband dedicated his life would never be forgotten by gaining recognition of King's birth in January as an American holiday.

Coretta King died on January 30, 2006, at the age of 78.

SAMMY DAVIS, JR.

Davis earned rave reviews from critics for his performance in the movie Tap. *One year later, he died from throat cancer.*

SAMMY DAVIS, JR., a consummate performer equally adept at singing, dancing, improvisation, and acting, was one of the first African American artists who had a legion of fans on both sides of the color line.

The son of black vaudeville star Sammy Davis, Sr., and Puerto Rican dancer Elvera "Baby" Sanchez, Davis was born on December 8, 1925, in Harlem. He started his career at the tender age of three, appearing with the vaudeville group Will Mastin's Holiday in Dixieland. When the act was threatened with closure because of child labor laws, Davis was given a cigar to hold and billed as "Silent Sam, the Dancing Midget." The act was later renamed Will Mastin's Gang Featuring Little Sammy. When he was seven, Davis appeared in the musical short *Rufus Jones for President,* his film debut. He later received tap dancing training from Bill "Bojangles" Robinson. In 1941, the Mastin Gang opened

for Tommy Dorsey at the Michigan Theater in Detroit, where Davis met singer Frank Sinatra. They began a lifelong friendship.

Davis joined the U.S. Army two years later, and he endured virulent racism while directing shows and visiting military installations. He returned to the Will Mastin Trio after leaving the army, and the group played clubs with entertainers that included Sinatra, Bob Hope, and Jack Benny. In 1946, the trio opened for Mickey Rooney, who encouraged Davis to include his comedic impersonations in the act. The same year, Davis signed with Capitol Records. His version of "The Way You Look Tonight" was chosen as Record of the Year by *Metronome* magazine, which also named Davis Most Outstanding New Personality.

During the 1950s, African Americans could perform in Las Vegas but couldn't stay in the hotels or even enter casinos through the front doors. Davis changed all that. Because of his friendship with Sinatra, Sammy was the first black performer to stay in the hotel where he performed. In this and other ways, he opened doors for other black performers.

In 1954, Decca Records signed Davis. The album *Starring Sammy Davis, Jr.,* was number one on the charts, and he followed it with a series of hit singles. Later that year, Davis lost his left eye in a car accident. He also converted to Judaism that year.

His religious choice, along with interracial romances, caused controversy in the black community. Some

African Americans also criticized Davis for his connection with the Rat Pack, a group of Sinatra associates that included Dean Martin, Joey Bishop, and Peter Lawford. They called him a sellout for allowing himself to be the butt of what some called subtly racist jokes. But Davis continued his kaleidoscopic career, making a series of Rat Pack movies. Davis starred in the Broadway show *Golden Boy* and earned a Tony Award nomination. The NAACP awarded Davis the Spingarn Medal for his 1965 autobiography, *Yes I Can.*

In 1973, Davis was hospitalized for kidney and liver problems due to alcoholism, but he returned to the stage in *Sammy on Broadway.* Davis starred in his own television show, *Sammy and Company,* from 1975 to 1977. During the 1980s, Davis published two more autobiographies, and he toured with Sinatra, Martin, and Liza Minnelli. Davis died of throat cancer in May 1990. When he died, the lights along the Las Vegas strip were turned off—the first time a performer was so honored.

Davis often performed with the Rat Pack, some of whom are pictured above, from left to right, Peter Lawford, Dean Martin, Davis, and Frank Sinatra.

JAMES BROWN

One of the most popular and influential performers in the history of American music, James Brown was also an astute businessman who owned fast-food franchises, record and publishing companies, radio stations, a booking agency, and a private jet. The two-time Grammy winner was also inducted into the Rock and Roll Hall of Fame.

JUST AS A DAM HARNESSES the raging currents of water to make electricity, James Brown captured the power of raw energy, pure feeling, and infectious rhythms to become one of the most influential performers of American popular music.

It's unclear whether this dynamo was born in 1928, 1933, or 1934. But it is known that he grew up in Augusta, Georgia, in abject poverty. He did whatever he could to earn extra money—shining shoes, picking cotton, and singing gospel and pop music he learned by ear and from local clubs. But when he took to crime in 1949, Brown was sentenced to reform school, where he served three and a half years. After his release, he joined the Gospel Starlighters in 1952. The group soon became known as James Brown and the Famous Flames, and they switched to rhythm-and-blues (R&B) music.

One story of Brown's discovery holds that before a Little Richard show in Toccoa, Georgia, the Flames took the stage and gave an impromptu performance. Richard's manager caught it and signed the group. However it happened, Brown's career began in 1956 with a contract with King Records.

The Flames released their first single, "Please, Please, Please," in 1956, which soon became one of Brown's signature hits. The group then began a grueling string of one-night stands across the country, where they honed their sound to razor-sharp precision.

Brown's rugged concert schedule, his insistence on rehearsing his band (which eventually grew to 40 members) until they reached his standard of excellence, and the enormous energy he expended dancing and singing earned him the nickname "The Hardest Working Man in Show Business."

Brown hit the top in 1963 with his unusual (at that time) concept of recording a live performance. His *James Brown Live at the Apollo* hit number two on the *Billboard* charts, and, along with his 1965 single "Papa's Got a Brand New Bag," catapulted him into international superstardom in the 1960s and 1970s.

Brown was the leading proponent of "soul" music, and his songs reflected growing racial pride among African Americans. His hit "Say It Loud, I'm Black and I'm Proud" became a new black national anthem.

His rhythmic arrangements featured tight, repetitious, almost hypnotic grooves, accented by heavy bass lines and flashy horns, with an unusual emphasis on the first beat. These arrangements created the foundations of funk music, which crested in the 1970s and 1980s. He is one of the most heavily sampled artists by rap musicians.

Brown won a Grammy Award in 1965 for best R&B recording with "Papa's Got a Brand New Bag" and another in 1987 for best R&B performance for "Living in America." In 1986, he was inducted into the Rock and Roll Hall of Fame. He died on December 25, 2006.

Brown was not just a phenomenal performer. He hit the charts with more than 100 songs as a writer and composer.

Brown uncharacteristically singing while sitting. His energetic, constantly moving stage show earned him the nickname "The Hardest Working Man in Show Business."

ALTHEA GIBSON

Gibson, in 1950, was the first African American player invited to the U.S. National Tennis Tournament in Forest Hills.

ALTHEA GIBSON'S life was one of struggle, perseverance, and redemption. Overcoming an early pattern of erratic behavior, inconsistency, and being easily frustrated, she became the first black player to win tennis championships at Wimbledon and the U.S. Open.

Gibson was born August 25, 1927, in Silver, South Carolina. She and her sharecropper parents relocated to Harlem while she was still a child. In New York, the pretty, gangly girl was frequently truant in school—prone to playing hooky and spending days at the movies.

Eventually placed in a foster home, Gibson was an embittered, restless malcontent who could not hold a job. But she showed remarkable prowess in street basketball, stickball, and table tennis. A New York City recreation department worker noticed her talents and introduced her to his friend Fred Johnson, a tennis pro at Harlem's elite Cosmopolitan Club.

Shortly after Gibson won her first tournament, the New York Open Championship in 1942, Cosmopolitan Club members pooled their resources to send her to more tournaments, where she did well. Gibson caught the eye of two black doctors who were leaders in the American Tennis Association, and they became her sponsors. Beginning in 1947, she won the first of ten ATA National Championships.

A restless, troubled youth, Althea Gibson found solace, success, and herself in tennis. She became the first black player to compete and win at both Forest Hills (U.S. Open) and Wimbledon—a feat she accomplished in 1957 and repeated in 1958.

Her tennis success made Gibson a better student. In 1949, she graduated from high school ranked tenth in her class and went on to Florida A&M College.

Gibson's tennis ability was not to be denied. She received invitations to play in eastern and national indoor championships and then, in 1950, became the first black woman asked to play in the U.S. National Championship Tournament at Forest Hills, now known as the U.S. Open.

Though eliminated in the second round of that tournament, Gibson traveled to Europe, Mexico, and Southeast Asia, winning 16 of 18 other tournaments. That secured her a bid to Wimbledon.

Gibson was defeated at Wimbledon and again that year at Forest Hills. It wasn't until 1957 that she won the U.S. National and her first Wimbledon title. In 1958, she won both tournaments again.

Surprisingly, at 30, Gibson gave up tennis to pursue other activities and make the money that tennis didn't provide. She recorded albums, briefly acted, toured with the Harlem Globetrotters, and became a celebrity endorser.

Gibson played pro golf from 1963 to 1967 as the first black member of the Ladies Professional Golf Association. Later she worked for the New Jersey State Athletic Control Board and served as special consultant to the New Jersey Governor's Council on Physical Fitness and Sports from 1988 to 1992. Gibson died on September 28, 2003.

Althea Gibson shows two young girls her first tennis racket, which she used when she played on the streets of Harlem. In 1973, she opened up a summer tennis program that brought tennis to 20,000 inner-city kids.

ELIJAH MUHAMMAD

FOR 41 YEARS, Elijah Muhammad, the controversial leader of the Nation of Islam, was the leading proponent in spreading the Muslim religion throughout black America. He was instrumental in creating a self-help movement through which many African Americans could determine and control their own destinies.

One of Muhammad's desires was to create an independent black nation located in the southern portion of the country, which he wanted ceded to the Nation of Islam by the U.S. government.

Born Elijah Poole in Sandersville, Georgia, on October 10, 1897, Muhammad was one of 13 children of former slaves. The major turning point in his life came when Poole, as a child, secretly witnessed the lynching of a black man by three whites.

This traumatic event may have led to Muhammad's ultimate belief that blacks and whites should live apart, independently. He created the Nation of Islam movement as a spur to the establishment of a separatist nation.

Poole moved to Detroit in 1923. In the 1930s, he became a follower of Wallace Fard, who preached that by practicing their "original" religion, Islam, blacks could overcome the conditions of degradation they experienced in America.

Fard encouraged Poole to reject his "slave" name and adopt an Islamic one; Poole became Elijah Muhammad. Fard then appointed Muhammad as supreme minister of the Nation of Islam, also known as the Black Muslims. When Fard disappeared in 1934, Muhammad preached that Fard had actually been Allah in disguise, who had shared secrets and teachings with Muhammad. This made Muhammad "The Messenger of Allah." Muhammad began traveling the country, spreading the teachings of the Muslim movement.

Arrested in 1934 for not sending his children to a public school (they attended a Nation of Islam school), Muhammad lived as a fugitive from 1934 to 1942. In 1942, he was jailed for three years for resisting the draft. After his release in 1946, he continued his influential reign as head of the Nation of Islam. About four years later, Muhammad recruited Malcolm X to be the national spokesman for the Black Muslims. The 13 years Malcolm X spent in that position were the organization's most fruitful. The newspaper, *Muhammad Speaks,* which he founded, carried stories about Africa and foreign affairs largely ignored by the mainstream press.

Muhammad and the Black Muslims earned grudging respect because of their comportment. They were self-reliant, highly moral individuals who did not smoke, drink, gamble, or take drugs. Self-disciplined and courteous, they maintained intact family units. They were particularly successful in reaching out to social outcasts, former addicts, and ex-cons.

Muhammad used his followers to show that every black person has the potential to reach the same level of dignity, with no assistance from white America. To support his ideology of separatism, Muhammad had his organization create and develop alternative institutions.

By the time of his death on February 25, 1975, Muhammad's Nation of Islam controlled a vast empire estimated at $80 to $100 million. The group's holdings included schools, a university, numerous farms and small businesses, a publishing company, an airplane, an import business, orchards, dairies, refrigerator trucks, apartment complexes, several mansions, and hundreds of houses of worship.

A Black Muslim member displays a copy of the Nation of Islam's Muhammad Speaks *newspaper.*

MALCOLM X

Malcolm called the assassination of President John F. Kennedy a "case of chickens coming home to roost"—an example of the kind of violence whites in America had long used against blacks.

PERHAPS NO ONE ELSE in the civil rights era gave as forceful a voice to the rage and frustration of black Americans as Malcolm X. As he passionately spoke to America, Malcolm brazenly challenged white domination and demanded change. In doing so, he struck a nerve with a large segment of the black population and helped many find self-respect and racial pride.

Malcolm's style and message stood in stark contrast to the leadership of the mainstream Civil Rights Movement, who favored nonviolent protests and integration to end discrimination. Malcolm's candid and often irreverent political views made him the most interviewed African American leader and, in 1959, the second-most sought-after college speaker.

Malcolm affirmed fighting back if attacked and felt integration was demeaning and that it would lead only to token accommodation by whites. He essentially concluded integration would have no effect on the urban black underclass. This made him a nationalist who believed that African Americans should control their own institutions, economy, and politics. He additionally preached that self-determination would have to be realized "by any means necessary."

He was born on May 19, 1925, in Omaha, Nebraska, as Malcolm Little. His family was forced out of Omaha by white vigilantes who burned down the family's house. The Littles resettled in Lansing, Michigan, where, in 1931, Malcolm's Baptist minister father was killed, supposedly by whites. After his mother was institutionalized from the strain of trying to raise her family, the children were separated and sent to various foster homes.

Malcolm went to Boston to live with a relative, but he fell into a life of crime—selling and using drugs, running numbers, and organizing a burglary ring. These activities landed him in jail for six years; he was only 21.

While imprisoned, he was introduced to the teachings of Elijah Muhammad, the leader of the Nation of Islam. Those teachings allowed him to vent his anger at the way whites had treated his family and denied him opportunities. Malcolm began to accept Muslim ideology. He improved his intellect by copying every word of the dictionary and reading voraciously before and after his parole.

Upon his release, Malcolm replaced his "slave name" with an X and rose to prominence as the Nation's representative (1952–1964). He proved to be a brilliant, powerful orator who attracted huge crowds on the university lecture circuit. He had a constant media following. He increased Nation of Islam membership by traveling the country and telling African Americans about their previously rich culture, which he said had been taken away by whites who had then brainwashed blacks into a mentality of self-hate. Malcolm pointed to Muslim separatists and Islam as the means to a better existence, using his own life as an example.

In 1954, Muhammad, whom Malcolm at first worshiped, made him a minister. Through the

At a rally in Harlem in 1963, Malcolm X talks about the integration efforts in Birmingham, Alabama. A person holds a picture of black men who were attacked outside a Black Muslim temple in Los Angeles in April 1962. After the Harlem rally ended, police were called to control the crowd, which had become violent.

years, Malcolm headed Muslim mosques in Boston, Philadelphia, and Harlem, in addition to organizing dozens of temples around the country. He also founded *Muhammad Speaks*, a newspaper in which a young Louis Farrakhan would later denounce him.

Malcolm's growing popularity became a source of contention within the Nation, and his discovery of Muhammad's alleged immoral personal behavior created a schism. Malcolm left the Nation of Islam in 1964 to form Muslim Mosque, Inc., in Harlem, New York.

To undergird his religious beliefs in opening his own mosque, Malcolm took a pilgrimage to the Islamic holy land of Mecca, Saudi Arabia. There he encountered worshipers of all colors who embraced him in the brotherhood of the orthodox faith. This pilgrimage awakened a new world, one of political unity and economic development between blacks around the globe, as well as social peace with whites. He turned away from the divisive canons on black-white human genesis and racial stereotypes underpinning the theology of the Nation.

As the primary spokesman for the Nation of Islam for a dozen years, Malcolm X captivated the country with passionate speeches about the anger and frustration felt by blacks because of the devastating effects of racism. He forcefully challenged white dominion, demanded change, and helped inspire racial pride in many African Americans.

BETTY SHABAZZ

After witnessing her husband's assassination in 1965, Betty Shabazz showed the world the greatness of simply living one's life fully. She quietly went about the business of supporting six girls, going to the University of Massachusetts for her doctorate in education administration, and keeping her husband's legacy alive.

Betty Shabazz, born Betty Sanders, shunned the media spotlight. In her first seven years of marriage, she rarely saw her constantly traveling husband, Malcolm X. Shabazz preferred to remain in the background raising their children.

Fate, however, had something else in store for her. Following her husband's death, she pursued her own set of goals, any one of which would have consumed the days of a less determined person. Yet, undaunted, Shabazz got it done.

With doctorate in hand, she served as a professor in health administration and communications director at Medgar Evers College in Brooklyn, guiding young minds for 20 years. The students at the college affectionately called her Dr. Betty.

Shabazz never lost sight of the battle for socio-economic rights and global peace for which her husband gave his life. She raised her low profile in 1995 by hosting a weekly radio talk show on WBLS-FM in New York City. She died in 1997.

Although she did not view herself as an American symbol of freedom, in death, Shabazz's life has become more than that. The life of this single mother is a symbolic affirmation that women can make the world a better place by proudly nurturing their children, their community, and themselves.

His political activities quickly grew beyond speeches. In Africa, Malcolm encouraged a show of solidarity by the Organization of African Unity (which was renamed The African Union in 2002) in passing a resolution denouncing racism in the United States. At home, he had already modeled the Organization of Afro-American Unity after its African counterpart. He continued lobbying the World Court and United Nations to support political and economic control of black communities by African Americans. He threatened to take America's racial policies to the world stage.

To solidify his newfound Islamic orthodoxy and ideological transformation, Malcolm renamed himself El-Hajj Malik El-Shabazz. In February 1965, before the Selma march, El-Shabazz spoke at Brown's Chapel in a display of respect for the civil rights activities in the South and to convey the common goals of blacks across the country. To Coretta King, he expressed regret for not being able to meet with Martin Luther King, Jr., who was in jail for a street protest.

Unfortunately, there was not enough time left for such a meeting. El-Shabazz was assassinated before it could take place. Threats from many corners of America had long been a way of life for El-Shabazz, but he came to believe that elements of the Nation of Islam and the United States government truly wanted him dead.

On February 21, a week after his home was firebombed, 15 bullets fired by three assailants entered his body. El-Shabazz died in the Audubon Ballroom in Harlem before medical services arrived. He left behind a loving family, an important social struggle, and an autobiography of audacity, conviction, and self-reinvention, which has become a classic of modern literature.

LORRAINE HANSBERRY

Hansberry was the first African American woman to have a play on Broadway. The title, A Raisin in the Sun, *came from a line in Langston Hughes's poem "Harlem," which noted that a dream deferred would dry up, "like a raisin in the sun."*

A BRIGHT STAR WHO BLAZED brilliantly but whose light died out too soon, Lorraine Hansberry wrote the play that is credited with giving birth to the modern black American theater.

A Raisin in the Sun opened on Broadway in 1959. It won the distinguished New York Drama Critics' Circle Award that year against heavy competition from plays by Tennessee Williams, Eugene O'Neill, and Archibald MacLeish.

This brilliant work, about the experiences and aspirations of a poor black family living in a Chicago ghetto, was Hansberry's first play. She began writing it at the age of 26, and when she received the Drama Critics' Circle Award at age 29, she was the youngest playwright, the fifth woman, and the first black to receive the honor.

The Broadway production, which ran for 19 months, starred such notable actors as Sidney Poitier, Diana Sands, Claudia McNeil, and Ruby Dee. This original cast also starred in the movie version of the work, which won an award at the Cannes Film Festival in 1961.

Unfortunately, *A Raisin in the Sun* was the height of Hansberry's short career—she died just six years after its debut on January 12, 1965, at the age of 34, from cancer.

Hansberry was born May 19, 1930, in Chicago, to a well-to-do family. Her parents opened a successful real estate firm and one of the first black banks in Chicago. The home of her youth was frequented by such luminaries as Walter White, Jesse Owens, Langston Hughes, Duke Ellington, and Paul Robeson.

Lorraine Hansberry is credited with beginning the modern era of black American theater because of the success of her Broadway play *A Raisin in the Sun*. In 1959, it became the first black production to win the prestigious New York Drama Critics' Circle Award.

Hansberry studied art, English, and stage design for two years at the University of Wisconsin before moving to New York in 1950. There she joined Paul Robeson's Harlem-based *Freedom* magazine. As associate editor from 1952 to 1953, she wrote articles dealing with Africa, women's issues, and social issues. While at the magazine, Hansberry

also wrote reviews of several plays, which provided the impetus for her to write her own plays.

After *A Raisin in the Sun,* Hansberry worked on a number of other projects, most of which remained uncompleted, including a novel and a collection of essays. Her last completed stage work was *The Sign in Sidney Brustein's Window,* about a Greenwich Village intellectual and his role in a local election. The play made it to Broadway in 1964 for 101 performances and was still running when Hansberry died.

After her death, her unpublished papers were assembled into the play *To Be Young, Gifted and Black,* which toured nationally from 1970 to 1971 and was later expanded into Hansberry's biography.

Actors Ruby Dee, Sidney Poitier, and Diana Sands starred in both the triumphant Broadway and screen versions of Hansberry's masterpiece.

BERRY GORDY, JR.

Berry Gordy's Motown Records produced the most popular sound in music in the 1960s and 1970s with such stars as Stevie Wonder, Michael Jackson, Marvin Gaye, Diana Ross, Smokey Robinson, and The Temptations. Gordy founded the company at the age of 30 with an $800 loan from his family.

BERRY GORDY, JR., parlayed his songwriting hobby into the most successful African American-owned record company in history, and along the way he changed the sound of pop music forever.

His Motown Records, started in 1959, became the world's largest independent record company, the first major black-owned company in the entertainment industry, and America's

largest black business in 1973, with sales of more than $50 million.

Through Motown, which became a music factory and produced hits as though they came off the assembly line, Gordy engineered superstardom for such talents as Stevie Wonder, Michael Jackson, Diana Ross, Marvin Gaye, Smokey Robinson, The Temptations, The Four Tops, Martha and the Vandellas, and Gladys Knight.

Born November 28, 1929, in Detroit, one of eight children, Gordy dropped out of high school in the eleventh grade to pursue a boxing career. That path ended when he was drafted into the army, where he earned his high school equivalency diploma while serving in Korea from 1951 to 1953.

Back in Detroit after the war, Gordy worked at the Ford Motor Company while writing songs when he had the chance. His breakthrough came when a young singer named Jackie Wilson recorded Gordy's song "Reet Petite" in 1957, which became Wilson's first hit. Over the next two years, Gordy wrote four more hits for Wilson, including "Lonely Teardrops" in 1958.

By then, Gordy had befriended another young singer named Smokey Robinson, who talked him into opening his own recording studio. With the aid of an $800 loan from his family, Gordy opened his company.

The hits began immediately. The Motown sound consisted of sophisticated rhythm-and-blues augmented by slick symphonic orchestrations. It not only appealed to African Americans but crossed over to white America as well.

Motown's first number-one pop hit came in 1958 with "Please Mr. Postman." In 1962, when the company had 11 R&B top 10 hits, it also had 4 singles in the pop top 10. The next year it

had six, with Stevie Wonder's "Fingertips, Part 2" reaching number one. In 1964, five Motown hits were number one on the pop charts. The legend of Motown was born.

In 1972, Gordy moved the company to Los Angeles and branched out into films, making the successful *Lady Sings the Blues,* for which star Diana Ross received an Academy Award nomination, and *The Bingo Long Traveling All-Stars and Motor Kings.* Gordy's TV special *Motown 25—Yesterday, Today, and Forever* aired in 1983. It was the most watched variety special in television history, and 1985's *Motown Returns to the Apollo* won an Emmy Award.

Gordy sold Motown Records to MCA Inc. in 1984 for $61 million, but he retained Motown's publishing company Jobete Music.

Smokey Robinson greets Gordy during a performance in 1981. Robinson started recording for Motown Records in the 1960s.

Gordy's contributions to the music industry are legendary. In 1988, he was inducted into the Rock and Roll Hall of Fame. Here he is shown with Diana Ross.

MARGARET BURROUGHS

Margaret Burroughs is founder and director emeritus of the DuSable Museum of African American History in Chicago, the nation's first and foremost black museum. With more than 50,000 artifacts, it contains Joe Louis's boxing gloves and W.E.B. Du Bois's graduation robe.

MARGARET BURROUGHS'S lifelong work has been in the creation, administration, and preservation of black art and history in all their varied forms.

Although this multitalented artist is renowned for her own painting, poetry, and sculpture, her greatest claim to fame is the DuSable Museum of African American History in Chicago, the nation's first major and still foremost black museum, which she founded in 1961.

Becoming keeper of the culture and heritage of a people was something Burroughs had aspired to since childhood. She was born Margaret Taylor on November 1, 1917, in Saint Rose Parish, Louisiana. Her family moved to Chicago in 1920. By the time she graduated from high school in 1933, Burroughs was participating in local art fairs.

In 1937, she earned her teaching certificate for elementary grades, and, in 1939, she earned her teaching certificate for upper grades, but she elected to pursue her art instead. It wasn't until Burroughs received her bachelor's degree in art education from the Art Institute of Chicago in 1946 that she combined her vocation and avocation as an art instructor at DuSable High School in Chicago, a position she held for 22 years.

In 1940, she had already become a charter member of Chicago's South Side Community Arts Center, which was created as part of the Works Progress Administration and dedicated by First Lady Eleanor Roosevelt. The Center was an important location for African Americans to take classes and display their art; Burroughs would remain there for 20 years as an officer and trustee. The Arts Center was the centerpiece of what Yale Professor Robert Bone dubbed "The Chicago Renaissance," which occurred between 1945 and 1960.

Meanwhile, she exhibited her own works throughout the country, including the annual national showcase of black art at Atlanta University. In 1947 and 1955, she won awards at the showcase for her print and watercolor works, respectively. In 1949, she married Charles Burroughs, a writer who had lived for 17 years in the Soviet Union. In the 1950s, she enjoyed international success in Mexico and Europe for her oils and acrylics.

In the late 1960s, after producing a series of works portraying great African Americans, including Harriet Tubman, Crispus Attucks, and Frederick Douglass, Burroughs wrote a poem to her grandson, Eric Toller, explaining her responsibility in producing the series. Another poem, "What Shall I Tell My Children Who Are Black?," became nationally famous, and it refers to a collection of African American folk expressions she had published in 1955.

In 1961, in order to "preserve, interpret and display our heritage," as Burroughs says, she opened the Ebony Museum of Negro History in her own home, across the street from the Southside Community Arts Center. Soon, she renamed the museum the DuSable Museum in honor of Chicago's first settler, a black man. An overwhelming grassroots response caused the city to donate one of the two remaining structures from the 1893 Chicago World's Fair, which in 1968 became the museum's permanent site.

Burroughs retired as a humanities professor at Chicago's Kennedy-King College in 1979 and has been director emeritus of her museum since 1985, when Mayor Harold Washington appointed her to the Chicago Park District Board.

In 2001, celebrating its 40-year anniversary, DuSable Museum presented the first full retrospective of Burroughs's work.

Burroughs started the DuSable Museum of African American History in her basement, which she initially called the Ebony Museum of Negro History.

WHITNEY M. YOUNG, JR.

WHITNEY M. YOUNG, JR., was a calming voice in the midst of the militant Civil Rights Movement of the 1960s. As executive director of the National Urban League, Young worked to keep the lines of communication open with white America's centers of financial and political power. He did so in order to give concrete help to African Americans. Critics feared Young had too many close ties to whites. Yet he brought millions of dollars to the Urban League, increased the number of branches, and gathered government support for many of their programs.

Young was born in Lincoln Ridge, Kentucky, on July 21, 1921. After receiving his bachelor's degree at Kentucky State College in 1941, he taught briefly before joining the U.S. Army during World War II. Young then studied electrical engineering at the Massachusetts Institute of Technology. His experiences with racism in the military turned Young toward the civil rights struggle.

Young received his master's degree from the University of Minnesota and started working with the Urban League. He worked at branch offices in two states at a time when the organization was focused more on housing and health issues than on civil rights. In 1954, Young became dean of the Atlanta University School of Social Work. The articulate and personable Young spent a year at Harvard University through a Rockefeller Foundation grant in 1960, then he began a brilliant career as executive director of the National Urban League.

Before Young's involvement, the group was training black social workers to fight for improvements in housing and sanitation, along with working on other self-improvement issues. The group left the civil rights fight to more militant African American organizations, such

Whitney M. Young, Jr., almost single-handedly put the National Urban League at the forefront of the struggle for civil rights and black economic equality.

as the NAACP. Young expanded the agenda of the Urban League. He dealt with social problems by influencing white decision-makers and becoming part of the process for change.

Critics called Young an "Uncle Tom," but he increased the Urban League's budget from $250,000 and 34 staff in 1961 to $3,500,000 and 200 staff by 1968. He created jobs and opened 90 new regional branches. Young, fighting to keep his credibility among blacks, proposed a national Marshall Plan in 1963 to help African Americans catch up. His book, *To Be Equal,* documents his vision. One quote

from his book is an example of that vision, "Good race relations—race harmony—is more than the absence of conflict, tension, or even war. *It is the presence of justice.* Nothing is more immoral than the suggestion that people adjust to injustice or that we make a god of 'timing.' The time is always ripe to do right."

During the 1960s, American leaders turned to Young and other leaders such as Dr. Martin Luther King, Jr., to calm the voices of more militant black leaders. Young stayed at the front of the struggle, helping to organize the 1963 March on Washington, D.C. Young published *Beyond Racism: Building an Open Society* in 1969, which explained that the black power era could help the nation move toward a more democratic society.

Young's brilliant career was cut short when he drowned in 1971 while attending a conference in Africa.

President John Kennedy meets with Whitney Young and Henry Steeger, both of the National Urban League, to discuss economic and social welfare issues. President Kennedy discussed these in his State of the Union message in January 1962.

CONSTANCE BAKER MOTLEY

IN A 1964 SPEECH ON African American political leadership, the Honorable Constance Baker Motley talked about how important it was for African American women to get into politics because it encourages young girls and young women to consider politics a career possibility. Certainly Motley did her part to open the doors for future generations of black women.

That same year, Motley became the first African American woman to serve in the New York State Senate. In 1965, she became the first woman to serve as Manhattan borough president. One year later, Motley was appointed a U.S. District Court judge for the Southern District of New York, which is the largest federal trial court in the country. The first black and the first woman appointed to the federal judiciary, Motley became the chief judge in 1982. She became the senior judge four years later. The hard work of women, including for-

Constance Baker Motley, the first female Manhattan borough president, smiles during a 1966 press conference at her office.

mer U.S. Senator Carol Moseley-Braun and Civil Rights Commissioner Mary Frances Berry, who have followed in her footsteps, proves that Motley's vision of the future was absolutely right.

Born September 14, 1921, in New Haven, Connecticut, Motley was the ninth of 12 children. Her parents, Rachel and Willoughby Baker, were from the Caribbean island of Nevis in the West Indies. Her father was a chef for an exclusive fraternity at Yale University. Motley first wanted to be an interior decorator but had decided she wanted to go into law by the time she graduated from high school with honors.

Motley's parents could not afford to send her to college, so she worked as a domestic before taking a job with the National Youth Administration. A white philanthropist, impressed by Motley, paid for her college education. She enrolled at Fisk University, then transferred to New York University, graduating with a degree in economics in 1943. While attending Columbia Law School, Motley met Thurgood Marshall, who hired her as a law clerk at the New York branch of the NAACP Legal Defense and Educational Fund. After earning a law degree from Columbia Law School, Motley became a full member of the legal staff, and she married real estate and insurance broker Joel Wilson Motley.

During her 20 years with the NAACP, Motley argued cases before the U.S. Supreme Court, one of the first women to do so. She won nine of the ten civil rights cases she argued. Motley played a prominent role in school desegregation and public housing cases in six states. She assisted in writing the briefs filed in *Brown* v. *Board of Education* (1954), and she person-

Constance Baker Motley with James Meredith. She successfully argued his case before the U.S. Supreme Court, which allowed him to enroll at the University of Mississippi.

ally argued the 1962 case that won James H. Meredith the right to be admitted to the University of Mississippi.

Motley, who represented Dr. Martin Luther King, Jr., and the Reverend Ralph Abernathy, also won Supreme Court cases that desegregated all recreational facilities in Memphis as well as a restaurant in the Memphis Municipal Airport. Motley argued several cases before the Supreme Court that involved sit-ins, including *Gober* v. *City of Birmingham* (1963), in which she defended ten African American students who sought service at store lunch counters.

Motley, the author of many articles on legal and civil rights issues, was awarded honorary degrees from Spelman College and Howard and Yale universities, among others. She was inducted into the National Women's Hall of Fame and received the NAACP Medal of Honor. She died on September 28, 2005.

MEDGAR EVERS

Evers's strongest skill was his ability to negotiate with various groups.

ONE OF THE MOST PROMINENT black leaders of the 1960s Civil Rights Movement in the state of Mississippi, Medgar Evers also became one of the Civil Rights Movement's earliest—and one of its most important—martyrs.

In 1962, *EBONY* magazine called him the bravest man in America. The first murder of a nationally known civil rights leader showed the world the continuing horror of racial violence in the South.

Evers's death led to increased participation in the movement by outraged Americans, which brought even more demonstrations and violence and was a motivating factor in President John F. Kennedy's decision a week later to ask Congress to enact comprehensive civil rights legislation.

Medgar Evers was born July 2, 1925, to strongly religious and hard-working parents in Decatur, Mississippi. Evers attended a one-room elemen-

tary school in Decatur; later he walked 12 miles to high school in nearby Newton.

After serving in Normandy and Germany during World War II, Evers returned home in 1946, and with his brother, also a war veteran, he tried unsuccessfully to vote. Having been blocked from doing so because of their color, they became members of the NAACP.

Evers enrolled in Alcorn A&M College where he was a popular student—a business administration major and school newspaper editor. Evers met his wife, Myrlie Beasley, there; they had three children. Following college, Evers sold life insurance, but seeing the results of a botched lynching drove him into the growing Civil Rights Movement in 1952. Evers became the NAACP Mississippi field secretary in 1954. Once the Supreme Court outlawed public school segregation that year, Evers actively sought its enforcement against the highly entrenched system in his state. He played a key role in helping James Meredith enroll as the first black student at the University of Mississippi in 1962.

Evers went on to spearhead a number of economic boycotts against downtown Jackson, Mississippi, businesses that practiced segregation. He also helped form the Jackson Movement, an umbrella group of black organizations that sponsored mass demonstrations for the integration of public facilities and institutions and for increased municipal job opportunities.

On June 12, 1963, as he returned home carrying T-shirts with "Jim Crow Must Go" on them, Evers was shot in the back by Byron de la

Beckwith, a fertilizer salesman and member of an old Mississippi family.

Despite the discovery of Beckwith's fingerprints on the weapon used in the crime, Beckwith denied being the assassin. He produced witnesses to corroborate his alibi. Mississippi jurors in two trials could not reach a unanimous decision in the case, but over the next 30 years Myrlie Evers demanded justice for her husband's death. It came in 1994 when Beckwith's conviction led to a sentence of life in prison.

In 1995, Myrlie Evers-Williams again stepped out of a quiet life in California, this time to help save the NAACP from eminent disaster. She defeated former chairman William Gibson by a one-vote margin. She brought integrity to a once-proud organization that was in the throes of nearly $4 million in debt and scandals.

The debt was eliminated by 1996, and the NAACP emerged even stronger with economic empowerment and affirmative action campaigns. Evers-Williams turned over the chair to Julian Bond in 1998.

Evers (facing the camera, right) and Roy Wilkins (facing the camera, left) are arrested in 1963 after trying to picket Woolworth's segregated lunch counter in Jackson, Mississippi.

JAMES BALDWIN

JAMES BALDWIN is perhaps the most widely read and best-known African American author of the middle 20th century. He was a prolific writer, popular with both black and white audiences worldwide.

He sensitively and honestly examined issues of race, gender, and class. And while he argued against racial injustice, Baldwin was more apt to stress the positive, life-affirming values of black culture than to simply blast a white racist hierarchy.

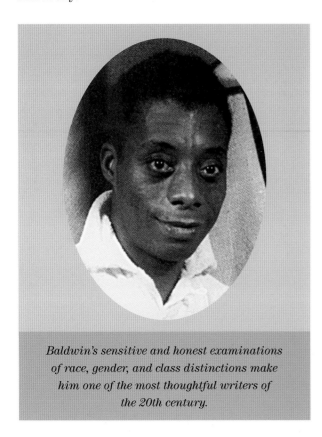

Baldwin's sensitive and honest examinations of race, gender, and class distinctions make him one of the most thoughtful writers of the 20th century.

Through six novels, four plays, and seven collections of essays, among his other works, Baldwin examined America's soul. His first novel, *Go Tell It on the Mountain,* is generally regarded as his best.

Released in 1953 to vast critical acclaim, it tells the story of a young black boy's battles with his minister father over the issue of worship. He took up the same theme in *The Amen Corner,* his play about a female evangelist, published in 1965. The theme is largely autobiographical.

Baldwin was born August 2, 1924, in Harlem, the oldest of nine children. Raised by a zealously religious minister stepfather, Baldwin preached from the revivalist pulpit from the ages of 14 to 17. But his real passion was writing. Editor of his high school newspaper, he eventually earned enough writing awards and accompanying cash prizes to move to Paris after graduation, where he lived for eight years, beginning in 1948.

While in Paris, he had his first novel published. He then wrote a collection of well-received essays, which he compiled as *Notes of a Native Son* in 1955. In 1956, he wrote *Giovanni's Room,* the first of two novels dealing with bisexuality; the other was 1962's *Another Country.*

Baldwin returned to the states in 1957 to work in the growing Civil Rights Movement. He made the cover of *Time* magazine in 1963, which discussed his eloquence as a spokesperson for black rights. His *New Yorker* magazine article on the Black Muslims and parts of the civil rights struggle was published in 1963 as a book titled *The Fire Next Time.* Baldwin was not a civil rights leader, but he was unquestionably the most eloquent writer on behalf of the cause of civil rights. The next year, his important play about racial oppression, *Blues for Mister Charlie,* opened on Broadway.

In 1968, Baldwin's popular novel *Tell Me How Long the Train's Been Gone* was released. Then in 1971, *A Rap on Race* was published, detailing a conversation with anthropologist Margaret Mead about world racism. In 1974, Baldwin enjoyed another best-seller with *If Beale Street Could Talk,* the tale of a pregnant, unmarried 19-year-old.

In 1982, after releasing more essay collections interpreting black and white relations in the United States, Baldwin became a professor of writing and African American history at the University of Massachusetts at Amherst. In 1987, he received the French Legion of Honor Award. Baldwin died in France later that year from cancer.

Though Baldwin's remarks delighted the crowd at this 1963 meeting of the Congress of Racial Equality, he maintained that he never intended to be a spokesperson for equality and was only expressing his personal thoughts.

ROBERT MOSES

IT CAN BE ARGUED that Robert Moses was second only to Dr. Martin Luther King, Jr., as the most important leader of the Civil Rights Movement. But Moses shunned the spotlight, playing a brief if crucial role in the Movement. His efforts at voter registration for blacks in Mississippi as a representative of the Student Nonviolent Coordinating Committee (SNCC) helped lead to the Voting Rights Act of 1965.

Born January 23, 1935, in Harlem, Moses earned a master's degree in philosophy from Harvard University and taught math in an elite, private New York high school. Stirred by the student sit-in movement of 1960, Moses went to Atlanta and joined the SNCC, which was spearheading the protests. He became the first full-time SNCC worker in the Deep South, assigned to register black voters in Mississippi. His job was extremely dangerous, and Moses was harassed, beaten, jailed, and almost killed.

In August 1961, he opened voter registration schools in two counties in southwest Missis-

Robert Moses works during a lecture at one of Mississippi's voter registration schools.

sippi. These schools taught blacks how to register, the power of community action to combat injustices, and how to shape current events. In October, Moses was jailed for leading a protest march. When he was released in December, nearly all the blacks he worked with had been intimidated into backing out of the registration efforts.

In the spring of 1962, the SNCC joined with other Mississippi groups to create the Council of Federated Organizations (COFO), with Moses as head, to unify registration efforts in the state. In 1963, the COFO staged the Freedom Election, a mock election open to all black adults, to show the country how strongly blacks in Mississippi desired the right to vote. More than 80,000 blacks cast votes on the Freedom Ballot.

The success of that effort led Moses to create the 1964 Freedom Summer Project, in which 1,000 volunteers entered the state to set up "freedom schools" and centers to work on voter registration. The summer was violent; there were a reported 35 shootings, 80 beatings, 60 bombings, and well over 1,000 arrests. Under such conditions, few blacks were registered, but the project gained national attention.

Moses helped create the Mississippi Freedom Democratic Party (MFDP) to challenge the segregated Democratic Party for seats at the 1964 Democratic National Convention. More than 60,000 people registered as members.

At the Atlantic City Convention in August, a compromise was offered: Only two MFDP members would be seated as at-large delegates. Moses's group rejected the compromise and staged a sit-in on the convention floor.

Moses was gaining a following that he did not want. He had no desire to be a leader; he

Moses was a quiet, courageous organizer who shunned the leadership limelight that he was pulled into. He left the Civil Rights Movement after a few years, but he made a significant impact in securing voting rights for African Americans.

just wanted to organize. He began going by the name Robert Parris, and in 1966, he left the SNCC and the movement for private life. As a conscientious objector, he refused to be drafted into the Vietnam War. He went first to Canada, then to Tanzania. He taught in Africa, before returning to the United States in 1976. President Carter's amnesty program soon freed him of any military obligation. Moses spent much of the next decade raising four children and completing his doctoral thesis.

Moses reentered the public arena with a MacArthur Fellowship in 1980 to establish the Algebra Project, a five-step program for encouraging underprivileged youth to become creative thinkers by translating their experiences into mathematical concepts. His innovative methods successfully improved students' standardized test scores.

JOHN ROBERT LEWIS

Congressman Lewis is hard pressed to remain silent about social injustice. He was a persuasive leader in the modern Civil Rights Movement and remains outspoken today.

IF COURAGE, FAITH, and perseverance have a face, then John Robert Lewis is the face you would see. As one of the foremost—and youngest—leaders in the Civil Rights Movement, he put his life at risk multiple times to fight for his belief in equal treatment for all.

Lewis was born February 21, 1940, to sharecroppers Willie Mae Carter and Eddie Lewis outside Troy, Alabama. As a young man, Lewis heard Martin Luther King, Jr., on the radio discussing the Montgomery Bus Boycott. Dr. King's inspirational words gave Lewis hope that the obstacles his family had faced due to racism could be overcome. Little did he know he would be instrumental in bringing about many of those changes.

After high school, Lewis applied to Troy State College, an all-white school near his home. When he didn't hear back from Troy State, he wrote to Dr. King for support in integrating the school. Lewis's parents disapproved of the plan, however, fearing white retaliation, so he enrolled in the American Baptist Theological Seminary (ABT) in Nashville, Tennessee. He became head of the student council at ABT but was unable to start an NAACP chapter on campus. Instead, he took part in civil rights discussions among students outside of school, which lit an irrepressible fire in him.

Lewis was finally able to express his unrest on the Freedom Bus Rides in the summer of 1961, which challenged equal accommodations on interstate bus lines. Not even a beating from staunch segregationists and his arrest in Montgomery, Alabama, could deter him from further protests. By that time, he had cofounded the Student Nonviolent Coordinating Committee (SNCC), which stepped up sit-ins at lunch counters and other public facilities until designated "White" and "Colored" signs came down.

While still a young man, Lewis became a well-positioned leader in the Civil Rights Movement. He helped organize the 1963 March on Washington, where he posed the question, "Which side is the federal government on?" He felt the nation had been waiting long enough for its elected leaders to establish equal economic opportunities. The 1964 Civil Rights Act governing equal opportunities became law soon after the nonviolent protest.

Somehow Lewis accomplished all of this while earning a bachelor's degree at Fisk University. Then, in 1964, the SNCC turned its sights on voting rights by launching the Mississippi Freedom Summer voter registration project. Lewis, always at the forefront of these campaigns, endured arrests and physical assault, as did other participants. The police beating he endured while leading marchers on the Edmund Pettus Bridge in Selma, Alabama, fractured his skull and could have ended his life. That March 7, 1965, known as "Bloody Sunday," had an impact on the passage of the Voting Rights Act.

In the midst of these heated days, Lewis never imagined himself in elected office. But after years of community service, he joined the ranks of policymakers on Atlanta's city council in 1981. Five years later he ran for the U.S. Congress and won. Denouncing the Persian Gulf War prompted his selection as Chief Deputy Whip of the Democratic Caucus in 1991. He also achieved a seat on the House Ways and Means Committee and became chair of its Oversight Subcommittee on Income Security and Family Support.

These positions did not stop Lewis from continuing to march for his beliefs. He joined the Million Man March in 1995 and in 2006 was arrested outside the Sudanese embassy while protesting genocide. His lifetime of dedication was honored with the Lincoln Medal, NAACP Spingarn Medal, and the John F. Kennedy Profile in Courage Award, among others.

Lewis placed his life at the head of demonstrations for equal opportunity during the Civil Rights Movement. Lewis, second from left, leads a march in 1964 to protest a speech by Alabama governor George Wallace.

FANNIE LOU HAMER

Hamer and others protested the regular Mississippi Democratic Party's all-white delegation at the 1964 Democratic Presidential Convention in Atlantic City.

FANNIE LOU HAMER was a farmer and educator who became a beacon of hope for the nation's poor and politically disenfranchised. Born in the rural South, Hamer became a powerful voice in the fight for black equality and self-reliance. Hamer's actions helped change some of the National Democratic Party's racist policies, and she increased black political power by registering voters in the South.

Hamer has said one of the things that made her so committed to helping poor people was watching her sharecropping parents struggle to raise their 20 children in rural Mississippi. Born in Montgomery County on October 6, 1917, she was working in the cotton fields by the time she was six years old. As early as 13, Hamer, who could pick 300 to 400 pounds of cotton per day, was troubled by the economic disparity between the black workers and the white plantation owners. But as a poor black woman

in the South, she had few options. She married Perry Hamer in 1942, and for 18 years she worked as a sharecropper.

But in 1962, Hamer burst upon the civil rights scene after attending a stirring rally for the Southern Christian Leadership Conference (SCLC) and the Student Nonviolent Coordinating Committee (SNCC). She volunteered to challenge voting laws, but she had to flee her plantation for trying to register to vote. Hamer was threatened and survived a gun attack. In 1963, she passed the literacy test many Southern states used to keep blacks from voting, and she registered.

A tireless drum major for African American political empowerment, Fannie Lou Hamer was a bright light in the firmament of the 1960s civil rights struggle. She spent her life fighting for equality.

Hamer's commitment to the movement caught fire. She became a field-worker for the SNCC. Hamer believed there was a link between lack of access to the political process and widespread black poverty. She helped start Delta Ministry, a community development program. Hamer continued to register voters, and, as a result, she was injured in a brutal beating in a rural Mississippi jail.

Since the state's Democratic party wouldn't allow black participation, Hamer helped found the Mississippi Freedom Democratic Party (MFDP) in 1964. That group made national headlines by challenging the seating of the all-

white Mississippi delegation to the Democratic National Convention in Atlantic City. Hamer spoke to the group in a televised hearing, telling the nation about the plight of blacks trying to exercise their right to vote. She was a delegate to the 1968 convention in Chicago.

Later, Hamer founded the Freedom Farms Cooperation, which helped needy families get food and livestock. She worked with day-care centers and developers building homes for the poor and spoke nationwide on behalf of black self-reliance. Hamer spoke for many oppressed African Americans when she told America, "I'm sick and tired of being sick and tired."

A lifelong source of strength for her people and an authentic American hero, Hamer died of cancer March 14, 1977.

When blacks were refused the right to participate in the '64 Democratic National Convention, Hamer vowed to get representation in the future. She succeeded—and served as a delegate to the 1968 convention.

SIDNEY POITIER

Poitier holds his Honorary Award Oscar, which he received for his lifetime body of work. The award is the highest honor given by the Board of Governors of the Academy of Motion Picture Arts and Sciences.

FOR ONE BRIEF PERIOD in his life, Sidney Poitier was a homeless teenager sleeping on Harlem rooftops. But he became a magnificent American film star and the first black actor to make it big in dramatic movies. He shattered the celluloid ceiling that had consigned blacks to roles as mammies and "Uncle Toms."

Despite a formal education of less than two years, Poitier polished his skills to the point that he won the Best Actor Oscar in 1963 for his touching performance as a handyman who helped a group of nuns build a chapel in *Lilies of the Field.* He was the first African American actor to win the award in that category, and he helped change the stereotypical presentation of blacks in movies.

Poitier was born February 20, 1927, in Miami, the seventh child of West Indian parents, who raised him in the Bahamas. Because of his family's poverty, Poitier returned to Miami to live with an older brother. He drifted to New York with little money. His lack of formal education made jobs scarce; he survived mostly by dishwashing, until he lied about his age to join the army.

After being discharged in 1945, Poitier returned to New York and auditioned for the American Negro Theater (ANT), which rejected him because of his thick Caribbean accent and poor reading skills. Undaunted, Poitier listened to the radio to learn how to speak without an accent and had a friend tutor him in reading. He applied to the ANT again in 1946, was accepted, and began working.

Poitier performed in the black Broadway production of *Lysistrata* and the Broadway and touring productions of *Anna Lucasta* in 1948. In 1950, he received his first Hollywood role in *No Way Out.* In the mid-1950s, roles in *Blackboard Jungle, Edge of the City,* and *The Defiant Ones* (for which he received his first Best Actor nomination) established Poitier as a box office draw.

Those roles also created a character that would become a Poitier trademark throughout his career—a sincere, sometimes angry, but generally good-hearted, highly moral, and intelligent black man of great dignity. This was typified by his role in 1967's *Guess Who's Coming to Dinner,* a story of interracial romance.

The biggest exception to that image was Poitier's brilliant portrayal of

Walter Lee Younger in the play and movie versions of *A Raisin in the Sun,* where he played a flawed black man distraught by the limitations placed on his life because of his race.

Poitier found additional success in the 1970s, directing and starring in the black western *Buck and the Preacher* and several comedies with Bill Cosby and other African American stars. He also directed Richard Pryor and Gene Wilder in *Stir Crazy* in 1980.

In 1992, the American Film Institute awarded Poitier the Life Achievement Award, its highest honor. In 2002, he was presented an honorary Oscar by the Board of Governors of the Academy of Motion Picture Arts and Sciences. Academy President Frank Pierson expressed his peers' gratitude for Poitier's contributions to the art of motion pictures. After an eloquent speech, Poitier witnessed Denzel Washington and Halle Berry win the Best Actor and Best Actress awards. Their triumphs were the sweetest affirmation of his pioneering legacy.

Poitier received a Best Actor Oscar for his performance in Lilies of the Field.

MUHAMMAD ALI

Ali was given the honor of lighting the Olympic torch to begin the 2002 Olympic Summer Games. Ali won his own Olympic boxing gold medal in 1960, when he was the winner in the light-heavyweight division.

THE COLORFUL PHRASE "Float like a butterfly, sting like a bee" perfectly sums up the boxing style of Muhammad Ali, the self-proclaimed and widely acknowledged "greatest fighter of all time!"

Ali's astonishing speed, punishing punching power, brilliant footwork, awesome defensive skills, and lethal left jab contributed to his boxing legend. To watch him was to see a dance of grace, skill, and strategy.

It was his prowess in the ring, boisterous personality, flashy showiness, and strong religious and moral convictions that first made Ali a figure of controversy. Those traits, in addition to an uncanny ability to spout poetry and pre-

dict the round in which he would vanquish his opponents, later made him a folk hero.

Born Cassius Marcellus Clay on January 17, 1942, in Louisville, Kentucky, Ali began boxing at age 12. Instead of taking the bus to school, he ran to build his endurance and dodged rocks thrown by his brother to improve his ability to slip punches.

Ali captured six Kentucky Golden Gloves and two national Golden Gloves titles before winning the Olympic light-heavyweight gold medal in 1960, setting the stage for his entrance into professional boxing.

Even with an undefeated record, Ali was a seven-to-one underdog against heavyweight champion Sonny Liston in the 1964 fight that brought Ali international fame. After seizing the championship, Ali announced his conversion to Islam with a name change. He then proceeded to defend his boxing title nine times until his 1967 refusal, as a Muslim conscientious objector, to be drafted and sent to Vietnam. Stripped of his title and boxing license for three and a half years, Ali became a worldwide symbol of moral consciousness.

In 1970, he returned to the ring for a series of legendary fights and substantial paydays. He suffered his first professional loss in the March 1971 heavyweight championship "Fight of the Century" with "Smokin'" Joe Frazier. It landed both boxers in the hospital.

Before his rematch with Ali, Frazier had lost the championship belt to George Foreman. In October 1974 in Kinshasa, Zaire, a slower Ali was ready to "Rumble in the Jungle" against the punching power of Foreman. After cunningly tiring Foreman out with his rope-a-dope technique, Ali launched a stinging counterattack that earned him an eighth-round knockout, a second championship title, and almost $5.5 million.

His worldwide reputation as "The Greatest" held up a third time against Frazier in the September 1975 "Thrilla in Manila" and against all takers until Leon Spinks upset him in 1978. Seven months later Ali defeated Spinks for a record-breaking third heavyweight championship title.

Ali retired from boxing in 1979. He came out of retirement for financial reasons twice, losing to Larry Holmes in 1980 and to Trevor Berbick in 1981. Pugilism had taken a devastating toll on his body, and Ali hung up his boxing gloves.

Despite the limits Parkinson's disease poses on him, Ali remains one of the most recognizable and popular people on the globe. Demand continues for public appearances at the Olympics and other venues worldwide. When he lit the torch at the 2002 Summer Olympics in Salt Lake City, the world cheered.

After the September 11, 2001, terrorist attacks on America, Ali expressed sorrow for the nation's enormous loss and denounced the violence by Muslim attackers as contrary to the teachings of Islam. Ali made sacrifices for peace in 1967, and his strong religious beliefs remain undiminished.

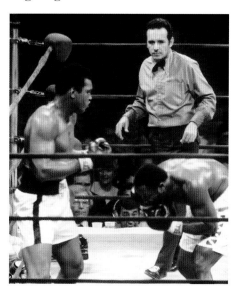

Ali could be punishing in the ring. He had lightning quick speed, agile footwork, and a lethal left jab. He only lost five times, and he had 56 victories in the ring.

MAULANA KARENGA

FOR THE PAST 30 YEARS, in the last week of December, many African Americans have celebrated the increasingly popular cultural holiday known as Kwanzaa. The ritual, a combination of ancient African traditions fused with the newer traditions of black Americans, was created in 1966 by Dr. Ron Karenga, chairman of the Black Studies Department at California State University at Long Beach. Karenga is known by the title of "Maulana," a Swahili word meaning "master-teacher."

Kwanzaa celebrates seven principles—one on each day of the holiday—that are rooted in African history and were selected by Karenga as keys to building the black family, community, and culture.

The principles, called Nguzo Saba, include *kujichagulia* (self-determination), *umoja* (unity), *ujima* (collective work and responsi-bility), *ujamaa* (cooperative economics), *nia* (purpose), *kuumba* (creativity), and *imani* (faith). The holiday begins on December 26 and concludes on January 1, as the word *kwanzaa* itself means "first." Africans have historically held celebrations at the occasion of the first harvests of the year. In the spirit of *umoja* (unity), Karenga deliberately selected the terms from the common Swahili language, which represents all of Africa, instead of any particular group or tribe. He wanted the Kwanzaa festival to be celebrated by all people of African descent in America and throughout the world, regardless of their individual religious and political beliefs and practices.

Karenga also created the popular red, black, and green flag as a symbol of the Kwanzaa celebration: red for the struggle, black for the people, green for their hope. The idea of the holiday caught on during the Black Power days of the Civil Rights Movement, as African Americans gained a heightened awareness of their heritage and their culture. Kwanzaa has since become ingrained in American culture.

Born in Maryland in 1941, Karenga holds two doctorates from the University of California at Los Angeles, one in social ethics, the other in political science. As a doctoral candidate in 1965, Karenga founded the United Slaves (US) Cultural Organization following the riots in Watts in Los Angeles.

Karenga believed that the key to helping black Americans was rescuing and reconstructing their original African culture and using it as a foundation for learning about and understanding who they are. While he was with the US, Karenga created Kwanzaa, after researching African cultures throughout history.

US disbanded in 1974, while Karenga was serving a four-year sentence on a controversial charge of assaulting one of the group's members. He used the time to begin a writing career. Since his parole in 1975, Karenga has written eight books, including *Introduction to Black Studies,* which is a staple of African American studies programs in colleges and universities.

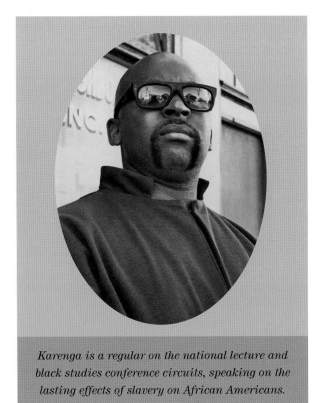

Karenga is a regular on the national lecture and black studies conference circuits, speaking on the lasting effects of slavery on African Americans.

A black nationalist, Karenga (middle foreground) has written on subjects ranging from feminism to Pan-Africanism to black art and culture.

BILL COSBY

Cosby's real gift to the world has been his gentle humor and likable nature.

BILL COSBY is well known to television audiences, both through award-winning sitcoms and his neighborly hamming with children in commercials. His life is a success story that has become a beacon for many African American comedians.

Cosby has acknowledged the pioneering role played by comedian Dick Gregory. But where Gregory often made racial observations, Cosby was a "nonracial" comedian whose gentle humor revolved around childhood and family themes. His humor is universal, his approach nonthreatening. He was the first African American comedian whom whites embraced without him getting the taint of "selling-out."

William Henry Cosby, Jr., was born July 12, 1937, in Germantown, Pennsylvania. He dropped out of high school to become a navy medic. Cosby later enrolled at Temple University, where he played football and tended bar at night. Pleased with his success at enter-taining customers, the tall, distinguished man with the expressive face left Temple in 1962 to try his hand in local clubs as a stand-up comic.

Cosby moved up to shows in New York's Greenwich Village. Audiences were thrilled, and within two years Cosby was performing at some of the nation's top comedy clubs. He also became a fixture on television variety shows and guest hosted for Johnny Carson on *The Tonight Show.* In 1965, Cosby made history as the first African American to get a network television drama show, *I Spy* with Robert Culp. *The Bill Cosby Show* followed in 1969, as well as appearances on the top-rated children's show *The Electric Company.*

Cosby appeared in several movies in the 1970s, including *Uptown Saturday Night,* and he returned to the silver screen in the 1980s and 1990s with features such as *Ghost Dad.* This expressive comedian also became popular at ritzy clubs in Reno, Las Vegas, and Lake Tahoe. Some of Cosby's most memorable work has been in television commercials, particularly the series with children produced for Jell-O.

Cosby's earnings skyrocketed after eight years as star and producer of *The Cosby Show,* a television sitcom focused on the antics of an upper-middle-class African American family. The show's positive values and its message that blacks can attain wealth and social status while retaining their cultural identity were powerful in the African American community.

Cosby has also shown a strong commitment to education with memberships in various civil rights groups and his activities with the United Negro College Fund. In 1977, Cosby went back to school, earning a master's degree and then a doctorate in education from the University of Massachusetts at Amherst at age 39. In the late 1980s, he donated $20 million to Spelman College, a black women's facility in Atlanta.

Cosby returned to TV in 1996, starring in and producing *Cosby.* A year later, his only son, Ennis, was shot and killed while changing a tire near an L.A. freeway. Cosby extends educational opportunities to youngsters and does other charitable works in his son's name.

The turn of the century brought better times for Cosby, who picked up another People's Choice Award in 1999 and an Image Award in 2001. *Men of Honor* in 2000 (he was executive producer) and a 2002 reunion of *The Cosby Show* cast were added to his credits.

In 2002, Cosby received the Presidential Medal of Freedom. President George W. Bush said of Cosby, "By focusing on our common humanity, Bill Cosby is helping to create a truly united America."

In December 1998, Bill Cosby, with his wife, Camille, arrive at the Kennedy Center Honors ceremony. Cosby was honored for his lifetime achievement in the arts.

ARETHA FRANKLIN

ARETHA FRANKLIN, with her molten-gold voice that oozes effortlessly over the octaves, is adored by generations of fans enamored of her ability to infuse songs with great passion and conviction. Franklin, winner of more Grammy awards than any other female artist, was named "one of the most influential people of the last century" by *Time* magazine. Her career has spanned more than 40 years, and she is known as "The Queen of Soul."

Franklin was born March 25, 1942, in Memphis, Tennessee, the fourth child of Baptist preacher C. L. Franklin and Barbara, a gospel singer. Her mother left when Franklin was six, and her father moved the family to Detroit, Michigan, where he became pastor of the New Bethel Baptist Church. Franklin's father gave her records to listen to and emulate. Visitors to the home included jazz pianist Art Tatum and legendary gospel singer Mahalia Jackson. Franklin credits gospel singer Clara Ward as a major role model who inspired her to sing professionally. The child, who already had a powerful voice, sang in the church choir. By age 12, Franklin sang solos in her father's traveling gospel revue. By age 14, Franklin recorded her first album for Chess Records, *Songs of Faith.*

At age 15, Franklin quit school after becoming the mother of the first of her four children, and she left Detroit for New York City three years later. This sultry woman with a soulful voice performed on many stages, from gritty clubs to large concert halls, singing rhythm and blues and jazz. Legendary talent scout John Hammond brought Franklin to Columbia Records in 1960, but he complained later that the company "misunderstood her genius." Despite her strong gospel roots, Columbia marketed Franklin as a jazz/cabaret singer. Her nine albums between 1960 and 1966 included

Aretha Franklin, "The Queen of Soul," has received many honors and awards. In 1986, the state of Michigan declared her voice a natural resource.

a tribute to her idol, Dinah Washington, but Franklin never had a big hit.

Franklin rocketed to stardom in 1966 after she signed with Atlantic Records, where producer Jerry Wexler encouraged her to let her voice free, while he added a sizzling rhythm section at an Alabama recording studio. The singer, with a voice the *Washington Post* wrote is "capable of a cornet's full brassy tone and agility over several octaves," was also named the top vocalist of 1967 by *Billboard* magazine. Franklin had a series of smash hits, including "I Never Loved a Man (The Way I Love You)," which sold a million copies. Her sisters, Carolyn and Erma, sang backup on the classic "Respect," a feminist/civil rights anthem that hit number one in June 1967. The chart busters continued with "Chain of Fools," and Carole King's "A Natural Woman (You Make Me Feel Like)." In eight straight years, Franklin won at least one Grammy.

The sassy performer, whose songs inspired the African American community during the golden age of soul and the civil rights movement, continued to top the charts in the 1970s. Her critically acclaimed albums included *To Be Young, Gifted and Black,* which featured the single "Daydreaming." Franklin won a Grammy for "Amazing Grace," with her father, Clara Ward, and the Reverend James Cleveland in the background. Franklin signed with Arista in 1980, the same year she appeared in the movie *The Blues Brothers.* In 1987, Franklin became the first woman to be inducted into the Rock and Roll Hall of Fame. The singer was awarded a Kennedy Center Honor, and she also won a Grammy Lifetime Achievement Award in 1994. She continues to inspire critics and fans with her work.

In 1998, Franklin transfixed the crowd with her performance at the Grammy Awards, subbing for tenor Luciano Pavarotti in the Puccini aria "Nessun Dorma," with only minutes to prepare. *Entertainment Weekly* magazine wrote, "now we know what D-I-V-A really stands for: Divine Incomparable Virtuoso Aretha."

Franklin performs at VH1's Divas 2001: The One and Only Aretha Franklin *tribute.*

Maya Angelou

In 1971, Angelou's screenplay Georgia, Georgia *was produced. That made her the first African American woman to have a feature film created based on one of her own stories.*

I N 1958, SINGER BILLIE HOLIDAY told Maya Angelou that she wouldn't be famous for her singing. But some critics have said the rhythmic, lyrical stories of this best-selling poet, actress, director, dancer, and professor are like the songs of a writer nourished on mother talk and the music of the black church.

Angelou, a cinnamon-colored woman who stands six feet tall, was born Marguerite Johnson on April 4, 1928, in St. Louis. At the age of three, she moved in with her paternal grandmother, Annie Henderson, in Stamps, Arkansas. When she was seven, Angelou left the town she called "mean and poor" to visit her mother. While there, her mother's boyfriend raped her. He was murdered before he could serve time for the rape, and Angelou didn't speak for almost six years because she thought her voice had killed him. She was sent back to Stamps, where her grandmother nurtured her toward becoming the woman we know today— a woman with a deep, rich voice and booming laugh who speaks six languages.

Angelou has worked a variety of jobs, ranging from the first female streetcar conductor in San Francisco, to a "madam" for two prostitutes, to a short-order cook. She became an unwed mother at 16 and says she educated herself so she could teach her son. Eventually, Angelou moved to New York City to study dance with Pearl Primus.

In the 1950s, she landed a role in the U.S. State Department–sponsored production of *Porgy and Bess,* which toured 22 countries in Europe and Africa. She became involved in the Civil Rights Movement in the 1960s, becoming northern coordinator for the Southern Christian Leadership Conference (SCLC). Angelou performed with actors James Earl Jones and Louis Gossett, Jr., in an off-Broadway production of *The Blacks,* then moved to Cairo with her son and South African activist Vusumzi Make. She was coeditor for the *Arab Observer* and later moved to Ghana, where she worked as a journalist and taught at the University of Ghana.

Angelou moved back to the United States in 1966 and wrote a ten-part television series called *Black, Blues, Black* about the role of black culture in American life. She also began work on a series of autobiographical books. *I Know Why the Caged Bird Sings,* published in 1970, became a best-seller. The book, the story of her childhood and Southern racism, was nominated for a National Book Award. Her screenplay *Georgia, Georgia* was made into a film, making Angelou the first black woman to have an original screenplay produced.

Since then, Angelou has continued to dabble in many aspects of the arts, appearing on Broadway, where she was nominated for a Tony Award, earning an Emmy nomination for her performance in *Roots,* and accepting a lifetime appointment as professor of American Studies at Wake Forest University in Winston-Salem, North Carolina. The NAACP awarded her the Spingarn Medal in 1994.

In 1993, at President Bill Clinton's first inauguration, Angelou delivered the poem "On the Pulse of the Morning." Not since Robert Frost read his inaugural poem for President Kennedy in 1961 has a poet become the subject of such widespread media attention. In 2002, Angelou launched a line of Hallmark greeting cards and accessories. In 2006, she began hosting a weekly radio program on XM satellite radio.

Actor/director/author Maya Angelou delivers a poem at the swearing-in ceremony for President Bill Clinton in 1993.

JESSE JACKSON

THE REVEREND JESSE JACKSON has spent more than 35 years in pursuit of economic justice and human rights for dispossessed Americans from all walks of life. He has also been instrumental in working for peace in various regions of the world. Jackson's activities have made him one of America's most important African American leaders and an international political leader.

Twelve years prior to his own run for the presidency, Jesse Jackson wears his People United to Save Humanity (PUSH) button at the 1972 Democratic National Convention in Miami.

In 1988, Jackson was, for a time, the front-runner for the Democratic nomination after winning six southern states, taking the state of Michigan with 55 percent of the vote, and finishing second in Illinois. Though he eventually came in a strong second behind nominee Michael Dukakis, Jackson's bid attracted almost seven million voters—a "rainbow coalition" from all across America. This allowed him to exert considerable power on the issues in the Democratic platform.

Being taken seriously as a presidential candidate was quite an achievement, given Jackson's humble origins. He was born October 8, 1941, in Greenville, South Carolina, to an unwed 17-year-old mother still in high school. They, along with his stepfather, lived in a three-room cottage with no indoor plumbing until he was in sixth grade. This environment may have produced in Jackson a strong need to prove himself and to succeed.

President of his high school class, Jackson won a college athletic scholarship to the University of Illinois, but racism there led him to transfer to North Carolina A&T College, where he became class president. He attended Chicago Theological Seminary and was ordained as a Baptist minister in 1968.

Jackson joined the Civil Rights Movement while at North Carolina A&T, and during demonstrations in 1965 in Selma, Alabama, he became an aide to Dr. Martin Luther King, Jr.

Jackson responds to the applause following his address at the 1984 Democratic National Convention. Jackson garnered a respectable percentage of the popular vote in 1984 and went on to run for the presidency four years later.

He is so firmly entrenched as a force for political and social change that in 1984, and again in 1988, he made the most successful bid by a black candidate in American history—until Barack Obama's run—to become president of the United States. In 1984, Jackson captured more than 3.5 million votes, 21 percent of the popular vote in the Democratic primary.

King appointed Jackson head of Operation Breadbasket in Chicago in 1966. As the economic arm of King's Southern Christian Leadership Conference, Operation Breadbasket used boycotts and selective buying strategies to induce white-owned businesses to carry black-produced products and to hire black workers.

In 1971, Jackson left the organization to found Operation PUSH (People United to Save Humanity), which expanded the economic mission of Breadbasket into the social and political arenas as well. In 1984, Jackson also founded the National Rainbow Coalition to address the problems of the disenfranchised. In July 1990, he was elected "shadow senator" to try to attain statehood for the District of Columbia. He was sworn into office in January 1991.

As he continues these activities, Jackson also mentors his son Jesse Jackson, Jr., who serves in the House of Representatives for Illinois's Second Congressional District.

SHIRLEY CHISHOLM

LIKE OTHER IMMIGRANTS who came to America in the 1920s, Shirley Anita St. Hill's parents left their daughter's birthplace of Barbados to better themselves. Although life for blacks was not easy in the United States, her parents insisted that their children would succeed despite the obstacles. They did, however, send the children back to Barbados to live with their grandmother in 1928.

Chisholm flashes a victory sign after defeating civil rights leader James Farmer to become the first black female member of Congress in 1968.

Shirley and her sisters returned to America to live with their parents in 1934. Shirley, the oldest, always seemed to stand out. She expressed herself forcefully and clearly even when her parents did not want her to. Meanwhile, this outspoken little girl excelled in her Brooklyn school just as she had in the demanding one back in Barbados. She was offered scholarships to Vassar and Oberlin colleges but instead stayed in more affordable Brooklyn.

With an education degree from Brooklyn College, Chisholm taught nursery school while she took courses at Columbia University toward a master's degree in early childhood development. She never lost sight of her aspirations; Chisholm continued to work to prove to men and to white America that women and African Americans were as capable as anyone. She fought against racism and sexism her entire life.

She married Jamaican private investigator Conrad Chisholm in 1949. Their life together was good, but Chisholm continued to show her concern for her friends and neighbors in her Brooklyn community. She started day-care centers for working mothers. Her biographer, Toyomi Igus, pointed out in the 1991 book *Great Women in the Struggle,* "The centers were so successful that Brooklyn residents chose her to represent them in the New York State legislature in 1964." Four years later, Chisholm was chosen to represent her community in Congress, becoming the first African American congresswoman. She served seven terms, from 1968 to 1982, and was elected using the slogan "Unbought and Unbossed," which later would be the title of her first autobiography. (*The Good Fight,* published in 1973, was her second.)

Chisholm was an advocate for the dispossessed and disenchanted and was always a champion for the poor. She wanted poor people to have the same opportunities other Americans had. So, in 1972, Chisholm looked at the political landscape and did not see anyone representing the interests she held so dear.

Shirley Chisholm, activist and educator, was the first woman and first African American to make a serious bid for the White House.

Her candidacy was a turning point. A decade before Jesse Jackson's first run, she was the first presidential candidate to address the dual "disabilities" of race and gender. She became the first African American woman to speak from a national platform about the discrimination black women face even within their own community. Chisholm noted that she often had to battle sexism more than racism to accomplish her goals. She lost her bid for the presidency, but to many women, African Americans, and poor people, Chisholm earned their respect by becoming a role model.

In 1993, President Clinton nominated Chisholm to be ambassador to Jamaica, but she declined due to poor health. She died in January 2005.

In 1972, Chisholm decided the country might just give credence to a black, female presidential candidate. She tossed her hat in the ring. Here she speaks at the Democratic Convention.

BARBARA JORDAN

BARBARA JORDAN would not be confounded or deterred by social traditions. She truly believed in the American dream—that she could become whatever she chose to be. Jordan had the confidence to break through racial and gender barriers, not with a battering ram but with poise and intellect.

Jordan's ability to negotiate with the staunchest conservatives at the top of the power spectrum, to wheel and deal with the best of them, yielded her greatest successes, but it drew sharp criticism from liberals.

Jordan became the first African American to serve in the Texas State Senate since 1883, the first black woman to serve as president pro tempore of an American legislative entity, the first black woman elected to the U.S. Congress from the South, and the first African American and the first woman to give a keynote speech at the Democratic National Convention.

Despite the criticisms leveled by liberals with whom she shared political beliefs, Jordan attained personal growth without sacrificing the interests of her constituency. She was pragmatic about her relationships with conservative power brokers. By mastering the game of *quid pro quo,* she killed a bill to restrict black voting rights in Texas and she opened the doors of the state legislature to people of color.

Barbara Jordan was born the youngest child of Arlyne Patten and Benjamin Jordan on February 21, 1936. Although household meals were often wanting, Barbara never wanted for encouragement. Her maternal grandfather counseled her to set high goals, and other family members offered support.

Following graduation from Boston University School of Law, Jordan paid her dues in private practice and by making legal inroads with the

NAACP. After two unsuccessful runs for the Texas legislature, Jordan's political career hit high gear. Some of her mentors included former President Lyndon Johnson, Robert Strauss, Robert Byrd, and Leon Jaworski.

Barbara Jordan garnered many awards for her years of public service, including the Spingarn Medal in 1992 and the Presidential Medal of Freedom in 1994.

In 1973, Jordan led freshmen Congressional Democrats in a move to oppose President Richard Nixon's flaunting of the laws of the land. Their outspokenness eventually spurred Congress to make the impounding of federally approved funds illegal and to establish the Congressional Budget Office and House and Senate budget committees, which are checks on misuse of federal finances by the executive branch.

Jordan went on to negotiate an extension of the Voting Rights Act, supported the Equal Rights Amendment, and worked to protect American privacy and curb other abuses by federal intelligence agencies.

The media provided Jordan a national following when she laid out the rationale for Nixon's impeachment before a television audience. This speech brought her national attention. Her image rocketed further after breaking the color barrier with a televised keynote speech that raised the 1976 Democratic National conventioneers to a fever pitch behind their nominee, Jimmy Carter.

Through the end of her life on January 17, 1996, Jordan continued to take on challenges beyond national politics while coping with multiple sclerosis. Beginning in 1979, she worked as a professor at the University of Texas Lyndon B. Johnson School of Public Affairs and later entered the international arena on a 1985 United Nations panel to examine ways corporations could support the anti-apartheid movement.

In sharp contrast to her no-nonsense public persona, Jordan could joke and socialize with the "best of the old boys' club," and those "old cronies" made a point of easing her path into their inner sanctum. From this vantage point, Jordan was able to achieve what she considered her greatest accomplishment—being an effective voice for sections of the American populace who had remained previously unheard in the halls of power. In doing so, her achievements exceeded the legacy of her great grandfather Edward A. Patton, who was run out of the state, thus ending its Reconstruction era as the last black voice in the Texas legislature.

This political dynamo also achieved a symbolic first. In Texas, the president pro tempore of the Senate participated in Governor for a Day festivities. After the elected governor and lieutenant governor left town on June 10, 1972, Jordan became the first African American to serve as governor of Texas for this celebration.

HANK AARON

I T WAS A RECORD that most baseball fans thought would never be broken: Babe Ruth's 714 career home runs. But on April 8, 1974, in front of 53,775 fans in Fulton County Stadium, 40-year-old Henry Louis "Hammerin' Hank" Aaron blasted a fastball from pitcher Al Downing 385 feet to surpass Ruth's achievement. Aaron went on to set new records for home runs (755) and runs batted in (2,297). Though Barry Bonds, Aaron's godson, eventually broke his home-run record, Aaron's accomplishments are unsurpassed.

Aaron appeared in 24 All-Star Games. He was the only National League player to hit 40 or more homers in eight seasons and was the first player to collect 500 home runs and 3,000 hits. No slouch defensively, Aaron won Gold Gloves as the top right fielder from 1958 to 1960. As soon as he was eligible, in 1982, Aaron was voted into the Baseball Hall of Fame—quite an

Hank Aaron received some of Major League Baseball's most prestigious awards during his illustrious career. Aaron added an honorary doctor of humane letters degree from Dartmouth College in Hanover, New Hampshire, on June 11, 2000, to his other awards.

accomplishment for a kid who originally didn't know how to bat correctly.

Aaron was born on February 5, 1934, in segregated Mobile, Alabama, where his high school didn't have a baseball team. While playing sandlot ball, Aaron batted with the wrong hand on top, but he had exceptionally quick wrists. He impressed the Indianapolis Clowns of the Negro Leagues, which offered the skinny 17-year-old a $200-a-month contract in 1952. His Negro League career would not last long, however.

When Jackie Robinson joined the Brooklyn Dodgers in 1947 (he had signed with the organization in 1945), breaking baseball's racial barrier, it was the beginning of the end of the Negro Leagues. By 1952, the financially strapped Clowns sold Aaron's contract to the Milwaukee (now Atlanta) Braves.

In his first year in the minors, Aaron batted .336 and was named Rookie of the Year. The next year, after moving up a level, he was named that league's Most Valuable Player (MVP). In 1954, Aaron was called to the majors after the Braves' second baseman broke his ankle. During Aaron's first game, he impressed the fans with three hits, including a mammoth home run. In 1955, he posted All-Star stats. In 1956, he led the National League in hitting with a .328 average and was considered one of the best players in the game.

Then, in 1957, he hit the home run that helped the Braves win the pennant and launched three more home runs to help the team capture the World Series. Aaron was also named league MVP that year, but 1957 was the only year he would win that award or a World Series championship.

Aaron's pursuit of Babe Ruth's home run record in 1974 should have felt wonderful. But it was marred by racist death threats against Aaron

and his family. Some of the hate letters vowed to hurt him while also threatening his family. It was sufficiently serious to trigger an FBI investigation and federal protection for Aaron's daughter, who was in college. Aaron also hired a bodyguard for himself.

Aaron retired after a 23-year career, rewriting baseball's batting record books along the way and holding more major league batting records than any other player in history. He currently serves as senior vice president of the Atlanta Braves and sits on the National Board of the NAACP and the Sterling Committee of Morehouse College. In 2002, Aaron was awarded the Presidential Medal of Freedom, the nation's highest civilian honor.

"Hammerin' Hank" had his eye on history as he hit his 715th home run on April 8, 1974.

TONI MORRISON

Morrison's third novel, Song of Solomon, *won the National Book Critics Circle Award in 1977 and became the first novel by an African American to become a Book of the Month Club selection since Richard Wright's* Native Son *in 1940.*

I
N 1988, WRITER TONI MORRISON won a Pulitzer Prize for her 1987 novel, *Beloved.* Five years later, the six novels she had written to that point earned her the honor of being the first African American to win the Nobel Prize for Literature. In announcing the $825,000 Nobel award, the Swedish Academy described how Morrison uses language to break the chains of racism.

Morrison is one of the most important writers in the nation's history and certainly one of the most significant novelists living today. Her primary focus has been on conveying the realities of life for black women and the physical and economic violence that affects them, along with the culture of the larger black community.

Morrison has had a three-pronged career as a writer, an editor, and an educator. Born Chloe

Anthony Wofford on February 18, 1931, in Lorain, Ohio, she was an intelligent child. The only black student in her first-grade class, she learned to read before her classmates.

After graduating from high school with honors, she attended Howard University as an English major and began using the first name Toni. Following her graduation in 1953, Morrison earned a master's degree in English literature from Cornell University in 1955. In 1957, she taught at Howard, where she married architect Harold Morrison. Her students at Howard included activist Stokely Carmichael and author Claude Brown.

In the mid-1960s, Morrison divorced and moved to New York to work as a textbook editor with Random House Books. A few years later, she was promoted to senior editor to work on black fiction. During her nearly 20 years with the publisher, she helped develop the careers of such luminaries as Angela Davis, Toni Cade Bambara, and Gayl Jones.

Morrison began writing more herself. In 1970, she turned an old short story into her first novel, *The Bluest Eye,* about a young black girl who wants blue eyes. *Sula,* her second novel, is about an intensely individualistic black woman and her relationships; it came out in 1973.

Morrison's third novel, *Song of Solomon,* about a middle-class black man searching through slavery for his ancestral roots, won her the National Book Critics Circle Award when it debuted in 1977. A fourth novel, *Tar Baby,* stayed on best-seller lists for more than three months and made Morrison the first African American woman featured on the cover of *Newsweek.*

She became the Albert Schweitzer Professor of the Humanities at the State University of New

York at Albany. There, she wrote her finest work, *Beloved,* published in 1987, which won the Pulitzer Prize for fiction. Morrison was inspired after reading the true story of Margaret Garner, who had escaped from slavery with her four children. Facing recapture, Garner killed one child and unsuccessfully attempted the same with two others rather than have them returned to slavery.

Morrison continued her string of successful novels with her sixth, *Jazz.* She also released a volume of literary criticism titled *Playing in the Dark* and followed that with the novel *Paradise* in 1998. She received the National Book Foundation Medal for Distinguished Contribution to American Letters in 1996. She still teaches and writes.

Morrison's fifth novel, Beloved, *won the Pulitzer Prize for fiction in 1988.*

ROBERT L. JOHNSON

ROBERT L. JOHNSON, founder of Black Entertainment Television (BET), the first cable network targeting African Americans, is the epitome of the term "entrepreneur." An enormously self-confident man with a deceptively quiet demeanor, Johnson tells those who want to be successful that they must "start with a fundamental belief that you can do just about anything you set your mind to." (Johnson was quoted from an article in *The Black Collegian,* written by Robert G. Miller.) Johnson, who was able to implement his vision for BET both through tenacity and his industry contacts, is a brilliant businessman who has created opportunities for black artists, writers, journalists, directors, and producers.

Born April 8, 1946, in Hickory, Mississippi, Johnson was the ninth of Archie and Edna Johnson's ten children. The family later moved to Freeport, Illinois. Johnson met his wife-to-be, Sheila Crump, while studying history at the University of Illinois. In 1972, Johnson earned a master's degree in public administration from Princeton University. He later launched his television career in Washington, D.C. After working for the Corporation for Public Broadcasting and the Washington Urban League, Johnson served as press secretary for then-D.C. Congressional Delegate Walter E. Fauntroy, before becoming vice president of government relations for the National Cable & Telecommunications Association (NCTA).

Realizing that it was possible to start a "niche service" for the black community using cable television, Johnson moved to launch his vision. NCTA President Tom Wheeler invested $15,000 in the concept. Johnson persuaded former Tele-Communications Inc. President John Malone to invest $500,000. The final component of the plan came when UA-Columbia Cablevision President Bob Rosencrans said he owned slots on a cable TV satellite that could be used for Johnson's channel. On January 8, 1980, BET hit the airwaves at 11:00 P.M. for two hours a week on Friday nights, broadcasting music videos. The company became the first black-controlled business listed on the New York Stock Exchange. Johnson bought back all the publicly traded stock and took the company private in 1998.

Viacom later bought BET for $2.3 billion in stock, with President and Chief Operating Officer Debra L. Lee and Chief Executive Officer and Chairman Johnson signing five-year contracts to stay in their positions. There was some criticism in the African American community about whether the company would continue its mission, but executives say the deal will allow for investment in better programming and more distribution opportunities. The company holdings include several major cable channels, along with a publishing arm, the lottery on six Caribbean islands, and a Web site. BET has 500 employees, reaches 65 million homes, and posted earnings of $225 million in 1999.

"All business is personal, so make your friends before you need them," Johnson says, adding that he doesn't approach anything as an obstacle. People, Johnson believes, should be able to communicate with anyone they need to in order to help achieve their goals. "It's everything from how you carry yourself, to how you arrange a meeting, to whether or not you show up on time. The way you dress, speak to someone, your handshake, body language, and tone of voice are all communication," he commented in the same article by Miller.

BET's founder says people of color should treat racism like rain—protect yourself but get on with life. Johnson says his top accomplishment has been creating an environment where African Americans can feel empowered.

Robert Johnson tells those who want to emulate his success to visualize it, then gather the resources to make it happen.

Johnson is also a political mover. Johnson (left) is seen here with President Bill Clinton, shown embracing Congressman John Conyers at a Conyers fundraiser.

SUSAN L. TAYLOR

Taylor has become the "face" of Essence—*an image of grace, beauty, dignity, and spiritual essence. These ideals are synonymous with the enduring black women's magazine.*

SUSAN L. TAYLOR began her public career in the 1960s as an actor with the Negro Ensemble Company. The birth of her daughter in 1969 caused her to give up acting so she could spend more time with her child. Taylor went into business, first becoming a licensed beautician and then creating her own cosmetics line, Nequai Cosmetics (named after her daughter).

In 1971, her expertise in cosmetology and the success of her business, along with her stunning beauty, caught the eye of the editors of *Essence,* a magazine marketed to African American women. That year she worked as a freelance writer for the magazine. A year later, she became the publication's beauty editor. From 1971 to 1980, she supervised both the fashion and beauty departments.

Since 1980, Taylor has served as the magazine's editor-in-chief. During her stewardship, circulation has grown. One of her chief responsibilities has been writing the monthly editorial, "In the Spirit," in which she shares her intimate thoughts on values and morals she feels are important. She talks about spirituality and, in doing so, touches readers in all walks of life. It is that positive message, along with her truly impressive track record, that has made her famous. "In the Spirit" also became the title of her first book.

Her 1998 book, *Lessons in Living,* is an exploration of intimate themes and issues. It's a celebration of her successes, failures, fears, and triumphs. But most of all, the book is a testament to her faith and commitment.

Susan L. Taylor went from being a single mother with a small cosmetics company to becoming an author, an inspirational speaker, and the editor-in-chief of *Essence* magazine.

In the early part of the book, Taylor confesses: "For years, I'd been racing through each day, not living my life, not owning it. I was driven, trying to cover all the bases at home and work while wrestling inwardly with insecurity. For some time, I'd been going round and round in tighter and tighter circles, arriving again and again at the same wordless pain. The people, places and predicaments changed, but the emotional landscape was always the same—stress, doubt and fear." Later on in the book, Taylor reveals how she found peace in her life and how

other people—famous and obscure—have also come to terms with calamity and triumphed.

She has received many awards, including the Women in Communications Matrix Award and an honorary doctorate of humane letters from Lincoln University. Since 1986, Taylor has served as vice president of Essence Communications, Inc. She launched a nationally syndicated television magazine show, which received rave reviews during its short time on the air. She has also added a personal touch in managing her magazine's editorial content, insisting that blacks worldwide get coverage.

Taylor's personal life and her career have intersected on one theme: nurturing the spirit for personal and community growth. In a passage in the last chapter of *Lessons in Living,* she talks about love being the only hope for the future and that contentment can only be found when we help others. Taylor continues to practice what she preaches.

Taylor is committed to and supports women's issues. Here she speaks at a 2002 event.

ALICE WALKER

WRITER ALICE WALKER paved the way for both black and women authors when her Pulitzer Prize–winning novel, *The Color Purple,* was developed into a Steven Spielberg film—a film that received 11 Academy Award nominations. Her books have sold millions of copies and have been translated into two dozen languages.

As a child, Walker wanted something far different than the sharecropping world she knew. She dreamed of being a painter or a blues singer.

While the controversial and popular book *The Color Purple,* which examines the effects of domestic violence and racism on three generations of southern black farmers, is her most famous work, it is one of many important pieces penned by this self-described "womanist" writer. Other noteworthy works include *The Temple of My Familiar, The Third Life of Grange Copeland,* and *Possessing the Secret of Joy.* Her book *Crossing the Same River*

Twice has received favorable reviews and lots of attention—something Walker enjoys professionally yet shuns in her personal life.

This reflective feminist writer was the youngest of eight children. She was born in 1944, in Eatonton, Georgia. Her father was a sharecropper, and her mother was a maid. Walker said both her parents were strong storytellers, and she remembers her mother toiling to make their humble shack spotless.

Like other important writers, Walker's childhood had pivotal events that changed her forever. At age eight, she was shot in the eye with a BB by one of her brothers. Because her family did not own a car, Walker was forced to wait a week before a doctor examined her. The doctor then told her she was permanently blind in her right eye. Self-conscious and shy, Walker, who had been an outgoing youth, retreated to a private world of words, ideas, and books. She started writing poetry and became so proficient that she was awarded several fellowships. She was also offered the opportunity to have her poems published.

Some critics speculate that Walker's own early injury helped her identify with Tashi, the main character in *Possessing the Secret of Joy.* Tashi is a tribal African woman who was genitally mutilated by the tsunga's knife and severely traumatized because of the experience. She spends the rest of her life fighting madness and is treated by disciples of both Freud and Jung and even by Jung himself. Finally, she regains her ability to feel. This book has generated much controversy: Critics of Walker say African cultural rituals are not America's concern, while feminists and many others say mutilation of women is not about culture but about control of women.

After high school, Walker attended Spelman College in Atlanta and Sarah Lawrence College in Bronxville, New York, where she graduated. Her first job after college was working in the Welfare Department in New York City. She hated the job and wrote feverishly at night. After leaving the Welfare Department, she was writer-in-residence and professor of black studies at Jackson State College and Tougaloo College in Mississippi. Her night writing paid off in 1970 when she published her first novel, *The Third Life of Grange Copeland,* about sharecroppers, a theme she would revisit in *The Color Purple.* Walker continues to write.

Walker ended up in the world of words and ideas. Her work with and mastery of words has earned her many awards, including a Pulitzer Prize.

OPRAH WINFREY

Winfrey is proof that the American dream is possible. In fact, in 2002 she was ranked number 10 on Fortune *magazine's first list of the 50 most powerful black executives in the United States.*

OPRAH WINFREY is an Emmy Award–winning talk show host, an Academy Award–nominated actress, and one of the highest paid entertainers in America. She uses her position as the country's best-known talk show host to tackle issues affecting people's daily lives. *The Oprah Winfrey Show,* handled by Winfrey's own production company, deals with social problems ranging from sexual abuse to racism and is watched by more than 17 million people daily. Winfrey is a testament to the resilience of the human spirit in the face of adversity and to the heights reachable through hard work. Her strength is her ability to make her guests and audience feel at home.

The bubbly, voluble Winfrey had a stormy childhood. Born in a small Mississippi town to unmarried parents, Winfrey spent her early childhood with her grandmother. She was an exceptional child, making her first speaking appearance in church at the age of three. At age six, Winfrey moved to Milwaukee to live with her mother, Vernita Lee, but she didn't fit into the subsistence-level existence Lee eked out on welfare and domestic work.

Winfrey lived briefly in Nashville with her father, Vernon, but soon returned to her mother's home. The next few years were among the darkest in Winfrey's life. She was repeatedly sexually abused by a cousin and friends of the family. Vernon Winfrey brought his daughter back to Nashville, and she began to bloom under his strict guidance.

Despite her troubles, Winfrey was destined for great things. She was reporting the news for WVOL radio in Nashville before graduating from high school and continued in broadcasting as she started at Tennessee State University. Winfrey was the first female television coanchor in town at WTVF-TV. A few months before graduation, Winfrey moved to WJZ-TV in Baltimore.

The talented Winfrey found her niche when the station made her cohost of its morning show, *People Are Talking.* Winfrey continued her meteoric rise in the field with a move to Chicago in 1984 to host WLS-TV's morning show, *A.M. Chicago,* which became the top show in the market within three months. The show was renamed for Winfrey, went into syndication, and consistently gets phenomenal ratings. She has also expanded into film, with a Best Supporting Actress Academy Award nomination for her first movie, *The Color Purple.*

Beloved was released in 1999, and Winfrey acted in and produced it. The movie received good critical reviews but did not do well at the box office. Winfrey started her own magazine, *O, The Oprah Magazine,* in 2000.

One of America's highest paid entertainers, Winfrey has contributed $1 million to Morehouse College, one of her many contributions to the community. She also uses her own company, Harpo Productions, to develop positive projects dealing with women and African Americans. She opened the Leadership Academy for girls in South Africa in 2007.

Winfrey has received numerous awards, including the prestigious Peabody Award, both for her talk show and for her philanthropic work.

Oprah has been an influential figure in publishing. She dons her special 50th Anniversary Gold Medal during the 1999 National Book Awards in New York City. Winfrey has galvanized millions of readers with her popular book club.

SPIKE LEE

Lee's success as a filmmaker has opened the doors of the movie industry for a new group of African American directors. Lee's movies portray the richness of black life and culture.

N 1986, SPIKE LEE enjoyed huge commercial success with his first major film, *She's Gotta Have It.* Lee proved that well-told stories from the black experience could be profitable and attract diverse audiences.

Born Shelton Jackson Lee on March 20, 1957, in Atlanta, and nicknamed Spike by his mother, Lee grew up in the Brooklyn section of New York City with an early interest in the arts. His father is noted jazz musician Bill Lee; his late mother, Jacquelyn, took the youngster to plays, museums, and galleries.

As a student at Morehouse College, Lee took an interest in filmmaking, which led to a summer internship at Columbia Pictures in 1979 after his graduation. He entered New York University's film school and, for his master's thesis, made the hour-long comedy *Joe's Bed-*

Stuy Barbershop: We Cut Heads, about a Brooklyn barbershop fronting for the local numbers racket.

The film won a student Academy Award from the Academy of Motion Picture Arts and Sciences in 1982 and was received with critical acclaim at film festivals from San Francisco to Switzerland. But with no offers from the Hollywood film industry, Lee decided to produce his movies independently.

Four years later, in 1986, he was able to complete *She's Gotta Have It,* which was shot in 12 days in a small Brooklyn apartment and nearby park. Financing was a major problem. Lee started with $18,000 and kept asking everyone he could for any money they could spare.

The film, about the hectic love life of an independent young African American woman, was completed for a relatively paltry $175,000 but went on to gross more than $7 million. For his efforts, Lee won the prize for the best new film at the Cannes International Film Festival and received the Los Angeles Film Critics Association Award for best new director in 1986. *She's Gotta Have It* was also named to many film critics' top-ten lists for 1986.

Columbia Pictures picked up Lee's second major film release, *School Daze,* a musical about life at a black college, for $6 million. The movie made *Variety*'s weekly list of the top-ten moneymaking films in March 1988. His third release, *Do the Right Thing,* about racial tensions between Italian Americans and African Americans, became a mainstream hit and cemented Lee's reputation as a bona fide major

American filmmaker. Lee was nominated for an Academy Award for his original screenplay, and many critics consider the movie the most important American film of the decade.

Lee's movies, though controversial, continue to be box office magic. He has gone on to make *Mo' Better Blues, Jungle Fever, Malcolm X, Crooklyn, Clockers, Girl 6,* and *Get on the Bus!,* the story of a group of men going to 1995's Million Man March on Washington, D.C.

Lee and Samuel D. Pollard's documentary *4 Little Girls* achieved critical recognition in 1998 with nominations for a Black Film Award and an Oscar. Lee followed that with a Black Film Award nomination for *He Got Game* in 1999. Then Lee returned to his controversial ways with the dramatic *Summer of Sam* feature film in 1999; *Bamboozled,* a bitter satire on the image of blacks in the media, in 2000; and *A Huey P. Newton Story* in 2001.

Accepting a teaching position at New York University's Tisch School of the Arts in 2002 did not slow Lee, who made *Jim Brown All American, The 25th Hour,* and *Ten Minutes Older* that year.

Brooklyn native Spike Lee does the right thing and spends time reading to children at a Brooklyn Head Start program in the summer of 1999.

AUGUST WILSON

Pulitzer prize–winning author August Wilson wrote a cycle of plays examining African American life in each decade of the 20th century.

Wilson, who wrote his first poem to a girl in the seventh grade, worked odd jobs and submitted poetry to black publications. In the late 1960s, he founded an African American theater company that focused on politicizing the community. He began writing serious drama in 1978 when he moved to St. Paul. He began hearing—and putting on paper—the infectious music in the cadence of the voices of black Pittsburgh.

Ma Rainey's Black Bottom, Wilson's first major play, opened on Broadway in 1984. It was about the effects of racism on a group of black musicians. He has since won seven New York Drama Critics' Circle Awards, several Tony awards, and two Pulitzer Prizes.

The first Pulitzer was for *Fences,* which opened on Broadway in 1987 and is the story of an athlete victimized by racism. Wilson won his

second Pulitzer in 1990 for *The Piano Lesson,* which tells of a family's conflict over selling an heirloom from the slavery era.

Wilson said he wanted to make an aesthetic statement with his work and put black culture on stage to demonstrate that it exists. Angry about the difference between being black and white in America, Wilson ignited a public debate in New York City in 1997 over the role of theater in illuminating African American life. He believed black theaters should be subsidized so people of color can have places to display their own vision of their culture.

Wilson died of liver cancer on October 2, 2005. Following his death, Virginia Theatre on Broadway was renamed in his honor. The August Wilson Theatre is the first Broadway theater to be named after an African American.

AUGUST WILSON WAS a self-educated writer who quit school at the age of 15 after confronting racism from both teachers and students in Pittsburgh's Catholic schools. He wrote a ten-part series of dramas that examine the issues facing African Americans; the series includes *Ma Rainey's Black Bottom* (1985), *King Hedley II* (2001), and *Radio Golf* (2005). Each play tells the story of a facet of black life, and each looks through the lens of a different decade.

Born Frederick August Kittel on April 27, 1945, in Pittsburgh, Wilson was named after his father, a German immigrant whom Wilson said was an alcoholic and rarely around. His mother, Daisy, was black, and Wilson says she gave him his sense of identity and his connection with African American culture. After dropping out of school, Wilson read books by writers ranging from Langston Hughes to Amiri Baraka.

ALVIN AILEY

Born impoverished in Rogersville, Texas, in 1931, Alvin Ailey managed to dance his way onto stages around the globe. His remarkable creative energies and inspirational choreography have entertained more than 15 million theatergoers.

In dances such as the acclaimed "Revelations," Ailey choreographed distinctive life lessons through incredible visual poetry using long, flowing, aesthetically spiritual movements that redefined the meaning of performance art.

Ailey's artistry first emerged in the form of the written word and drawings he made as a child in Texas. Greater cultural exposure in Los Angeles, where his mother relocated, brought forth his gifts for poetry and singing. A high school excursion to Ballet Russe de Monte stirred his interest in music and dance.

Enamored with the performances of black ballerina Jane Collins, Alvin Ailey timidly took

the plunge into dance classes with Lester Horton in 1949. Ailey assumed leadership of that dance group following Horton's death in 1953, but his early creative works left the critics unimpressed.

Recognition as a masterful artist did not come until he had absorbed the physical grace of Hanya Holm, Martha Graham, Charles Wiedman, Katherine Dunham, and every other choreographer on the New York scene. This experience gave way to Ailey's exotically photo-perfect choreography.

Years of hard work took shape in 1958 with the premiere of "Blues Suite," a dance reminiscent of the finger-popping joys and devastations found in Texas roadhouses. The composition may have been equally reflective of the mental conflicts that Ailey constantly battled. Ailey's creative genius was extinguished when he passed away on December 1, 1989.

COLIN POWELL

The son of Jamaican immigrants became one of the most powerful men in the United States. Along the way, he earned two Purple Hearts during his military service.

THAT COLIN POWELL SO successfully crossed color barriers into some of the greatest political assignments in the nation is a credit to his unlimited abilities. Becoming the first African American national security advisor to the president propelled him to America's highest military position, chairman of the Joint Chiefs of Staff. As a civilian, he continued to walk where other blacks have never gone in a presidential cabinet—after the 2000 election he was appointed Secretary of State under President George W. Bush.

More amazing has been Powell's sphere of support across political party lines; enthusiastic politicos attempted to draft him into a presidential candidacy in 1996 and in 2000. Despite his strong results in opinion polls, Powell decided the time was not right for him and his family to seek that top position.

Colin Powell was born April 5, 1937, near the end of the Great Depression, in Harlem. His parents labored in blue-collar jobs. His education was a product of integrated public schooling from elementary through college in New York City, during which his performance was less than stellar. While at City College of New York, he liked the discipline and structure of the ROTC (Reserve Officers Training Corps). Powell worked six years part-time in his Bronx neighborhood at a baby furniture store, where he picked up Yiddish from owner Lou Kirshner.

After graduating from college as a newly commissioned second lieutenant, he served two years in Germany, then was sent to Massachusetts. There he met and married Alma Johnson. Powell was transferred to Vietnam in 1962. He received the Purple Heart for an injury caused by a booby trap that was rigged with a sharpened punji stick, which drove through his left foot. After completing his tour of duty, he enrolled in the prestigious U.S. Army Command and General Staff College in 1967, which gave his career a dramatic boost. He served another tour in Vietnam in the summer of 1968, earning another Purple Heart and the Soldier's Medal for rescuing injured soldiers from a downed helicopter. A decade later, he was a brigadier general. His skills were augmented with several upper echelon military courses as well as a master's degree from George Washington University. Following that, a succession of Pentagon jobs headed his way.

Powell came to the attention of America when he became national security advisor under President Reagan in 1987. He was appointed chairman of the Joint Chiefs of Staff under President George H.W. Bush, a year before Operation Desert Storm in Kuwait. Powell emerged from Desert Storm a hero.

During that offensive, the Powell Doctrine yielded military success. The doctrine is a decision tree for after diplomatic approaches have failed; it determines the best possible outcomes from well-supported military intervention with the least loss of troops. During The War on Terrorism and the fighting in Afghanistan, most portions of the doctrine appeared to remain in active use.

In civilian life, Powell released a best-selling autobiography in 1995. He also promotes national charities, such as the Boys and Girls Clubs of America. During lecture tours, he shares his inspiring blueprint for positive growth and volunteerism with seasoned corporate executives as well as with young minds.

When America embarked on The Global War on Terrorism, Powell, as Secretary of State, was at the forefront of leadership as he has been with every major military action in this age. Powell stepped down as Secretary of State on January 26, 2005.

Powell has served both Bush presidents. He served under the elder President Bush, and he served as Secretary of State for President George W. Bush.

MICHAEL JORDAN

MICHAEL JORDAN was cut from his high school basketball team but came back as an upperclassman to become an All-American. He helped North Carolina win the NCAA championship in 1982, was named College Player of the Year in 1983 and 1984, and was the third player selected in the 1984 NBA draft.

Jordan demonstrates his amazing ability to soar through space, which is how he got his nickname, "Air."

No one ever played the game of basketball as fluently as Michael Jordan, nicknamed "Air" because of his ability to float off the ground longer than seemingly possible in order to perform his scoring magic. The Chicago Bulls' shooting guard led the team to six National Basketball Association (NBA) championships from 1991 to 1993 and from 1996 to 1998.

The strength of his game is his completeness as a player. Jordan is adept at scoring, defending, passing, and rebounding. Along with his limit-less physical talents are an intense focus, fierce determination, and inspired leadership.

The achievements Jordan has collected include Most Valuable Player for five seasons (1988, 1991, 1992, 1996, 1998), in six NBA Finals (1991 to 1993, 1996 to 1998), and in three All-Star Games (1988, 1996, 1998); Defensive Player of the Year in 1988; and Rookie of the Year in 1985. He also helped the U.S. team win two Olympic gold medals (1984, 1992).

Attesting to his all-around game, Jordan was named to eleven All-NBA first teams and the All-Defensive First Team nine times. He was the second player in league history (Wilt Chamberlain is the other player) to win seven straight scoring titles (1987 to 1993). Three more titles, from 1996 to 1998, make him the record holder. His presence with the Bulls was worth an estimated $5 million to Chicago's economy.

Jordan was a virtual scoring machine from both two- and three-point range, in addition to having the pizzazz to raise public interest in the NBA. After ending his retirement a second time, he joined the elite group of NBA players (Kareem Abdul-Jabbar, Karl Malone, and Wilt Chamberlain) who have scored 30,000 career points. He hit this mark playing with the Washington Wizards in 2001 against the Bulls.

Other notable achievements include his career high 69 points scored against Cleveland in 1990 and a play-off record 63 points against Boston in 1986. Jordan holds the NBA record averages of 31.5 points per game during his career, 21.3 points in All-Star Games, and 33.4 points in playoff games. In the 1993 finals against Phoenix, Jordan scored 41 points per game, an NBA finals record.

Born February 17, 1963, in Brooklyn, New York, Jordan grew up in Wilmington, North Carolina. In 1993, after the Bulls' third championship and the murder of his father, Jordan retired to play professional baseball. After batting .202 as a minor leaguer, Jordan reentered basketball late in the 1994–95 season. Starting in 1996, he led the Bulls to a second "three-peat" (three more consecutive NBA championship wins), after which he retired again.

Jordan bought into part ownership of the Washington Wizards, hoping to show them the art of winning. In 2001, Jordan returned to play for the Wizards. Although he had to divest his interest in the Wizards, he demonstrated that he was still one of the best in the game until his comeback was cut short by injury.

Jordan's efforts are not all made on the basketball court. He remains an example to children, working to help underprivileged families with the James R. Jordan Boys and Girls Club and Family Life Center, named for his late father.

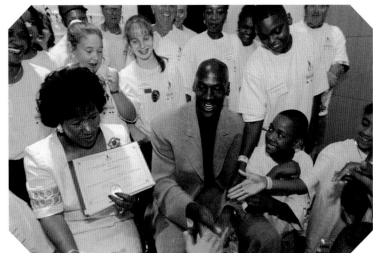

Jordan, with his mother, Delores, sits amid a group of children at Reidsville Middle School, in Reidsville, North Carolina, in 1996. Jordan's foundation works to help at-risk children.

MAE JEMISON

IN HER BIOGRAPHY, *Find Where the Wind Goes,* published in 2001, Jemison tells about a discussion with her kindergarten teacher: "'What do you want to be when you grow up?' Without hesitation, I answered emphatically, 'I want to be a scientist.' The kindergarten teacher may have felt her job was to help her

Dr. Mae Jemison has two bachelor's degrees, one in chemical engineering and the other in Afro-American studies, along with a medical degree.

students set realistic goals. In 1961, being a scientist was not in the realm of possibility for most people. So she replied, 'Don't you mean a nurse?' I simply put my hands on my hips and said, 'No, I mean a scientist.'"

Jemison became much more than a scientist: She is a chemical engineer, physician, and teacher. She also rocketed into orbit as the first African American female astronaut. The space shuttle *Endeavor* took off on September 12, 1992, with Jemison aboard as a science mission

specialist. Since then, she has focused on using science and technology in a socially responsible way to help educate children and to improve health-care delivery in developing countries.

Jemison was born October 17, 1956, in Decatur, Alabama, the youngest of three children. Her parents, Charlie, a maintenance supervisor, and Dorothy, a schoolteacher, moved their family to Chicago. Jemison entered Stanford University on a scholarship and graduated in 1977 with two bachelor's degrees, in chemical engineering and Afro-American studies. She then spent time working in Cuba, in rural Kenya, and at a refugee camp in Thailand while studying at Cornell's medical school, earning her medical degree in 1981.

After working as a general practitioner in Los Angeles, Jemison joined the Peace Corps as a medical officer in Sierra Leone and Liberia in West Africa. Jemison also wrote manuals and developed guidelines for health and safety issues, which she helped implement.

In 1985, she returned to practice in Los Angeles and began taking graduate courses in engineering before applying to the National Aeronautics and Space Administration (NASA). She wasn't accepted the first time. But her 1987 application was accepted, and Jemison became one of 15 astronaut candidates chosen from among 2,000.

Jemison began her career with NASA representing the astronaut office at the Kennedy Space Center in Cape Canaveral, Florida. She helped prepare space shuttles for launch before serving aboard the *Endeavor* on a joint United States/Japan mission. She spent 190 hours in space, conducting experiments in life and material sciences and was coinvestigator in the Bone Cell Research experiment. This experi-

ment was used to determine the effects of zero gravity on humans and animals.

In 1993, she resigned from NASA to start the Jemison Group. The company researches, develops, and implements technological projects. One project, Alafiya, which means "good health" in Yoruba, is a satellite-based telecommunications system aimed at improving the delivery of health care to West Africa. The company also runs The Earth We Share, a science camp for students. Jemison believes that scientists should consider the impact of their research and that people should understand how technology affects everyday life.

Jemison was a member of Dartmouth College's faculty in the Environmental Studies Program from 1995 to 2002. She directed The Jemison Institute for Advancing Technology in Developing Countries at Dartmouth. She also hosted and served as technical consultant to the "World of Wonders" series, produced by GRB Entertainment and seen on the Discovery Channel.

Jemison was the first African American female astronaut. She sits aboard a shuttle trainer at the Johnson Space Center in 1987.

BEN CARSON

Education was very important to Carson's mother. Carson later realized his mother couldn't read, despite making her sons read two books a week and write reports on them.

D R. BEN CARSON, an African American pediatric neurosurgeon, believes that people create their own luck. But it is hard work and caring that has made this doctor internationally known for his innovative techniques to successfully separate twins conjoined at the head and to help children suffering from brain tumors and chronic seizures.

This intense man with elegant hands and strong religious faith transcended his poverty-stricken youth to become director of pediatric neuro-surgery at the Johns Hopkins Medical Institutions in Baltimore. He performs hundreds of surgeries a year, and he says he loves to be able to walk out of an operating room and tell a devastated family that their child is awake and asking for them. Carson, who has written several books, including *The Big Picture* and *Gifted Hands,* both autobiographical, tells chil-

dren about his life to encourage them to succeed through academic achievement. He and his wife, Candy, started the Carson Scholars Fund that gives college scholarships to students who strive for excellence.

One of Carson's biggest successes came in 1987, when he led a medical team of 70 to separate seven-month-old German twins conjoined at the back of the head. The children shared the major cerebral blood drainage system. The operation, which took 22 hours, is believed to be the first time hypothermia (lowering body temperature) was used with circulatory bypass and deliberate cardiac arrest. The boys returned to Germany seven months later, though they still suffer from severe disabilities.

In 1997, Carson led another team of doctors in South Africa to successfully separate twins who were conjoined vertically at the head. After the 28-hour operation, the 11-month-old boys showed no problems. Carson also performs hemispherectomies, in which half the brain of a chronic seizure victim or neurologically diseased patient is removed to alleviate seizures.

Born Benjamin Solomon Carson in Detroit, on September 18, 1951, he was raised by his mother, Sonya, who worked several jobs to support Ben and his brother, Curtis. Though Carson had decided at age eight that he wanted to be a doctor, he was a problem student. His mother made her sons read two books a week and write reports on

them. Carson said it wasn't until years later that he realized she couldn't read. By eighth grade, his teacher at Carson's mostly white junior high school was berating his classmates for having allowed an African American to win the outstanding student award.

But Carson's temper nearly derailed his future. At 14, he tried to stab another student in a dispute over changing a radio station, then he locked himself into the bathroom to pray. Carson, a Seventh-day Adventist, says that changed his life. He went on to win a scholarship to Yale in 1969, where he got a B.A. in psychology, and he earned a medical degree at the University of Michigan in 1977. Carson did his internship and residency at Johns Hopkins, then went to Sir Charles Gairdner Hospital in Australia for two more years of intensive training. At age 33, he became the youngest director of pediatric neurosurgery in the United States. Carson is currently professor of neurosurgery, plastic surgery, oncology, and pediatrics at Johns Hopkins University School of Medicine.

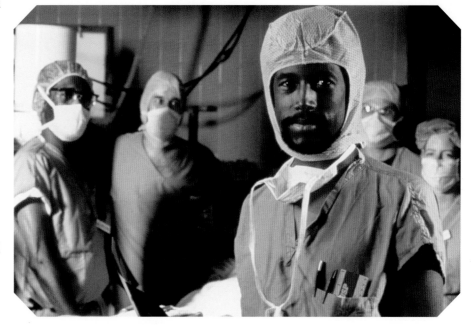

Carson in the operating room with a medical team ready. He is a pioneer in separating conjoined twins.

CAROL MOSELEY-BRAUN

CAROL MOSELEY-BRAUN, former U.S. senator and former ambassador to New Zealand, has lived a life of firsts. She made history in 1992 as the first African American woman elected to the Senate. She was the first black to serve as assistant majority leader in the Illinois House of Representatives, where she spent ten years fighting for schools and against discrimination, and she was the first woman and African American to hold executive office in Illinois Cook County government.

Moseley-Braun speaks during a press conference in 1997. She and Senate Minority Leader Tom Daschle proposed legislation to put money into the nation's deteriorating school buildings.

Moseley-Braun was born August 16, 1947, in Chicago. She is the daughter of Joseph, a police officer, and Edna, a medical technician. She attended public schools in Chicago. She received her law degree from the University of Chicago; she then worked as a prosecutor in the U.S. Attorney's office, winning the Attorney General's Special Achievement Award.

In 1978, Moseley-Braun, a Democrat, was elected to the Illinois House of Representatives. For seven of her ten years there, she was the chief sponsor of all school funding bills that affected the city of Chicago, including a 1985 bill that created parent councils in public schools. As legislative floor leader for the late Mayor Harold Washington, she sponsored bills to ban discrimination in housing and at private clubs.

In 1988, Moseley-Braun was elected Cook County Recorder of Deeds as part of Mayor Harold Washington's "Dream Team" ticket. Feminists and civil rights activists urged her to do the unthinkable: challenge the powerful incumbent senator Alan Dixon, who had never been defeated. Despite limited funding (her opponents outspent her 20-to-1), she was determined to run because she was angered by Dixon's support of Supreme Court nominee Clarence Thomas. She upset Dixon in the primary, and she won a historic victory when she was elected senator. She became the first black female senator and only the second black elected to the Senate after Reconstruction.

While in the Senate, she battled for youth job training and for issues affecting senior citizens. She became the first woman to serve on the powerful Senate Finance Committee. Her battle with Republican Senator Jesse Helms over the Confederate flag also garnered her much press coverage.

Moseley-Braun lost her re-election battle in 1998, partly because of allegations of mis-

conduct and for associating with Nigerian military dictator General Sani Abacha.

In 1999, President Clinton nominated Moseley-Braun to be the United States ambassador to New Zealand. At her swearing-in ceremony, Vice President Al Gore called her an embodiment of America in our most diverse and democratic spirit.

Moseley-Braun was a visiting professor at Morris Brown College. She continues to speak out for fairness and justice. After the terrorist attacks in New York City and Washington, D.C., on September 11, 2001, Moseley-Braun defended President Bush's War on Terrorism, saying it is important that the rest of the world understand that Americans stand for the essential goodness of humanity; she also castigated the Taliban for their treatment of women. She briefly ran for the Democratic presidential nomination in 2004.

Candidate Carol Moseley-Braun joins President Bill Clinton and Vice President Al Gore at a Chicago rally. Moseley-Braun became the second African American elected to the U.S. Senate since Reconstruction.

LOUIS FARRAKHAN

Minister Louis Farrakhan in 2000. He is a powerful speaker and is known to rile his detractors, but he has a very loyal following.

Louis Farrakhan is the leader of the Nation of Islam and a spellbinding orator who preaches black self-reliance, independence, and economic self-sufficiency.

L OUIS FARRAKHAN is the Honorable Minister of the Nation of Islam, based in Chicago, with mosques in more than 120 cities. An intense speaker with a strong belief in black independence, Farrakhan has been seen as a religious extremist since converting to Islam in 1955. He advises his followers to buy black, live clean, and take care of their own. But Farrakhan's anti-Jewish remarks have made him unwelcome in some quarters, and many people, African Americans among them, consider him a racist.

The eloquent, magnetic Farrakhan was born in the Bronx, New York, on May 11, 1933, to parents who supported black nationalist Marcus Garvey. Farrakhan attended Winston-Salem Teachers College in North Carolina. He married in 1953 and has nine children.

Farrakhan, an accomplished musician, was performing in Chicago in 1955 when he first heard Nation of Islam leader Elijah Muhammad speak. After sampling the fiery oratory of Malcolm X, Farrakhan joined the Nation that same year. He ran the Boston temple, then took over in Harlem after Malcolm X was murdered. There have been questions as to whether Farrakhan was involved in the assassination, which he vehemently denies.

In 1975, Farrakhan took over the Nation's leadership. He has worked to restore many of their businesses, he reopened the Chicago mosque, and he opened a school that teaches Muslim traditions.

But Farrakhan's speeches exhorting blacks to defend themselves against white racism and economic repression, stressing the importance of the black male and family structure, and his raging against whites (especially Jews) for their crimes against African Americans, have made him a controversial figure.

Since 1986, the government of Great Britain has banned Farrakhan from that country, arguing that he is a threat to community relations and public order because of his anti-Jewish views, which they consider racially divisive.

With the Reverend Benjamin Chavis, Jr., Farrakhan initiated and co-organized the Million Man March on Washington, D.C., in October 1995. Black men were asked to atone for the mistakes of the past.

In 1996, Farrakhan took his message of reconciliation to 23 Arab and African countries, including Libya and Nigeria, saying money and support from the nations would help him revitalize black urban communities. The U.S. government threatened Farrakhan with an investigation, believing he may have compromised national security. Farrakhan remarked that he was trying to link the interests of blacks and Muslims worldwide.

After a bout with cancer, Farrakhan toned down his rhetoric somewhat, though he still remains controversial. He continues to lead the Nation of Islam.

Farrakhan speaks at the Million Man March in Washington, D.C., on October 16, 1995. This was the largest assembly of African Americans since the 1963 March on Washington, D.C.

RUTH SIMMONS

Within the elite circles of Ivy League academia, few have done more to elevate the presence and focus of women and people of color than Dr. Ruth Simmons.

RUTH SIMMONS'S ascent to president of Brown University is a genuine and inspiring story of excellence. Born in 1945, Simmons traveled a remarkable distance, culturally and economically, to Brown University; her beginnings were on a cotton farm in the tiny Texas town of Grapeland. She is the youngest of 12 children born to sharecropper parents, a fact even she marvels at.

"I would not have thought it possible for a person of my background to become president of Brown University," Simmons acknowledged in her acceptance speech on November 9, 2000.

It was clear early on that education would be her vehicle out of poverty. After high school, Simmons won a scholarship to the historically black Dillard University in New Orleans, where she earned her bachelor's degree and graduated summa cum laude in 1967. She then pursued her master's and doctorate degrees in Romance languages and literature at Harvard University in 1970 and 1973, respectively.

Simmons spent one undergraduate year as a visiting student at Wellesley College in New England, and it was there that she experienced a period of empowering self-awareness that affected the course of her life. The attitudes and social atmosphere of the North were more progressive than those of the South, where Simmons was reared. This atmosphere proved to be more conducive to free-thinking for women and African Americans.

Simmons never abandoned her determination to succeed, which is evident in the diverse contributions she has made at several universities around the country. Her career began at the University of New Orleans, where she was an assistant professor of French and then assistant dean of the College of Liberal Arts. She also graced the faculties of California State University at Northridge and the University of Southern California.

In 1983, Simmons landed at Princeton University, where she served as acting director of Afro-American Studies Program and then associate dean of the faculty. That led to a two-year term as provost at Spelman College and a return to Princeton as vice-provost. In 1995, Simmons was named president of Smith College in Northampton, Massachusetts.

Simmons established an outstanding legacy during her tenure at Smith College. Her dedication to presenting educational opportunities to students of color and women was the driving force behind such unprecedented initiatives as the establishment of the first engineering program at a women's college in the country; the

DARLENE CLARK HINE

Her current position of John A. Hannah Distinguished Professor of History at Michigan State University and the presidency of the Organization of American Historians for 2001–2002 represent the tip of Darlene Clark Hine's illuminating search for historical truths. Her exploration began with questions about the origins of the racism she has experienced and also the haunting images of black Americans struggling for freedom through the modern Civil Rights Movement.

Hine's drive to unearth the contributions of black Americans, often omitted from national textbooks, led her into the very foundations of America. As the editor of volumes of books, she has presented not just the worth of African American men but also the value of black women who have shaped the world. And Hine did this during a time when many felt there was no interest in the subject. Thanks to Hine, "Stagecoach" Mary Fields, the western, gun-toting, mail-carrying African American has become a female hero, for both black and white women.

Hine's reputation as the preeminent scholar on the legacy of black women was already sealed by the time she completed editing two volumes of *Black Women in America: An Historical Encyclopedia*. The second edition of *The African-American Odyssey*, written with William C. Hine and Stanley Harrold, is one of her latest works.

In 2002, she was the second African American woman elected president of the prestigious Organization of American Historians.

Meridians journal, which explored the concerns of minority women; and a significant rise in the college's endowment. The scores of honors and awards bestowed on Simmons are a testament to a remarkable career.

TIGER WOODS

GOLF PRODIGY TIGER WOODS became the youngest—and the first person of color—to win the U.S. Masters tournament. His 1997 showing, finishing 12 strokes ahead of the rest of the field, was one of the most dominating performances in the history of professional golf.

By age 26, the 6′1″ golfer with a charismatic style had won seven major championships. In 1999 and 2000, Woods took the U.S. PGA championships. He won both the U.S. and British Opens in 2000. With his 2001 Masters title, Woods became the first pro golfer to hold all four major championships at one time. In April 2002, he won his third Masters—becoming only the third player in history to win back-to-back championships.

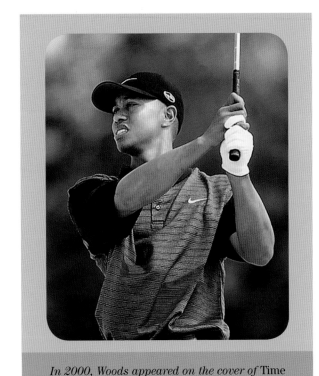

In 2000, Woods appeared on the cover of Time *magazine, 40 years after Arnold Palmer became the first golfer to be so honored.*

Born Eldrick Woods on December 30, 1975, in Cypress, California, he was nicknamed "Tiger" in honor of a South Vietnamese soldier his father had become friends with during the Vietnam War. Earl Woods is half black, a quarter American Indian, and a quarter Chinese. Woods's mother, Kultida, is half Thai, a quarter Chinese, and a quarter white.

Tiger started swinging a sawed-off golf club in his garage at 10 months. By age 2, Woods was putting against Bob Hope on the *Mike Douglas Show*. At age 3, Woods shot 48 for 9 holes, and he was featured in *Golf Digest* at the age of 5. He also won the Optimist International Junior Tournament six times, at ages 8, 9, 12, 13, 14, and 15.

Woods was the youngest winner of the U.S. Junior Amateur golf championship, which he won in 1991, 1992, and 1993. He then won the U.S. Amateur golf championship in 1994, 1995, and 1996. Woods dropped out of Stanford University to turn pro in 1996. In his first pro tournament, the Greater Milwaukee Open, Woods tied for 60th place. He went on to play in eight official PGA tour events that year, winning two and earning almost $800,000.

Woods, a Buddhist, says his religion has taught him calmness, inner peace, and the ability to stay focused while on the course. He's also learned that the perfection he desires takes time and discipline. But he does more than just play golf. Woods and his father created the Tiger Woods Foundation, including the Tiger Woods Learning Center, which helps people of color and disadvantaged youth get involved in golf and other activities so they can reach their potential and make their dreams come true. Woods has said that being a good role model is important to him and that he wants to influence kids in a positive way.

Woods is doing much more than that. His third Master's victory in 2002 brought CBS its third

Golf prodigy Tiger Woods, during his first visit to China in November 2001, acts as a role model for a young boy.

highest rating in the 47 years the network has covered the championship; 34.3 million people tuned in to watch the final round. But Woods, the world's number-one-ranked golfer, downplays speculation on how many championships he plans to rack up before he retires.

Woods won the 2005 Masters and British Open. He won the British Open again in 2006 as well as the PGA Championship. By August 2007, he had won his fourteenth World Golf Championship.

Woods has impressed the world with his talent, generosity, and goodwill, and where his career will take him remains to be seen. His determination and commitment to improving his game is an inspiration to many.

CONDOLEEZZA RICE

BEING A GIFTED OVERACHIEVER brings out the highest qualities in Condoleezza Rice, whose capabilities in foreign policy made her the first female to head the National Security Council (NSC) and the first African American female Secretary of State.

As senior fellow at Stanford University's Hoover Institution, Rice crossed multiple barriers to become the youngest, first female, and first African American provost for the university. Those incredible milestones preceded her leave of absence to take to the campaign trail with then-Governor George W. Bush as his foreign policy advisor. Given media and public concerns about Bush's presidential fitness for international diplomacy, her position became indispensable to the campaign.

Bush's selection of Rice for National Security Advisor followed a controversial election victory and was met with additional public complaints about her experience. Detractors believed her expertise was limited to the Soviet Union and Cold War politics, both having crumbled with the Berlin Wall.

Rice has proven her ability to grasp and execute the complex since birth. She was born in 1954 in segregated Birmingham, Alabama, to teachers Angelena and John Rice. Her mother named Condoleezza after *con dolcezza,* a musical direction meaning "with sweetness." Rice was a musical prodigy at age three.

In school, she was also gifted. She breezed through school and skipped two grades. At 15, she enrolled in the University of Denver, where her father was vice chancellor, and she graduated cum laude and Phi Beta Kappa by age 19.

Initially intending a career in music, Rice decided her talent did not meet her self-imposed standard of greatness. Rice then pur-

sued studies in political science, receiving a master's degree from Notre Dame and a doctorate from Denver. She arrived at Stanford with a

The fluid intellect, gifted articulation, international expertise, and velvet-glove delivery of Condoleezza Rice made her an indispensable asset during the 1999–2000 presidential campaign of George W. Bush.

fellowship in arms control and disarmament. Real-life experience with Washington politics came in 1986 when she served as special assistant to the director of the Joint Chiefs of Staff and worked on nuclear strategic planning. She returned to in Washington for three years as the director and later senior director of Soviet and East European Affairs in the NSC during the administration of George H.W. Bush. This gave Rice a higher profile because she was frequently consulted throughout the upheaval stemming from a waning Soviet Union during the period of 1989 through 1991.

Back at Stanford, Rice soared from senior Hoover fellow to university provost in 1993.

Becoming the chief budget and academic officer entailed managing $1.5 billion annually, 1,400 faculty members, and 14,000 students.

On January 22, 2001, Rice became National Security Advisor; one of her first tasks was to trim the NSC by one-third. She showed her teamworking ability by directing the remaining staff to Bush administration priorities.

Some Americans have speculated that this shift in focus could have allowed the terrorist attacks on the World Trade Center and the Pentagon to go unchecked on September 11, 2001. There can be no doubt, however, that Rice moved immediately on the War on Terrorism, offering reasoned counsel and coordinating daily meetings with the president and the highest leaders in his cabinet. She continues to be one of Bush's most trusted advisors.

Condoleezza Rice, the first female national security advisor to a president, believes the world of politics does not have to be bereft of morality.

BARACK OBAMA

BARACK OBAMA'S remarkable bid for the U.S. presidency has inspired many, especially younger voters, to get involved in the democratic process. His speech on race on March 18, 2008, may become one of the foundation documents in 21st-century American history.

Obama was born in Honolulu, Hawaii, on August 4, 1961. Financial upheavals and seeing poverty in Indonesia as a young boy left Obama passionate about lessening the divide between the haves and the have-nots. Even so, it is doubtful his white American mother, Stanley Ann Dunham, and black father, Barack Obama, Sr., had envisioned their son running for the U.S. presidency.

His father returned to Africa when Obama was two years old. American racism and culture grew intolerable for the independent Kenyan father who held high expectations for himself and the people around him. Obama was confused by his father's abandonment and where he, a person of mixed heritage, stood in American society. He was raised in a white culture, but society viewed him as an African American. Reconciling the two seemed impossible, and he tried to cover disillusionment with drugs. That is until he stopped dwelling on past losses and began to value his life and the lives of others with hope, compassion, and ethics.

Even if Obama did not yet fully understand these driving values, he acted on them after graduating from Columbia University in 1983. He worked to organize the impoverished Chicago community of Altgeld, which meant training residents to demand the resources they needed to improve their lives and their community.

Employment programs and business development plans were moving forward in Altgeld

by the time Obama sought further education at Harvard Law School. He became the first African American president of the *Harvard Law Review* before graduating in 1991.

After law school, he returned to Chicago and directed a voter registration drive. In 1992, he met fellow lawyer Michelle Robinson. They wed, and both pursued law careers while raising their two daughters.

Obama is a family man with the uncommon skill of inspiring people to action. The nation saw that at the 2004 Democratic Convention.

His focus at Miner, Barnhill & Gallard continued to be community legal services, and he taught constitutional law at the University of Chicago.

These life experiences made him well-suited to uphold constitutional principles and set policies as a legislator in the Illinois Senate. In the state senate, Obama chaired the Health and Human Services committee. He supported numerous bills on behalf of ordinary citizens, including

the Illinois Earned Income Tax Credit and the expansion of early childhood education.

He bounced back after Bobby Rush defeated him in a race for the U.S. House of Representatives. Obama ran for the U.S. Senate in 2004; he trounced ultraconservative Alan Keyes. Obama sits on the influential Health, Education, Labor, and Pensions Committee and Foreign Relations Committee, committees that shape domestic and foreign policies. The senator also promotes the safety and welfare of Americans, including military veterans, through work on the Veterans' Affairs Committee and Environment and Public Works Committee.

Obama stole the show at the 2004 Democratic Convention. His speech captured the hearts of people nationwide and garnered him enormous political capital, which catapulted him to the Democratic presidential nomination in 2008.

Political ethics and campaign finance reform rank high on Obama's list of important issues. His presidential campaign enjoyed unprecedented financial support without donations from corporations and special interest groups.

Obama's appealing messages of hope and human compassion, of military restraint and political negotiations, have resonated with voters of all ages and colors. The entire story of Obama's political life has yet to be written. Many doubted his chances for success after he announced he would run for the Democratic presidential nomination. But public enthusiasm abounded, arising from his speeches and his two best-selling books. Obama inspired a nation to get involved in the political process. How he has done so is reflected in the title of his second book, *The Audacity of Hope.* In 2008, the audio version of that book earned him his second Grammy Award.